Studies of Religion in Africa

Supplements to the Journal of Religion in Africa

Edited by

Paul Gifford

School of Oriental and African Studies, London

VOLUME 35

Migration and Christian Identity in Congo (DRC)

by

Emma Wild-Wood

BRILL

LEIDEN • BOSTON
2008

On the cover: The front cover shows an evangelistic procession during the centenary celebrations of 1996. David Asiki is leading, behind him to the right wearing a dog collar is Munege Kabarole, to the left is Sinziri Onadra, also in a dog collar. All three were interviewed for the book. Used with the permission of Nigel Pearson.

This book is printed on acid-free paper.

Library of Congress Cataloging-in-Publication Data

Wild-Wood, Emma.
  Migration and Christian identity in Congo, (DRC) / by Emma Wild-Wood.
    p. cm. — (Studies of religion in Africa, ISSN 0169-9814 ; v. 35)
  Includes bibliographical references and index.
  ISBN 978-90-04-16464-2 (hardback : alk. paper) 1. Church work with immigrants—Anglican Communion. 2. Emigration and immigration—Religious aspects—Anglican Communion. 3. Identification (Religion) 4. Anglican Communion—Congo (Democratic Republic) I. Title. II. Series.

  BV639.I4W55 2008
  261.8'36—dc22

                                                    2008025430

BV
639
.I4
W55
2008

ISSN 0169 9814
ISBN 978 90 04 16464 2

Copyright 2008 by Koninklijke Brill NV, Leiden, The Netherlands.
Koninklijke Brill NV incorporates the imprints Brill, Hotei Publishing,
IDC Publishers, Martinus Nijhoff Publishers and VSP.

PRINTED IN THE NETHERLANDS

To Peter
and to the community of ISThA
—past, present and future.

CONTENTS

List of Illustrations, Maps and Diagrams ix

Acknowledgements xi

Abbreviations xiii

Glossary xv

A note on African names and language xvii

Chapter One   Of Roots and Routes: An Introduction 1

Chapter Two   "Their Own Church:" *L' Eglise Anglicane du
Congo*, 1896–1960 20

Chapter Three   Being at Home in a New Place: EAC
Growth Through Rural-Urban Migration 49

Chapter Four   Returning Home to a Strange Land: EAC
Growth Through Trans-border Migration 80

Chapter Five   Contesting Unity and Order: Inter-church
Conflict 111

Chapter Six   Homeless and Free for the Gospel: Revivalists
in the EAC 127

Chapter Seven   Weak Vessels or Church Foundations?
Women in the EAC 144

Chapter Eight   "Young People, Keep Your Faith:" Youth,
Spirit and Contemporary Christian Expression 171

Chapter Nine   Migrant Anglican Identity in Congo 203

Bibliography 219

Index 231

Contents

LIST OF ILLUSTRATIONS, MAPS AND DIAGRAMS

1 Map of North-east Congo from the University of Texas
   Library 16

2 Photograph of Apolo Kivebulaya teaching, about 1930.
   Used with permission of Cara Frost-Jones 23

3 Diagram of Rural-urban Migration 52

4 Photograph of Four Archdeacons at Apolo's grave. Used
   with permission of Isingoma Kahwa, Bishop of Boga 77

5 Diagram of Trans-border Migration 84

6 Photograph of Mothers' Union Members processing during
   the centenary celebrations, 1996. Androsi Kasima,
   interviewed for the book, is front right. Used with
   permission of Sarah Roberts 149

7 Photograph of Imani ya Kweli choir performing during
   the centenary celebrations, 1996. Used with permission of
   Sarah Roberts 180

ACKNOWLEDGEMENTS

This book is a result of collaboration between myself and those who gave their time, stories, advice, friendship and their financial and moral support. Without them it could not have been written but the responsibility for its content is entirely mine.

To the Pew Charitable Trust with the Overseas Ministries Study Centre I am grateful for awarding me a Research Enablement grant to facilitate the investigation of church archives and the recording of oral history interviews in Congo. I am appreciative of the financial support of St. Luke's College Foundation, the Whitfield Institute, the Church Mission Society, the Pollock Trust and New College, Edinburgh University. I offer my thanks Jack Thompson, David Kerr, Kevin Ward, Andrew Ross, those at the Centre for the Study of Christianity in the Non-Western World at Edinburgh University and in the African History Group at Cambridge University for their thoughtful guidance, advice and collegiality. Fred Mukungu of Uganda Christian University assisted me with archives in Uganda. Fred Ngadjole transcribed a number of the interviews. Cara Frost-Jones, Bishop Isingoma Kahwa of Boga, Nigel Pearson and Sarah Roberts allowed me to use their photographs.

Many of those to whom I am indebted have their names listed as sources at the end of the book. I am grateful to the members of the Dioceses of Boga and Nord-Kivu for allowing me to carry out this research. They told me their stories with patience and good humour, gave me hospitality and helped me gather information. Some added to this by correcting my Swahili, challenging my interpretation of events, and being willing correspondents on matters of minutiae. I am particularly appreciative of all I learnt from the students and staff of the *Institut Superieur Théologique Anglican* over several years, most especially Titre Ande, colleague, friend and fellow researcher, and Maturu Ande, for hours of patient Swahili conversation.

My family has been a source of encouragement and necessary distraction. Parents, Diana and Roger, sister, Vicky, and in-laws, Mary and Eric, helped with child-care and proof reading. Peter, my husband, has been unfailingly supportive, whilst our children, Ruari, Cara and Cameron, have provided a healthy perspective on research and writing by being largely oblivious to it. Thank you to you all.

ABBREVIATIONS

AIC	African Initiated Churches
AIM	African Inland Mission
CBFMS	Conservative Baptist Foreign Missionary Society (previously UAM).
CECA 20	Communauté Evangélique du Centre de l'Afrique, member no. 20 of ECC.
CER	Chosen Evangelical Revival
CMS	Church Missionary Society
COU	Church of Uganda
CPC	Congo Protestant Council
EAC	Eglise Anglicane du Congo
ECC	Eglise du Christ au Congo
IM	Immanuel Mission
MPR	Mouvement populaire de la Révolution
MU	Mothers' Union
UAM	Unevangelised Africa Mission (subsequently CBFMS).

GLOSSARY

The words below are in Swahili, unless otherwise stated in brackets.

Abanyoro—heads of clans (Hema).
Balokole—saved ones, revivalists (Luganda).
Furaha—joy, pleasure, satisfaction.
Heshima—respect, honour, dignity, ceremony, distinction, politeness, reputation. Used in the Anglican Church to refer to behaviour expected in worship and towards those in authority.
Kanisa—church
Kimya—quiet
Maendeleo—development, progression, advance, improvement. Used by Anglicans to denote that which encourages both material and spiritual improvement.
Mwalimu (s)—teacher in a school or in a church. The lowest rank of church worker in charge of a chapel. Translated either as teacher or catechist.
Mwangalizi (s)—A church worker in charge of a chapel or sub-parish. Usually translated as evangelist.
Omukama—chief, king, lord (Hema).
Uhuru—freedom, liberty, liberation. Used by some Anglicans to refer to the way in which the Revival movement or the institutional church has enabled them to take alternative social and religious routes in their area.
Upole—gentleness, slowness, smoothness, sympathy, moderation, calm. In the EAC it is used to refer to the way of worship or a characteristic of a good church worker.
Utaratibu—order, system, method, organisation, regime. Anglicans often use it refer to the hierarchical structure of the EAC and the liturgical order of the Prayer Book.
Vijana (pl)—young people
Walimu (pl)—Teachers, see *mwalimu.*
Wangalizi (pl)—Evangelists, see *mwangalizi.*
Wokovu—literally, salvation, used to refer to revivalists.

A NOTE ON AFRICAN NAMES AND LANGUAGE

As far as possible personal names have been spelt as they were given to me by the person interviewed. Different ethnic groups have different traditions and it is common for a person to receive a large number of names. Mobutu's regime attempted to impose a universal structure using the personal name followed by the father's name, rejecting the use of European or Biblical names. The present popular use of names is not systematised. Where possible I have used the most common order in Congo—personal name, family name, baptismal name, e.g. Sinziri Onadra Christophe—which means subverting the order usually given to me by those brought up in Uganda. When referring to an individual more than once it is the personal name that is given e.g. Sinziri. Where this is not possible I have tried to respect the order given by the individuals themselves. Many of the women interviewed have chosen to be known by a European or Biblical name e.g. Janette Sinziri. Janette is her given personal name and thus the name used when she is referred to by only one name.

Current place names, their spellings, and current political divisions of territory have been used to aid clarity. Congo has been used throughout, although during most of Mobutu's long presidency the country was known as Zaïre. Kisangani and Kinshasa are used instead of Leopoldville and Stanleyville, which were the names given by the Belgians.

To avoid confusion I consistently refer to the Anglican Church of Congo as *Eglise Anglicane du Congo* or EAC. It has also been known, at various times and circumstances, as CMS Mission, Native Anglican Church, Boga Mission, Diocèse de Boga-Zaïre, Church of Uganda, *Communauté Anglicane du Zaïre/Congo* (CAZ or CAC) and the *Province de l'Eglise Anglicane du Zaïre/Congo* (PEAZ or PEAC). Likewise I consistently use Church of Uganda (COU) to refer to the Anglican Church in that country.

CHAPTER ONE

OF ROOTS AND ROUTES: AN INTRODUCTION

Introduction

On May 30th 1933 Revd Apolo Kivebulaya died in Boga, Congo. As a Ganda evangelist and Anglican priest, Apolo[1] had introduced Christianity to the village of Boga and the surrounding area from 1896. On his deathbed he is reported to have said, "Bury me with my head towards the West so that the work of the Lord will continue," so, contrary to Ganda custom, he was interred pointing away from his home and towards the Congo forest. The burial request is repeated in the opening paragraph of a pamphlet published for the centenary of the *Eglise Anglicane du Congo* (EAC) in 1996.[2] In the text it is interpreted as a prophecy of African agency in the migratory growth of the EAC. This particular narration of Apolo's death indicates the roots of identity among Congolese Anglicans and acknowledges the centrality of migratory routes in the church's expansion. Reverence for Apolo was fertile soil in which to root Anglicanism in Congo and, most particularly, in Boga. To change metaphors, Boga became the home of the Congolese Anglicanism, its place of origin and the place believed to define it. Reverence for Apolo influenced the contested making of a home-from-home by migrant Anglicans and ultimately led to the growth of the EAC.

This book provides a contemporary social history analysis of the complex interaction between the social change occurring in relocation/dislocation and the religious change in the expansion and altering expression of a Christian church. It hypothesises that migration brings or hastens change by providing migrants with a new set of life experiences that, in dialogue with the old set of experiences, negotiate an altered identity. In this interaction religious identity provides migrants

---

[1] Apolo Kivebulaya was born 'Waswa', that is, one of twins. 'Kivebulaya' means 'one from Europe', referring to the jacket he wore over his Gandan *kanzu*. 'Apolo', his baptismal name, is used in Congo with affection and reverence when referring to him by only one name. This usage is followed here.

[2] *Esquisse historique de l'Eglise Anglicane du Zaïre 1896–1996* (Bunia, ISThA, 1996), 1.

with a framework for stability and flexibility during migration. Thus migration alters religious identity. The study uses oral narratives related by EAC members to understand migrant and religious identities. The varying usage of particular words and phrases provide hermeneutical tools with which to examine shifting and interconnecting identities.

Christianity in Africa

The consideration of the influence of migration on religious identity makes an important contribution to the growing body of work on mainline African Christianity as a locally accepted religion. Migration is widespread on the African continent but its relationship with Christianity has had little attention. Examining migration innovates within the field by exploring a dynamic that alters the agency of African Christians in relation to their Christian affiliation. A number of studies demonstrate, as I do, that the adoption and alteration of Christianity in Africa depended upon the way in which Christian belief and practice were perceived to meet local spiritual, social and political needs. For example, in *The Realm of the Word*, Paul Landau[3] presents a social history of the impact of the London Missionary Society on the Tswana people. He recognises Tswana agency and initiative in the localisation of Christianity because it provided opportunities for greater self-determination, thus departing from the view of Jean and John Comaroff[4] who saw the Tswana as manipulated objects of missionary hegemony. David Maxwell's *Christians and Chiefs in Zimbabwe: A social history of the Hwesa people, c. 1870s–1990s* is another example.[5] It studies the interplay of political and religious change among the Hwesa during colonialism and independence. They accepted those mission churches that presented the Christian message in local terms. Maxwell recognises the transformation of group identities as Hwesa chose between traditional cults and various Christian options. He briefly acknowledges returning migrants as one of several facilitators of change but does not explore the issue further. I take the conclusions of the impact of Christianity

---

[3] Paul Landau, *The Realm of the Word: Language, Gender, and Christianity in a Southern African Kingdom* (Cape Town, David Philip, 1995).

[4] Jean and John Comaroff, *Of Revelation and Revolution: Christianity, Colonialism and Consciousness in South Africa* (Chicago, University of Chicago, 1991).

[5] David Maxwell, *Christians and Chiefs in Zimbabwe: A social history of the Hwesa people, c. 1870s–1990* (Edinburgh University Press, Edinburgh, 1999).

on local cultures and the localisation of Christian belief and practice further into the contemporary sphere of mixed Christianities as migration brings those of different denominations and ethnic backgrounds face to face. In taking this approach I demonstrate the mobility and hybridity of African contexts.

In the studies mentioned above, Landau and Maxwell follow convention by examining one ethnic group. They focus on the conversion process before analysing the further development of Christianity among the group chosen. I question the position of ethnic identity as the essential staring point for a discussion of contemporary African socio-religious history, recognising that "ethnic identities are merely a small fraction of the many identities mobilized in... everyday life".[6] This is particularly obvious when studying the plural societies developed through migration. In these societies the discreet boundedness often presented by ethnic groups and those who study them is demonstrably variable and mythical. Any particular expression of ethnicity is seen as relational and situational.[7]

In this book I innovate by focusing on the development of a single mission denomination, decades after the first introduction to Christianity in the area. This enables an analysis of the effect of church membership and its correlated life experiences on EAC members from a number of culturally and historically distinct ethnic groups who are affiliated to it. In African Christian Studies, scholars have studied single African Initiated Churches (AICs)[8] and, more recently, Pentecostal churches,[9] but there has been a wariness of studying a mainline western mission church. This unbalanced interested has been fuelled by a fascination with the exotic, a distaste for institutions perceived to be linked to colonialism, and an awareness that early mission and church histories were often uncritical, elitist and spiritualised. As Ogbu Kalu suggests, early historical accounts of mission churches did not sufficiently deal with the political, social and cultural elements surrounding conversion

---

[6] Richard Werbner, "Introduction: Multiple Identities, Plural Arenas," in *Postcolonial Identities in Africa*, ed. Richard Werbner and Terence Ranger (London, Zed Books, 1996), 1.

[7] Thomas Eriksen, *Ethnicity and Nationalism* (London, Pluto Press 2002), 58.

[8] For example, Carol Ann Muller, *Rituals of Fertility and the Sacrifice of Desire* (Chicago, University of Chicago Press, 1999).

[9] For example, David Maxwell, *African Gifts if the Spirit, Pentecostalism and the Rise of a Zimbabwean Transnational Religious Movement* (Oxford, James Currey, 2006).

and commitment.[10] My approach, however, does not assume that a denomination is a single closed unit but is rather an alliance of different social units that can be identified by ethnicity, gender, generation and so on; units that can be further deconstructed.

This study also analyses the response made by members of a denomination to the continuing change of post-independence African society sometime after initial Christian conversion had taken place. As such it focuses on the socio-religious factors of contemporary identity and touches only in the first chapter on issues of primary conversion and its relationship with indigenous worldviews. The penultimate chapter focuses on the interaction between the EAC and the growing Pentecostal movement. This contemporary approach demonstrates that the dichotomy between some mission-initiated and some African-initiated churches is much less striking than has sometimes been assumed.

Migration and Christianity

If the identity of Christianity on the African continent is to be understood, frequent and widespread migrations and their relation to the Church should be studied thoroughly as both results of, and catalysts for, rapid religious change. Africa possesses large migrant populations who move as labourers, traders and refugees. They are affected by economic differentials and political instability that are the consequence of broader social change.[11] Migration is part of life for many Africans and is a factor that informs their identities. Some migrants cover large distances and settle in cultures very different from those in their place of origin. Small-scale migration, however, is much more common and directly affects more people. Those intent on improving their lifestyles often migrate to their nearest town. Refugees fleeing war usually cross the nearest international border or are internally displaced. If, as I hypothesise, migration provides a catalyst for rapid change, then change often occurs in the common place and unpublicised movement of people.

---

[10] Ogbu Kalu, "African Church Historiography," in *African Historiography: Essays in Honour of Jacob Ade Ajayi*, ed. Toyin Falola (London, Longman, 1993), 166–167.

[11] Aderant Adepoju, "Links between Internal and International Migration: the African Situation," in *International Migration Today*, vol. *1* ed. Charles Stahl (UNESCO/University of Western Australia, 1988), 38.

An emphasis on missions and church institutions from historians and an interest in rites and ritual practice from anthropologists has often obscured from view the movement of ordinary church members and the initiation of church workers in Africa. Bengt Sundkler, however, recognised the role of migration in the spread of Christianity. He called for "a new key" to African Christian history that emphasised the role of "the highly mobile African communities" of refugees and migrant workers.[12] Meredith McKittrick noted the potential for change present in migratory movements. In *To Dwell Secure: Generation, Christianity and Colonialism in Ovamboland* McKittrick studied the convergence of Christianity and labour migration in Namibia's history.[13] She argues that both these elements provided young people with security and seniority, aspirations that they took from indigenous culture but which, influenced by migration and Christianity, challenged that same culture. Similar issues emerge in this study as migrant members of the EAC reconfigured their identities and that of their church thus diversifying the possible identities available within the EAC and challenging the dominant identity.

The EAC grew numerically and spread geographically through relatively short migratory routes. This study is limited to the EAC in North-east Congo which provides the researcher with a compact area and a small institution on which to carry out detailed microanalysis of the impact of migration and the shifting identity issues at work during a time of transition. Ethnically the area of Ituri and Nord-Kivu is very diverse, being peopled by Sudanic and Nilotic groups in the north and Bantu and Pygmy groups in the south.[14] Most of the migrants interviewed for the research came from five groups, although the EAC in the North-east is also present among at least eight others. The study focuses on two routes that have led to the establishment of the EAC in new areas. Firstly, the route from the Semeliki escarpment area to the towns of Ituri and Nord-Kivu, taken mainly by the Hema and Nande. Theirs was a voluntary, rural to urban migration with the aim of an improved life-style. It led to the contested urbanisation of migrants and

---

[12] Bengt Sundkler, "African Church History in a New Key," in *Religion, Development and African Identity*, ed. Kirsten Holst-Peterson (Uppsala, Scandinavian Institute of African Studies, 1987), 75.

[13] McKittrick (Portsmouth, Heinemann, 2002).

[14] Jan Vansina, *Introduction à l'ethnographie du Congo* (Bruxelles, Universitaires du Congo, 1965), 213–214.

their institutions. The second migratory path is the sudden migration of refugees from Uganda to the Aru and Mahagi zones of Congo, taken by the Kakwa, Lugbara and Alur.

These migrations are simply the latest in an age-old saga of mobility and socio-religious change. Colonial rulers, themselves migrants to Africa, discouraged the westward drifting of population in search of new land thus changing the nature of the migration which had been occurring for centuries. This action frequently precipitated over-population and labour migration. All the peoples in this study lived along colonial boundaries and their corporate identities were, to some extent, re-formed by them. By the late 20th century, perceptions of ethnic groups, particularly their boundedness and hierarchy, had been influenced by colonial policies with the inevitable consequence of inequality in divisions of power between different groups rooted in colonial demarcations of identity. Social and geographical mobility became more structured as colonisers attempted to systematise a variety of social groups within their controlling framework of a unitary bounded state. Belgian colonial policy effectively reinvented or clarified different ethnicities,[15] thereby dismantling slowly established social and political bonds and ossifying linguistic, ethnic and geographical boundaries. Boundaries of *collectivités* were to be observed even in situations of high population density. Furthermore, the Belgian authorities made assessments about the relative merits of different ethnic groups. They believed certain ethnic groups, like the Alur and Hema, to possess a superior civilisation and greater ability to lead than others. As a result they preferred Alur and Hema to work for them and encouraged them to migrate to commercial or mining centres. The migrations studied here provide another chapter in the movement of people within the continent.

This study pays particular attention to the micro-, informal, socioreligious factors of relations, beliefs, rites and aspirations through which migrants adapt to their new situations, becoming to varying degrees assimilated into, or remaining separate from, their host societies.[16] Micro-factors provide a way of understanding new, migratory interconnections between places and peoples and a way of examining the

---

[15] Crawford Young, "Nationalism, Ethnicity and Class in Africa: A Retrospective" *Cahiers d'Etudes Africaines*, 26 (1986): 442.

[16] Monica Boyd, "Family and Personal Networks in International Migration: Recent Developments and New Agendas" *International Migration Review* (1989): 641.

complex relationship between migration and religious identity. They permit an exploration of belonging as people are unsettled from, what Nadje Al-Ali and Khalid Koser in their article "Transnationalism, International Migration and Home" describe as, their "bounded, singular and stable conceptualizations of home."[17] Micro-factors also indicate why religion is often a cohesive force during the dislocation that occurs during migration.

Identity

Central to identity for many Congolese interviewed during research was the sense of corporate belonging: "Someone without identity is nowhere. It's good to belong to a particular family, a particular group," pronounced Muhindo Tsongo. This idea resonates with a common African proverb on being-in-relation: *Mutu ni Watu* (a person is people). Belonging is primarily studied here in terms of attachment to a religious community, the EAC, in which ultimate belonging is to God within the body of Christ. Yet the way in which members belong is complex and shifting and reflects their influence, or lack of it, within the group. In studying this particular group identity I acknowledge the influence of multiple identities that at times coalesce and at times contradict each other. The issue of belonging is particularly acute for migrants who may pose questions previously taken for granted; to what, whom or where do I belong when I am dislocated from the familiar? Where or how can I be 'at home'? Such questions are asked by Congolese Anglicans. As the centenary pamphlet puts it, many "...are looking for an identity by gathering together scattered parts of a collective memory".[18] Many members of the EAC are interested in their history as a means of understanding the foundations of their identity.

In this search for belonging, many use the word 'home' to describe their attachment to the EAC. Since the publication of an early work on AICs, *A Place to Feel at Home*,[19] denominations birthed on the African continent have been understood to provide a 'home' for their adherents

---

[17] Nadje Al-Ali and Khalid Koser, "Transnationalism, International Migration and Home", in *New Approaches to Migration? Transnational Communities and the Transformation of Home*, ed. Al-Ali and Koser (Routledge, London, 2002), 7.

[18] *Esquisse historique*, 2.

[19] F. B. Welbourne & B. A. Ogot, *A Place to Feel at Home, A study of Two Independent Churches in Western Kenya* (London, Oxford University Press, 1966).

in a way that western mission denominations could not. This study questions that assumption and suggests that members of western initiated denominations have also developed a sense of homeliness within their churches. It asserts that it is the attachment to the EAC as home that allowed it to spread, and its growth that caused members to contest the meaning of home. Migrants are forced to re-assess their bounded and stable ideas of home. In their article Al-Ali and Koser recognise the dynamic and pluripresent use by migrants of the word 'home' to refer to a physical dwelling place, a community, or nation, *inter alia*. Al-Ali and Koser define 'home' as "the place where personal and social meaning are grounded."[20] However, for EAC members, whose sense of belonging is grounded in worship of the Almighty, this definition is deficient; 'home' is also where their *spiritual* meaning is grounded. This enhanced definition will be employed as the different meanings given to 'home' by EAC migrants are explored to provide an understanding of their religious identity.

The focus of this study is the observation of a changing corporate religious identity through the analysis of a particular historical process. Identity signifies a network of connecting ideas about the self/group and the other/s. It is a construction of, firstly, how one views oneself/group and, secondly, how one's group is viewed by others, and the complex and dynamic interplay of these viewpoints. This construction is affected by the situation and by the relation of others with the group. 'The others' in this study are members of another denomination present in the North-east of Congo. 'Others' are also different groups within the EAC, whether they be Revivalists, older leaders or young women, who contest group identity from different positions of power and influence within a broad consensus of Anglican identity.

Religious identity can be defined briefly as a construct of faith-practice and discourse in a particular social, economic and political situation. The sense of the supernatural, the supportive belonging to others, the belief system and rituals which make sense of the world, and the social activities of religious experience are powerful and cohesive idioms in which to develop identity. Membership of a specific Christian group provides its members with a particular expression of belief and belonging and a particular way of being within society in a specific historical, social, political and religious context. Furthermore, specific

---

[20] Al-Ali and Koser, 7.

identity perceptions entail particular responses to situations, engender interpersonal relationships and develop communities.

Those in search of roots can dig very deep but, for the purposes of this study, the starting point for religious identity is the rural Anglican identity germinating on the Semeliki escarpment from 1896. As the next chapter demonstrates it flourished by grafting itself onto the social and religious order already present as well as through the introduction of new skills and services provided through the church. This identity both flourished and decayed as a result of migration.

Hybrid identities

Any individual or group is made up of many identities that vary in significance for the subject at any given time or circumstance.[21] Migrant members of the EAC also have ethnic, national, gender, and generation identities, *inter alia*, which are variously configured among different people in different places. Their identity is a shifting construct of the elements of personal and cultural identity brought from the place of origin, and the negotiated choices made on arrival and settlement in the new environment. These choices are limited by such factors as access to power, perceptions by those amongst whom they settle, the extent to which the expectations of the migrants are fulfilled on arrival in the new location, and the success of their integration. All these factors are influenced by the historical turn of events. Migration is a good event through which to study identity precisely because these issues are brought to the fore. If historical analysis ensures a respect for the dynamic of change within identity, the study of migration recognises the mobility and hybridity of identities.

During research, gender, generation, ethnicity and nationality appeared to be particularly pertinent to the context when religious identity was deconstructed. These factors were then further deconstructed and their fluidity and pluriform nature were examined. Generation indicates social age rather than biological age. It governs status in society, signalling to whom respect is conferred. Personal character, or more often, familial connection with elites, may confer seniority on one

---

[21] Cookie White Stephan and Walter Stephan, "What are the Functions of Ethnic Identity?" in *We are a People: Narrative and Multiplicity in Constructing Ethnic Identity*, ed. Paul Spickard and Jeffrey Burroughs (Philadelphia, Temple University Press, 2000), 238.

person much earlier in their life than someone else less well-connected. As long as young people aspire to the characteristics of a particular social configuration of seniority, unequal generation identities function smoothly. When this is no longer the case generational conflicts often occur. Generational issues are also gendered. Women and men have different roles in society but gender is not usually an 'isolated factor' in determining social-religious roles. As J. D. Y. Peel demonstrates in his article, 'Gender in Yoruba Religious Change', gender interacts with other 'social attributes,' It does not '...exist as a factor outside time but as one whose significance is likely to change and develop.'[22] In the EAC gendered roles were influenced over time by Anglican and indigenous traditions, migration, education and ethnicity. In the EAC, for instance, an older clergyman—particularly if he were from a prominent Hema family—had a potential for greater influence than a young woman. Yet, as chapters six and seven show, groups of young people and women began to influence the EAC precisely because they did not possess ecclesiastical authority. Thus the effect of migration on EAC identity was ultimately to question the generational and gender norms of the pre-migration church.

Ethnic and national identities were also identified as important identity factors. They are recognised by those interviewed as an important part of their selves. Ethnicity has been described as "...an arrangement of people who see themselves as biologically and historically connected with each other, and who are seen by others as being so connected."[23] This definition places the self-understanding of people first. Members of ethnic groups in Congo generally see themselves as belonging 'essentially' or 'primordially' to one group; that is, membership is a matter of land or blood relations.[24] This is different to an emphasis on instrumentality considered by many anthropologists to be a more accurate understanding of ethnicity; that is, ethnic groups are politically and socially constructed associations created and shaped by shared interests, institutions and culture.[25] The ethnic identity of most

---

[22] J. D. Y. Peel, "Gender in Yoruba Religious Change," *Journal of Religion in Africa* 32 (2002): 152.

[23] Paul Spickard and Jeffrey Burroughs, "We are a People: Narrative and Multiplicity in Constructing Ethnic Identity," in *We are a People*, 2.

[24] Francisco Gil-White, "The Cognition of Ethnicity: Native Category Systems under the Field Experimental Microscope," *Methods* 14 (2002): 161.

[25] Charles Keyes, *Ethnic Change* (Seattle, University of Washington Press, 1981), 10.

Anglicans was often related in some way to their expression of national identity. Migrants first conserved and then challenged the ethnocentric norms that had developed in the EAC, attempting to replace them with an ethnic pluralism situated within a national identity. This appeared both to make more sense in the new locations and to fit more closely with prominent Christian teaching. National identity provided a larger unit of belonging that cohered with belonging to an international denomination. Nationalism has, in African studies, often been seen as opposite, weaker, and 'synthetic' in comparison to ethnicity when assessing group identity, particularly as many nation-states in Africa are deemed 'weak' or 'failed'.[26] However, a number of studies have shown that national sentiment is often demonstrated amongst ethnic groups straddling national boundaries.[27] All the ethnic groups included in this research are found on both sides of the Uganda-Congo border and those interviewed exhibited strong feelings of national identity. These narratives of national identity participate in state rhetoric but interpret it to respond to local socio-religious needs which rely heavily upon the commonplace nationalism of national music, languages, dress, different administrative and educational systems *inter alia*. A detailed examination of the complexities of ethnicity and nationality is beyond the scope of this study. However in the internal war which started in 1998, and which only directly effected the EAC at the end of 2000, ethnocentricity was a tool used by warlords to gather militia and demand loyalty.[28] Thus the interplay of ethnic and national socio-political constructs in religious identity becomes particularly acute at the very end of the period under study and will be examined in some detail in the final chapter.

---

[26] George De Vos, and Lola Romanucci-Ross, "Ethnic Identity: A Psychocultural Persective," in *Ethnic Identity: Creation, Conflict and Accommodation*, ed. De Vos and Romanucci-Ross (Walnut Creek, AltaMira, 1995), 352.

[27] For example, Paul Nugent, and A. I. Asiwaju, "Introduction: The paradox of African Boundaries," in *African Boundaries: Barriers, Conduits and Opportunities*, ed. Nugent and Asiwaju (London, Pinter, 1996), 10.

[28] Johan Pottier, "Emergency in Ituri, DRC: Political Complexity, Land and Other Challenges in Restoring Food Security" (paper given at FAO International Workshop, 'Food Security in Complex Emergencies' Tivoli, Italy, 23–25 September 2003), 6–7.

Methodology[29]

This study relies on the analysis of oral narratives of Anglicans and non-Anglicans who told their stories with enthusiasm and generosity. My interpretation of these taped interviews is based on a narrative method that accepts that people recount events and actions to express those things that are important to their sense of self. Narrative identity analysis understands that even in the most 'artless' conversations three steps of 'narrativisation' have taken place: the *selection* of certain elements of the past, and the ignoring or forgetting of others; the *plotting* of these elements to link them together; and the *interpretation* of these events by claiming for them specific significance.[30] Oral interviews already have a performance element to them; that is, they are not natural conversations and thus are highly 'narrativised'. When Congolese Anglicans recounted events and actions of their lives as they related to the EAC they were providing a narrative of their identity. These narratives were analysed to discover common expressions of identity and to observe difference of selection, plotting and narration by individuals or groups.

I further analysed the narratives using a two-pronged approach in order to adequately present clusters of belonging and, thus, a plurality of EAC identities in North-east Congo. Firstly, I explored a number of words in Swahili that were frequently repeated in interview as migrants sought to express their sense of home within the EAC during the process of migration and resettlement. These words provide a hermeneutical group of identity signifiers held by almost all Anglicans from which the various religious identities of different groups within the EAC can be ascertained. They appear in interview narratives embedded in stories that demonstrate their worth as identity signifiers. They indicate a range of events and ideas through which identity is signalled. Analysing the terms made it evident that some words were selected by a large and diverse group of Anglicans for describing Anglican belonging. Others were used by smaller groups. More significant was the variety of cross-interpretation of these words through which different groups asserted their alternative identities. These hermeneutical terms and the events

---

[29] For more detail on research methods used see Emma Wild-Wood, "Se Débrouiller or the Art of Serendipity in Oral Research," *History in Africa* 34 (2007) and "An Introduction to an Oral History and Archive Project by the Anglican Church of Congo," *History in Africa* 28 (2001).

[30] Stephen Cornell, "That's the Story of our Life," in *We are a People*, 42.

they indicated had particular social meanings for EAC members that they variously plotted together depending on circumstance. For example, hierarchical and liturgical order was selected to provide a base of belonging for most Anglicans but the meaning of such an order was contested through the plotting of it with various identity signifiers which were used to interpret this order.

The second prong of my approach was to use the contested interpretation of the hermeneutical group of words to problematise the identity issues of migration, gender, generation, ethnicity and nationalism as they impinged on religious identity and its convergence with migration. Religious identity highlights contested issues of power between groups within the EAC and thus provides an entrance to the analysis of social divisions of power. The detailed analysis of the interviews from historical and hermeneutical perspectives demonstrates that religious identities are subjective, personal, hybrid and open to change.

The Anglican Church of Congo

> . . . when [Anglican] Christianity did establish itself . . . it came not as the conquering world religion but in its popular form, in the hands of . . . migrants responding to locally based need and struggles.[31]

Add the word "Anglican" to David Maxwell's words and his description of the establishment of Christianity among the Hwesa is equally valid for the development of the EAC in the North-east of Congo. It is the "popular form" of Anglicanism spread by migrants and the local "needs and struggles" which are the subjects of this study. The Anglican Church has often been understood to migrate with British interests around the world and has frequently been seen as "incorrigibly English."[32] The parish structure of Anglicanism is founded on bounded geographical space over which a bishop and priests have oversight. Thus it can be perceived to be static rather than fluid, more influenced by roots than by routes. Its expansion has rarely been associated with the mass movement of people, or of grassroots commitment to its governance and liturgy, or as a response to local issues.[33] This study attempts to address

---

[31] Maxwell, *Christians and Chiefs in Zimbabwe*, 53.
[32] Kevin Ward, *A History of Global Anglicanism* (Cambridge, Cambridge University Press, 2006), 2.
[33] Ibid., 9.

that balance. It attempts to understand the socio-religious dynamics among members rather than critique its theology, liturgy or governance, issues that have been addressed by Congolese scholars themselves.[34] It analyses the corporate identity of EAC members and their articulation of EAC identity and identities rather than the official pronouncements of the EAC as an institution. It recognises the dilemma faced by many Anglican migrants who desired the familiar, static and bounded but whose lives were influenced by movement and change. The church grew through the initiative of its members who made of it a 'home' from which they expressed their religious beliefs and practices, accepted or changed their cultural customs, and located them in their immediate social milieu. One response to these local needs was the expression of pride in membership of the global network of Anglican provinces. Although this study emphasises local rather than transnational belonging, attachment to the Anglican Communion will be shown to inform EAC identity. Thus a brief explanation of the EAC in its national and international context is appropriate here.

The EAC was introduced to the peoples on the Semeliki escarpment from 1896 through the ministry of Apolo Kivebulaya and other Ganda. They had become Anglican Christians because of the work of the Church Missionary Society (CMS), an agency founded by Church of England members that had been working among the Ganda since 1878. Many Ganda accepted Christianity and took it, with all its spiritual, social and political associations, to neighbouring kingdoms,[35] including the area west of the Semeliki River that was loosely under British influence until 1910 when it came under the jurisdiction of the Belgians. For fifty years after 1910 the EAC remained a small church with close links to the Church of Uganda (COU) and the Episcopalian Churches of Rwanda and Burundi. The growth of the EAC from the 1960s was, largely, the result of the migration of members. In 1992 it became an independent province within the Anglican Communion with its own Archbishop. By 2000 it had spread through Ituri, North and South

---

[34] For example, Dirokpa Balufuga Fidèle, "Liturgie anglicane et Inculturation, Hier, Aujourd'hui et Demain: Regard sur la Célébration eucharistique en République Démocratique du Congo" (PhD, Université Laval, 2001) and Titre Ande, "Authority in the Anglican Church of Congo: The Influence of Political Models of Authority and the Potential of 'Life-Community Ecclesiology' for Good Governance" (PhD Birmingham University, 2003).

[35] Louise Pirouet, *Black Evangelists, the spread of Christianity in Uganda: 1891–1914* (London, Rex Collings, 1978).

Kivu, Maniema, Katanga and the Kasaïs and around Kisangani and Kinshasa, from where it spread to Brazzaville. Current EAC membership is approximately 500,000 in a country of about 52 million people. Two EAC dioceses cover the area of the migrations studied in this book: the dioceses of Boga (Ituri and Haut Uélé) and Nord-Kivu.[36] The area is over 100,000km², stretching from the Sudanese border in the north to Lake Edward in the south, along almost the entire length of Uganda. It encompasses the Congo side of the Rwenzori Mountains and Lake Albert, and the Ituri forest as far west as Isiro. It is a fertile, mineral-rich area with a population impoverished by colonial occupation, dictatorship and war.

The EAC is a member of the Protestant 'umbrella' organisation, the *Eglise du Christ au Congo* (ECC) which has a membership of about 29% of the population of Congo. Roman Catholics are estimated to account for 49% of the population and 18% of the population are African Initiated Church (AIC) members, with a large number of these being Kimbanguists.[37] Political and economic mismanagement and corruption during the dictatorship of President Mobutu Sese Seko (1965–1997) caused decline in the country's infrastructure and services. By the 1990s, the churches in Congo were the most effective vehicles of civil society. Religious institutions ran 85% of schools and half the health zones, as well as many hospitals and clinics outside those zones.[38] They often offered only the most basic of services but for the Congolese it connected religious identity, which had always been public, with modern civic identity. The EAC played its part in providing health care, education and agricultural development in the areas in which it operated. By 2000 Congo was in the throes of factionalised, internal warfare which killed an estimated four million people,[39] and further eroded services and infrastructure. The war was at its most acute in Anglican areas of the North-east from 2001 to 2004 and, therefore, is mentioned only briefly in chapter eight.

---

[36] Boga diocese was divided to form Aru diocese in 2006. Nord-Kivu diocese is smaller than the province of the same name.

[37] David Barrett, et al., *World Christian Encyclopaedia: A comparative study of churches and religions in the modern world, AD 1900–2000, vol. 1.* (Oxford, Oxford University Press), 211–216.

[38] Winsome Leslie, *Zaire: Continuity and Political Change in an Oppressive State* (Colorado, Westview, 1993), 78 and 84.

[39] International Rescue Committee, "Mortality in the Democratic Republic of Congo: Results from a Nation-wide Survey" (April 2003), ii.

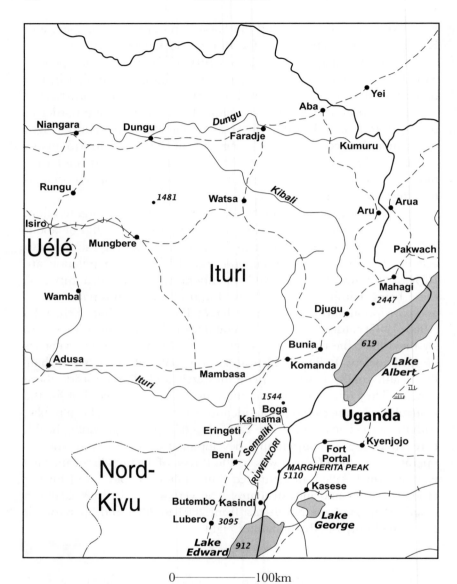

Illustration 1 Map of North-east Congo[40]

[40] Adapted from http://www.lib.utexas.edu/maps/africa/congo-demrep-rel97jpg University of Texas libraries.

Chapter outlines

The book is divided into eight further chapters. The next chapter analyses the rural identity of the EAC in Congo between 1896 and 1960. It outlines its historical beginnings and social context. It shows that the EAC, geographically constrained to a small, isolated area developed a local ecclesiastical identity which bolstered the local influence of the Hema among neighbouring groups and allied church adherence closely with ethnic identity. It is this expression of Christian identity that influenced migration, this identity that was understood as 'home' for many migrants, and yet this same identity that was contested through the effects of migration.

Chapters three and four continue a chronological study of the EAC after independence and introduce themes that emerge when identity was renegotiated as a result of migration. Chapter three traces the spread of the EAC from the late 1960s as a result of the migration of Anglicans from the Semeliki escarpment to the growing urban centres; a move encouraged by the modernising elements of Christian identity. Ethnic identity as a narrative of belonging and group cohesion was heightened during this period and expressed through an attempt to build a home-from-home and replicate the conservative elements of the rural EAC. Second generation migrants wished to assert a religious identity that better fitted with their urban identity. They challenged their parents' sense of 'home'. The chapter ends with an analysis of their use of national identity in their discourse of religious belonging. The study of contrasting narratives of parents and their children demonstrate that migrant congregations often became the site of a generational struggle to define the identity of the Anglican Church.

Chapter four shows the effects of trans-border migration on the north-eastern border of Congo by those who fled Uganda with the fall of Idi Amin in 1979 and returned to their villages of origin. Their experience of prior labour migration meant these northern migrants were less conservative in their attachment to Anglicanism than migrants from the escarpment. They established the EAC in response to their need for a religious expression that allowed them freedom to develop socially and spiritually. The development of a religious identity within the EAC enabled them to negotiate a sense of belonging and to re-order their home. Their appropriation of an Anglican identity in order to address their local concerns further widened the possibilities for belonging within the EAC.

The growth of the EAC caused external and internal conflicts. Chapters five and six examine the competing identities that emerged as a result of two of these conflicts. Chapter five shows the influence of the difficult relationship with the Communauté Evangelique du Centre de l'Afrique (CECA 20) church on the identity of the EAC. Migrants reordered their sense of 'home' in response to their reception by CECA.

Chapter six provides an analysis of the consensual and contested expressions of faith altered by migration as radical Revivalists challenged EAC assumptions about religious identity from within the church. For Revivalists the experience of migration prompted reflections upon its possible divine purpose. They redefined the value of relocation by expressing Christian life as one of migrating for the Gospel rather than establishing an earthly home, whilst other EAC members expected the church to offer unity, stability and homeliness in the context of their mobility in a disordered society.

Chapters seven and eight emphasise the discrepancies of gendered and generational power within the EAC in the late 1980s and 1990s and demonstrate the ways in which women and young people used migrant experiences to challenge practices and power structures and thus alter EAC identity. Migrant women used Christian women's groups to negotiate new roles for themselves or cling to old ones. A significant event that highlighted the emergence of a new identity for Anglican women is recounted and deconstructed in chapter seven. It reflects attachment to different locations as 'home'. It demonstrates that second generation migrants became increasingly reluctant to see denominational loyalty as being an exclusive factor in their identity and made significant alliances with other Christians. Anglican youth developed their identity through the youth group, contemporary music and charismatic manifestations. They sought spiritual freedom and development and challenged the increasingly ethnocentric public discourse in the 1990s. Chapter eight analyses different aspects of the youth movement employing songs as well as narratives to chart identity shift in response to the growing ethnocentricity in the violence at the end of the 1990s and in order to embrace contemporary Pentecostal forms of worship.

The final chapter summarises the influence of migration upon African Christian identity, underscoring its place as a force for change and not simply for growth. It examines the way in which identity is narrated and 'home' is constructed, through negotiated positions on ethnicity, nationality, gender and generation. It studies the contested relations between the global, national and local and between the traditional and the modern. It discusses the place of Anglican identity within contemporary Congolese expressions of Christianity.

Conclusion

As the succeeding chapters follow the EAC from its roots on the escarpment along the migratory routes taken by its members, a story of the development of a particular Christian identity unfolds. It is unique to Congo and yet it highlights issues pertinent to Christian identity elsewhere in Africa. Migration aided the growth of the EAC and altered its identity. It encouraged greater denominational diversity in the areas to which members migrated, and heightened generation and gender tensions, whilst creating an atmosphere of greater co-operation between different ethnic groups. Its study will, I trust, enable an appreciation of the socio-religious dynamics in the commonplace but largely untold story of shifting populations and altering religious identities in Africa.

CHAPTER TWO

"THEIR OWN CHURCH:"
L' EGLISE ANGLICANE DU CONGO, 1896–1960

Introduction

In 1960, when Congo gained independence from Belgium, the *Eglise Anglicane du Congo* (EAC) was a small, rural church at the edge of the forest on the Semeliki escarpment overlooking the Rwenzori Mountains. Within Congo, it was geographically isolated and socially marginal. Members of the EAC, however, regarded the church with affection and pride. They had moulded its rites and tenets, appropriating them into their culture, and they appreciated the education and health care that was introduced alongside Christian worship.

This chapter provides an historical understanding of the making of EAC identity between 1896 and 1960. It analyses the introduction of the Anglican Church into Congo and demonstrates the place of the EAC in the wider context of church affairs in Congo. It provides a background to the issues of gender, generation, ethnicity and nationality that will be discussed later and introduces the first hermeneutical words of Anglican self-identity. Finally, it argues that the Christian message initially appeared new and contrary to escarpment culture but that, within a generation, Anglican Christianity became part of the dominant culture. To use the prominent metaphor of this study, it made itself at home on the Semeliki escarpment whilst also reshaping that home. It is this Christianised escarpment culture which was altered by the migrations studied in subsequent chapters.

A background of movement

The events of this chapter take place in the colonial period against a background of flux among Congolese societies. Geographical mobility and interaction with emerging powerful social forces continually altered the identity of the peoples living along the escarpment. The influence of Christianity on their socio-religious structures and practices should be understood in this light.

About 1800, as a result of an internal dispute, a group now known as the Southern Hema[1] migrated from Bunyoro to the Semeliki escarpment area, south-west of Lake Albert. The Hema are Nilotic pastoralists who originally migrated from the Nile basin to Bunyoro. They speak a Bantu language, Hema or Runyoro. Migration to the escarpment led to a greater dependence on agriculture. Like other immigrant aristocracies,[2] the Hema gained influence over ethnic groups with less stratified political structures, the Ngiti (Lendu-Bindi), Lese Mbuti (pygmies), Nyali, and Talinga, who were already present in the area, establishing client relations with them. Their southern neighbours, the Nande, are a Bantu group who also migrated to the Rwenzori region from Bunyoro. Their society was led by clan heads who were rain-makers and diviners, and who, by the nineteenth century, had achieved a greater hierarchy of power and a royal class similar to that of the Hema. Thus both groups held notions of stratified governance and subordination as vital social values.[3]

In the nineteenth century all the peoples of the area had to contend with the effects of European and Arab migration. Nande and Hema who allied themselves with Arab ivory traders operating between Maniema and the Semeliki plain possessed new power in the form of arms and commodities and negotiated positions of political and territorial influence.[4] Mutinies, border disputes and ethnic antagonism stirred up by colonial policy brought more violence and uncertainty in the region. Between 1910 and 1912 the escarpment peoples came under effective Belgian rule and their social systems were institutionalised, with chiefs expected to perform colonial functions for the political ends of the colonisers. The influence of the church brought further change. Missionaries challenged cultural norms, brought new ideas and skills and established new institutions. In presenting the historical background to the post-independence migration this chapter will introduce themes of change and movement, contested interests and shifting identities.

---

[1] The Northern Hema, or Gegere, live north-west of Lake Albert. They have intermarried with neighbouring Lendu and speak their language. They are not prominent in this study.

[2] Aidan Southall, *Alur Society: A Study in Processes and Types of Domination* (Cambridge, W. Heffer & Sons, 1953), 229.

[3] John Beattie, *The Nyoro State* (Oxford, Clarendon Press, 1971), 121–122.

[4] J. E. Nelson, *Christian Missionizing and Social Tranformation: A History of Conflict and Change in Eastern Zaire* (New York, Praeger, 1992), 20.

"Books as spears": Apolo Kivebulaya's mission

Apolo Kivebulaya, a Ganda evangelist and, later, priest, is credited
with the foundation of the EAC. He was in the employ of the Church
Missionary Society (CMS), an evangelical Anglican society founded
in 1799, which had been working in Buganda since 1877. As a result
of this the EAC became part of the Anglican Church in Uganda.
CMS had overseen the rapid growth of an indigenous church that
had spread into neighbouring kingdoms through the work of a large
body of Ganda evangelists like Apolo.[5] Apolo first visited the Hema
of Boga on the Semeliki escarpment in December 1896 when the area
was under British jurisdiction.[6] Although he was not the first missionary to the area west of the Semeliki River,[7] Apolo's ministry there was
the longest and most successful. His life and work were the subject of
numerous missionary biographies which heralded Apolo as an example
of the success of 'native agency' in spreading Christianity and proof
of the maturity of the Ugandan church.[8] His imprint on the EAC
influenced its development for the next century and he is venerated as
a saint in Uganda and Congo. The myth-making of his life and work
has enhanced the EAC's strong sense of identity.

Apolo followed the pattern of evangelism he knew from Buganda;
a pattern which fitted the culture of the ruling class. He targeted
Omukama[9] Tabaro and his entourage through living with and teaching
children of family heads in a manner analogous to the Ganda custom
of educating young men by sending them to the household of a chief.[10]

---

[5] Louise Pirouet, *Black Evangelists, the spread of Christianity in Uganda: 1891–1914*
(London, Rex Collings, 1978), 12–19.

[6] A. Tucker, "The Spiritual Expansion of Buganda; the Narrative of a Journey to
Toro", *Intelligencier* (February 1899), 108–111.

[7] Sedulaka Zabunamakwata and Petero Nsugba worked in Boga for a few months
earlier in 1896 but strained relations with *Omukama* Tabaro curtailed their stay. Sedulaka
went to Boga with Apolo but later returned to Toro. Popular biographies imply that
Apolo found little in the way of Christian faith when he and Sedulaka arrived. However,
A. B. Fisher mentions that during an 'itineration' to Boga in 1896 he found 'twenty-
five men and women who could read a New Testament and a number of learners'.
A. Fisher, *Extracts from the Annual Letters of Missionaries* (London: CMS, 1897), 237.

[8] A. B. Lloyd, *Apolo of the Pygmy Forest* (London, CMS, 1923); *More About Apolo*
(London, CMS, 1928); *Apolo the Pathfinder—Who Follows?* (London, CMS, 1934); W. J.
Roome, *Apolo, The Apostle to the Pygmies* (London, Morgan & Scott, 1934); P. Yates, *Apolo in
Pygmyland*, (London, Highway Press, 1940); Margaret Sinker, *Into the Great Forest* (London,
Highway press, 1950); Anne Luck, *African Saint* (London, SCM, 1963).

[9] *Omukama* or *mukama* is variously translated as chief, lord and king.

[10] W. A. Anderson, *The Church in East Africa, 1940–1974* (Dodoma, Central Tanganika Press, 1988), 23.

Illustration 2   Photograph of Apolo Kivebulaya teaching—about 1930.
Taken by A. T. Schofield.

He taught them to read in Luganda until reading sheets were available
in the vernacular of Runyoro/Rutoro about 1900.[11] He introduced
new approaches to health, sanitation and ascetics by promoting western medicine, well-ventilated houses and the growing of flowers. He
advocated a new moral and spiritual code that challenged polygamy,
drinking, smoking and the veneration of ancestors. In the first few
months of evangelism some Hema responded positively to instruction.[12]
The first baptisms took place as early as 4th April 1897.[13] Within two
years there was a small church in Boga with literate members, a sizeable group of adherents and a sympathetic chief.

From Boga Apolo evangelised the surrounding peoples who had client relationships with the Hema. Apolo kept a diary in Luganda that
provides insights into the priorities of his ministry and the practices
he introduced to the area. The excerpts below from 1925 are typical
of many entries:

> April 13th: I started my journey to the forest to go and spread the Gospel.
> I reached Bukogwa...I prayed with them in the church and there were
> 32 people.
>
> April 14th: We reached Bwakadi. We found the teacher with 15 people
> waiting for us on the way. We had prayers with them in the church.
>
> April 15th: We saw them reading. I talked with them to encourage
> them...Then I went to teach the Pygmies. I found them waiting for us,
> so I started teaching them. There were 15 of them...I then went on to
> Kainama. At the teacher, Edward's, we found them waiting for us, and
> there were 30 people. We had prayers with them in the church.[14]

Apolo established chapels over an area of a radius of three days walk, or
about 60 km, from Boga. Praying and reading were the activities Apolo
oversaw; praying followed the *Book of Common Prayer* and reading was
based on the liturgy and the Bible. These two activities were central
to Apolo's understanding of Christianity. His own preaching came out
of his praying and reading. Apolo believed they provided security for
life. He says that he told one group:

---

[11] MU, Anne Luck file, letter from R. Fisher, 17 November 1957.
[12] MU, Apolo Kivebulaya's diary, 25 December 1896.
[13] RDO, Baptismal Register, Book One.
[14] MU, Apolo's diary, 14–16 April 1925.

...that they should love books as they are the spears which protect us. Therefore the one without a book was really without a spear.[15]

In the political and social upheaval of the region at the time his audience understood the value of trying a new skill to face the challenges of living in a disordered colonial state.

Apolo also founded schools, built and maintained small church buildings, prayed for the sick, handed out medicines and accompanied British missionaries.[16] The Christian message Apolo preached came as a package; 'the Gospel of Christ' was explained firstly through literacy, but also through new ways of healing, and the construction of community buildings, all of which followed the Ugandan pattern. Those who accepted his message accepted a new set of priorities in their lives. The young church learnt, as an integral part of the new religion, to aspire to literacy and health care as modern services, introduced by Europeans, which were expected to improve the quality of life. Elsewhere,[17] I have suggested that the underlying appeal of the Christianity Apolo brought was its appeal to both spiritual and temporal power and its offer of modern skills and practices to tackle the rapidly changing sociopolitical situation. It corresponded with the escarpment worldview that considered all power to come from God and thus believed that social influence was divinely ordered.

Using the Ganda evangelism model meant that Apolo attracted a following of young people whom he catechised and taught to read. They worked alongside him, accompanying him in his journeys into the forest and becoming *walimu* (teachers) in the small chapels.[18] Growth in the early EAC was largely driven by young people with a strong personal loyalty to Apolo. Basimasi Kyakuhaire, mentioned in Apolo's diary,[19] provides an example of the life of these young *walimu*. In interview in 2000 she explained that, because her father was in the first group to be baptised in Boga, she was baptised almost immediately after her birth in 1906. Probably about 1916 she went daily to Apolo's house

---

[15] Ibid., 3 June 1925.

[16] Ibid., 14 December 1915, 12 April 1917, Rose Kaheru, Bunia, Swahili, 16 September 2000.

[17] Emma Wild-Wood, "Saint Apolo from Europe or 'What's in a Luganda Name?'" *Church History*, 77 (2008), 105–127.

[18] Ndahura Bezaleri. "L'Implantation de l'Anglicanisme au Zaire, 1896–1972" (Licence en Théologie, Faculté Protestante de Kinshasa, 1974), 60.

[19] MU Apolo's Diary, 17 July 1924.

for lessons, early in the morning and in the late afternoon. There were
between twenty and thirty girls alongside the boys. Her father later sent
her to Fort Portal to study and she returned to Boga as a *mwalimu*. She
married another *mwalimu* and both of them continued working in their
different chapel/schools until after Apolo died. Her life illustrates the
intimate connection between Christianity and the new skills of literacy
and book learning. The word *mwalimu* is used both for catechist and
school-teacher because, in the early days, the tasks were interchangeable.
Basimasi also insisted that, so complete was her family's conversion to
this modern Christian lifestyle, she had no experience of traditional
Hema religious or healing practices.[20] Such an assertion suggests that
another attraction of the new socio-religious system for the first converts may have been its difference from the old.[21] Basimasi's story also
demonstrates that women were accepted as leaders in the early years
of the church alongside men.

A report by the Bishop of Uganda, John J. Willis, after his visit to
the EAC in 1931 provides an overview of the church situation. He
was full of praise for Apolo and the other teachers. He mentioned six
ethnic groups within a three day walk from Boga who had forty-two
churches between them, with fifty-eight teachers and 1,426 baptised
Christians.[22] Willis confirmed 274 people, 116 of whom were peoples
living in the forest; the rest are presumably Hema. From this description it is clear that the EAC was a predominantly lay church and that
leadership was predominantly local. Most of the fifty-eight teachers
had been children whom Apolo had befriended. However, Willis noted
that the Christian development seen in Uganda, even in places where
the work started later than in Boga, was not apparent in this corner
of Congo. By that he meant that there were no 'native born clergy',
or even senior *walimu*, the school was of a lower level and there was
no continuous medical work. The translation of the Bible and the
Prayer Book had not been carried out in the languages of the other
escarpment peoples. Although Apolo seems to have facilitated some
translation,[23] the process of vernacularisation, through which Biblical
concepts are transformed into local ideas during translation and usage,[24]

---

[20] Basimasi Kyakuhaire, Komanda, Swahili, 21 September 2000.
[21] Pirouet, *Black Evangelists*, 198.
[22] COU. 2bp10.1, 1931. In 1933 Willis claimed that there were eighty teachers.
[23] MU. Apolo's Diary, 14 March 1926.
[24] Lamin Sanneh, *Translating the Message: The Missionary Impact on Culture* (Maryknoll,
Orbis, 1989), chapter five.

had effectively stopped with the Hema. Willis considered that the kind of change he had experienced in Uganda was hampered by the socio-political situation in Congo.

"Under particular observation:" the socio-political situation

Conversion took place on the cusp of colonial control. In 1896 the Semeliki escarpment was part of a contested area under the British sphere of influence but outside effective colonial control. A degree of social and political disorder buffeted the area. The Hema elite sought alliances with larger and more influential social units. *Omukama* Tabaro who, in the 1890s, invited Ganda evangelists to Boga, was seeking to ally himself with the ascendant Toro kingdom where the evangelists were based.[25] Bunyoro's regional influence was waning and Toro, with its Christian *Omukama*, Kasagama, and its good standing with the British and the Ganda, was the rising regional power.[26] It is likely that Tabaro regarded the political and religious interests of Kasagama as indivisible. Tabaro's own eventual conversion must be understood in this light.

As *omukama*, Tabaro's political role was seamlessly integrated with his social and religious roles. He was the active symbol of personal, social and spiritual meaning for the Hema. He was the representation and the protector of home. Thus corporate, spiritual well-being was for Tabaro intrinsic to political manoeuvring. He incarnated God's (*Ruhanga*) rule, uniting his people by being the intermediary between them and their ancestors. He ensured the continuation of ancestral rites, and protected sacred objects, like the royal drum, around which notions of corporate identity were formed.[27] The *omukama* and the royal class were expected to provide ritual, military and social organisation to the ordinary people who in turn provided tribute through agricultural labour. However, Tabaro's attempts at providing protection and maintaining unity were undermined by the European forces in the area. In 1897, 2,000 mutineers from Maniema fled their Belgian commander, twice passing through the area, looting and raping as they went. In 1899 King Leopold claimed the area as part of his Congo Free State. His

---

[25] Pirouet, *Black Evangelists*, 52.
[26] S. R. Karugire, *A Political History of Uganda* (Nairobi, Heinemann, 1980), 19–22.
[27] Isingoma Kahwa Henri, "La Notion traditionelle de la Communauté en Afrique noire et son Intergration dans la Vie ecclesiale (Cas de Banyoro en Republique du Zaïre)" (Maitrise en Théologie diss., Faculté de Théologie Evangélique de Bangui, 1989), 31.

Force Publique soldiers increased instability by forcing tribute from the local population. In 1901 Boga was temporarily under British control once again. The Congolese believed the British to be less harsh colonial masters than their Belgian counter-parts and many people moved into the area to escape taxation, forced labour and looting by the *Force Publique*.[28] Boga seems to have become a centre of rubber and ivory trade at this time.[29]

By 1910, however, the boundary commission had decided definitively that the colonial border should be drawn along the Semeliki River with the result that Boga came under Belgian government administration. The Belgians installed Sulemani Kalemesa as sub-chief of Boga under Bomera, chief of Irumu. This marked the introduction of the unpopular 'great chief' system as part of the Belgian policy of 'indirect rule'. It changed the local political landscape by adding greater stratification and solidified the internal and external relations of ethnic groups. Kalemesa was unsupportive of the EAC accusing it of British sympathies. This took its toll on the EAC. Between 1899 and 1915 Apolo only had brief visits to Boga. When he was permitted to stay in 1916 he found the small Christian community very much depleted and disheartened.[30] From then until his death in 1933 he spent much of his time on the escarpment but his work was hampered by government concerns over the legitimacy of the EAC.

The Belgian colonial authorities were suspicious of dealing directly with Africans and of permitting Protestants to work in the country. Their activities were subject to close surveillance. Government fears were heightened after the brief independent healing and preaching ministry of the Baptist, Simon Kimbangu, in Bas-Congo in 1921 which was seen as politically subversive.[31] The *Ministre des Colonies* sent a circular letter to the provinces warning of the Protestant tendency to "…organise indigenous churches, independent of the authority and control of missionaries from the white race."[32] The administrator

---

[28] Ndahura, "L'Implantation de l'Anglicanisme au Zaïre," 54.

[29] Foreign Office, "Official Report of the British Section of the Uganda-Congo Boundary Commission: 1907–1908" (London, Foreign Office, 1909), 8.

[30] MU Apolo's Diary, 12 January 1916 and 05 March 1916.

[31] M.-M. Munayi, "La Déportation et le Séjour des Kimbanguistes dans le Kasaï-Lukenie (1921–1960)" *Zaïre-Afrique* (1977): 555–6. Kimbangu's followers went underground emerging as a large African Initiated Church after independence.

[32] Quoted in G. Samba, "Tolérance religieuse et Intérêts politiques belges au Kibali-Ituri (1900–1940)," *Etudes Zaïroises* (1973): 106.

of Ituri reported back that Apolo was the only African church leader among the Protestant missions in the area and he would be "particularly observed".[33] Although nothing untoward about him was ever reported, the colonial administrators considered that there was now justification for a lack of co-operation with Apolo and the Boga mission.[34]

Legal representation of an organisation could only be made by westerners and, therefore, with no white missionary presence, Boga mission's legal status was at best ambiguous. The church suffered harassment by colonial authorities and British CMS missionaries were prevented from making regular pastoral visits until the 1930s.[35] The authorities were both fearful of independent minded Protestant Congolese and worried that they might lose their population to a neighbouring colonial power. The EAC was Protestant of British origins and African led—all deemed potential threats to Belgian control of Congo. Once the ban on CMS missionaries was lifted, and in order to legitimise the mission in Belgian eyes, at least one British missionary was resident in Boga for most of the years between 1934 and 1960. Most evangelism and teaching in small chapels continued to be done by Ugandans and Congolese.

The pre-independence context of the EAC engendered an identity different to that of the quasi-established COU of which it was still a part. It often had to act independently of its mother church and adapt to different local and national circumstances. When the escarpment became Congo territory the connection between Anglicanism and Britain was detrimental to its growth. Its geographical position rendered it remote but colonial boundaries made it seem alien. It is to these different circumstances, particularly the ecclesiastical circumstances of the colonial context, that we turn now.

Colonial trinity

The Roman Catholic Church was the largest religious institution in colonial Congo and was closely allied to the Belgian administration. The situation of unequal patronage from the state affected the religious demographics of the country. Between 1885 and 1908 King Leopold II of the Belgians ruled Congo Free State as his personal property. To

---

[33] Ibid., 107.
[34] COU 2bp10.1, letter 2 March 1926 & report 1931.
[35] COU 2bp10.1, letter 27 October 1925.

ensure loyalty he supported Belgian Catholic mission societies by grant-
ing them large and numerous land concessions and funding. Protestants
received few concessions, were expected to pay heavy taxes, and were
impeded by local authorities.[36] With the Belgian bias for its own Catholic
societies, companies operating in Congo invited Catholic societies to
provide chaplaincies and work in their schools. There developed what
has been termed the 'trinity' of Belgian control, a close and mutually
beneficial relationship between state, business and the church.[37] In 1908
the governance of Congo passed to the Belgian government. There
were fluctuations in the details of colonial policy but the Catholic
Church remained dominant.[38] Government and business relied on the
Catholic missions to educate the majority of clerks and company agents
they employed. Congolese were aware of the advantages for personal
advancement in education, health care and employment available by
allying themselves with the Catholic Church. For Congolese wanting
to make the best of the colonial situation, the Catholic Church offered
the most acceptable way to personal development and modernisation.
However, it took the Catholic Church some time to establish a presence
in north-east Congo.

Catholic missionaries in Toro observed the progress of the EAC with
concern[39] but their trip to Boga in 1897 met with the consequences of
the Maniema mutiny and the area was considered too volatile for a
mission.[40] It was not until 1906 that the first small mission was founded
in Nord-Kivu, by the Fathers of the Sacred Heart. Ituri was part of
the prefecture of the Missionaries to Africa, better known as the 'White
Fathers.' Their first station in the area was at the mines in Kilo in
1911.[41] Schools, hospitals, agricultural and vocational centres sprung
up rapidly. Many mission stations in the area were established in direct
competition to the Protestants. Mgr. Alphonse Matthijsen, who worked

---

[36] Leopold favoured a few Protestant societies that supported his claim on Congo
territory. M. D. Markowitz, *Cross and Sword: The Political Role of Christian Missions in the
Belgian Congo, 1908–1960* (Stanford, Hoover Institution Press, 1973), 4–6.

[37] Patrick Manning, *Francophone Sub-Saharan Africa, 1880–1995*, 2nd ed. (Cambridge,
Cambridge University Press, 1998), 76.

[38] These fluctuations depended on the politics of the parties in power in Belgium.
M. D. Markowitz, *Cross and Sword*, 32–37.

[39] Gerard Malherbe, "La Mission au Lac Albert (Ituri-Zaire) 1911–1934" (PhD,
Louvain la Neuve, 1976), 1342.

[40] P. Van Roy, *Vie de son Excellence Mgr. Alphonse Matthijsen, Evêque de Bunia, 1890–1963*
(Bunia, Diocese of Bunia, 1970), 6–8.

[41] Ibid., 10–11.

in the area between 1916 and 1963 was concerned about the influence of the Protestants and the heresies he believed they propounded, colourfully comparing them to the many crocodiles swallowing fish at the mouth of the Semeliki River.[42]

In the last years of colonialism the Catholic Church became less antagonistic towards its Protestant rivals. It was so influential in the country that it had little need to compete with Protestant missions and largely ignored them. Thus it does not feature greatly in this study, although its presence remains a backdrop to the subject because of its influence on the majority of Congolese. By independence over half of Congolese in Ituri considered themselves Catholics,[43] with a similar amount in Nord-Kivu. There was little sign of religious independency in the region until the stringent colonial laws governing religious adherence were lifted at Independence. Most of the rest of the population considered themselves Protestants. It is to their missionary societies that we turn now.

Crocodiles swallowing fish

The relationship between the EAC and neighbouring Protestant churches, and the role of the Congo Protestant Council are significant in the historic shaping of Congolese Anglican identity. King Leopold's efforts to hobble Protestant work in Congo did not prevent a large number of Protestant missions entering the country. The EAC had three neighbouring missions with which it would interact and which would increasingly affect the definition of its own identity. The Unevangelised Africa Mission (UAM), subsequently the Conservative Baptist Foreign Missionary Society (CBFMS), established a station at Katwe near Butembo in 1928. The Immanuel Mission (IM) created by American Brethren in 1926 was based in Nyankunde, 45 km west of Bunia,[44] and established other stations in the Ituri forest. The largest and most influential Protestant Mission in the area was the African Inland Mission (AIM) whose church became known after independence as *Communauté*

---

[42] Gerard Malherbe, "La Mission au Lac Albert," 1329. Apolo Kivebulaya believed that a Catholic priest was spreading stories that he was a British spy, MU Apolo's diary, 07 June 1917.

[43] Samba, *Phenomène d'Ethnicitie et Conflits ethno-politics*, 230.

[44] E. M. Braekman, *Histoire du Protestantisme au Congo* (Bruxelles, Librarie des Eclaireurs Unionistes, 1961), 261–2.

Evangelique du Centre de l'Afrique (CECA 20). AIM was established in the USA in 1895 and had started work in Congo from its base in Kenya.[45] It established a mission station among the Alur near Mahagi in 1912, among the Lugbara in 1917, and the Kakwa in 1924. In 1932 it took over the Oicha mission in Nord-Kivu from UAM.[46] AIM was the first Protestant missionary society to work in Bunia, preaching regularly to migrant workers from 1935.[47] It had a Congolese catechist there and a plot of land on which to build a chapel by 1937. It was in this chapel that most of the early Anglican migrants to Bunia were to worship on Sunday mornings. After independence Anglicans established their own churches in all these areas, a situation that sparked the conflict analysed in later chapters.

There were some obvious similarities between CMS and the other three missions. They were all evangelical, all desirous of evangelising Africans. They all upheld the importance of being able to read Scripture, and aimed to produce vernacular translations of the Bible. They all provided services for local people beyond simple evangelism. They were all, at this time, antagonistic to the Catholic Church and concerned about its influence. Missionary personnel in all societies had a similar code of personal morality and had been influenced by the Holiness Movement that emphasised faith in victory over sin, enabling a 'higher life' of intense piety, and a radical trust in God rather than one's own efforts. This spirituality encouraged support for Revivals and Faith Missions.[48] As a result they, at times, would collaborate closely together. An example of missionary co-operation pertinent to this study was that between CMS and AIM. In 1918 AIM accepted an invitation by CMS to work in West Nile in Uganda among the Alur, Lugbara, Kakwa and Mardi provided it followed Anglican structures. West Nile Protestants all became Anglicans in the COU brought up with the Prayer Book, priests and bishops within a conservative evangelical ethos, which emphasised primary evangelism, instilled strong discipline into the church, and provided fewer social services than elsewhere in

---

[45] Dick Anderson, *We Felt Like Grasshoppers* (Nottingham, Crossway Books 1994), 17–19.

[46] Kenneth Richardson, *Garden of Miracles: A History of the African Inland Mission* (London, Victory Press, 1968), ix–xi.

[47] Muzuro Kana Wai, "Croissance de l'Eglise locale de la Communauté évangelique an Centre de L'Afrique, Section de Bunia" (Diplôme de Graduat diss., ISTB, 1982), 21–23.

[48] D. W. Bebbington, *Evangelicalism in Modern Britain: A History from the 1730s to the 1980s* (London, Unwin Hyman, 1989), 150–159.

Uganda. On the Congolese side of the border AIM worked with Alur, Lugbara, Kakwa and others providing a similar ethos but without an episcopalian structure.

AIM, IM and CBFMS all came from a new wave of missionary societies which emerged from the late nineteenth century. They were Faith Missions influenced by the North American fundamentalist movement that upheld belief in biblical inerrancy and criticised the materialism and modernity of western culture. These missions were anti-clerical and anti-establishment: attitudes that made them ecclesiastically and missiologically wary of the episcopalian Church of England and its societies, like CMS. They emphasised the importance of evangelism above all other missionary activity and held strict standards for their African converts.[49] Individuals were expected to make a personal 'decision for Christ' and demonstrate this by an obvious life-style change. Infant baptism, as practised by Anglicans, could not be countenanced. This ethos demanded of the first converts a more radical break with their own culture than was expected in the EAC.

These missions built dispensaries but they regarded further education as a distraction from evangelism and as an enticement to 'worldliness'.[50] In North-east Congo, at least, government bias towards the Catholic Church was not the only reason why Protestant educational standards were low. When government subsidies became available to Protestant missions in 1946, AIM applied for them reluctantly and after much delay, worried that this course of action might distract them from their priorities of evangelism and Bible teaching.[51] CBFMS did not change its schools in accordance with State requirements. It wanted to maintain the separation of Church and State and feared sullying education with worldly interests, like good job prospects and salaries. The issue resulted in an acrimonious dispute that split the church in 1963 because many Congolese wanted an education recognised in secular employment.[52] The missions were concerned about the evils of modernity and development. They did not want to change African culture by introducing western ideas or technology which they believed had affected European

---

[49] Stephen Morad, "The Founding Principles of the Africa Inland Mission and their Interaction with the African Context in Kenya" (PhD, Edinburgh University, 1997), 119–120, 218–219.

[50] Ibid., 333.

[51] Richardson, *Garden of Miracles*, 162.

[52] Syaikomia Nganza, "Les Principes d'Organisation de la Communauté baptiste au Kivu" (Diplôme de Graduat diss., ISTB, 1982), 12–14.

and American culture adversely. The three missions developed a rigorous church discipline in which excommunication and physical punishment were meted upon converts who broke the strict moral code or returned to traditional lifestyles.[53]

The most striking difference during the colonial period between CMS and the Faith Missions was the issue of indigenous leadership. Concerned to maintain what they considered the highest moral and spiritual standards the Faith missionaries were unwilling to hand over control of the church to Africans whom they feared were not mature enough to lead.[54] Even though colonial policy dictated the presence, from 1934, of white missionaries in Boga, the EAC was given a great deal of autonomy in running its pastoral affairs. In Congo, by 1955 there were only 452 ordained Protestant Congolese pastors compared with 2,052 western missionaries.[55] The tiny EAC had four ordained Congolese pastors, one ordained Ugandan, and a British missionary couple in this year. The indigenous leadership of EAC was vital in shaping its identity (as shall become apparent later in this chapter) and stood in stark contrast to the neighbouring mission churches.

Despite their differences, Protestant missions throughout Congo worked together from 1902 in the Congo Protestant Council (CPC), the precursor to the post-independence *Eglise du Christ au Congo* (ECC). Protestant missionaries perceived the need of presenting a united front before the colonial state and the Catholic Church. They also wanted to establish greater collaboration in their common goal of spreading the gospel. Protestants often claimed that they did not intend to spread denominationalism whilst evangelising Africa.[56] To avoid it, the CPC facilitated the division of Congo into geographically distinct Protestant spheres of influence. This missionary comity meant, for example, that the EAC could not operate in the areas designated for AIM or IM. Breaching the 'no overlap' principle by working in an area designated for an another organisation was considered to be competitive rather than ecumenical, a waste of resources, and a threat to inter-Protestant

---

[53] Edjidra Leko, "Histoire du Catholicisme dans la Zone d'Aru de 1925 à 1990" (Licence, ISP, Bunia, 1996), 33.

[54] Morad, "The Founding Principles of the Africa Inland Mission," 421–422.

[55] Markowitz, *Cross and Sword*, 112–4.

[56] Philippe Kabongo-Mbaya, *L'Eglise du Christ au Zaïre: Formation et adaption d'un protestantisme en situation de dictature* (Paris, Karthala, 1992), 55.

relationships. The outworking of comity agreements, however, had a different effect to what was intended; denominational adherence was made along ethnic lines and so the Hema from Boga became Anglicans, whilst the Lugbara became CECA members. Ethnic and religious identities coalesced, reinforcing the colonial administration's ossification of what had been more fluid ethnic boundaries.

"A tradition like our one:" the EAC 1933–1960

Having studied the external church and state relations in Congo, analysis is now resumed of the Anglican Church on the Semeliki escarpment in the latter part of the colonial period. How did the peoples who had accepted Apolo's ministry develop the church in the years leading to political independence? What effect did indigenous leadership have on ecclesiastical identity? It will be shown that, faced with the limitations of geographical spread and colonial legitimacy outlined above, EAC members looked inwards, aiming to maintain the tradition which had been given to them by nurturing the ecclesiological model of Apolo's ministry but also adapting it to their own culture. This process, variously known as inculturation, contextualisation, localisation or indigenisation, is a complex phenomenon in which a new or alien structure or system is re-coded sufficiently for those who have adopted it to feel that it is part of their own culture. For the EAC, inculturation involved developing a local expression of an international movement. This process included the vernacular re-coding of Anglican structures and rites, the maintenance of power for traditional leaders and thus the continual marginalisation of disempowered groups. It is this indigenised form of global Christianity that the first migrants would call home and which other migrants found less homely.

Boga remained the centre of the EAC and, as a result, the Hema had a preponderant influence on leadership and decision making. The EAC adapted itself to the life of the peoples on the escarpment but through the dominant culture and language of the Hema. Until the 1970s the liturgy and the Bible remained in Runyoro/Rutoro, otherwise known as Hema, and thus there was a closer association with Hema culture than with any other. That the EAC was mediated through Hema meant a greater sense of ownership of the church for the Hema. One Hema explained:

> They know well the history of the first evangelist...how he learnt how
> to speak their own language—since at that time study was in their own
> language and they considered it their own religion.[57]

Escarpment leadership and vernacularisation were uneven from the
start, even though Apolo and others worked to make it less so. Christian
concepts and Anglican culture took more of a Hema form and less of
a Lese or Giti one. The school operated in Hema until 1950 when,
following colonial policy, Swahili was introduced.[58] The issue of language also favoured Hema catechists. A good knowledge of Hema was
essential to anyone who wanted further training in church work. Many
Nande, whose language and culture is similar, did learn the language
and became catechists. There were fewer Lese, Nyali, Ngiti and Talinga
catechists. Ven. Tabu Abembe, a Lese, learnt the catechism in Runyoro
and explained how the language was viewed:

> Runyoro was regarded as a biblical language, like Hebrew or Greek
> [laughs]...but the drawback was that the people who didn't know Runyoro
> considered the Anglican religion as a Hema issue.[59]

The lack of other translations and the subsequent maintenance of Hema
dominance re-enforced the client relationships between people groups.
Parish structure also played a role in this inequality. The first two
Congolese priests, Nasani Kaberole and Yusufu Limenya, were ordained
in 1937 and the large parish of Boga was divided in two. Kabarole, a
Hema, took over Boga parish, which included Hema, Ngiti and Lese.
Liminya, a Nande, had oversight of the new parish based in Kainama,
the centre of a Nande *collectivité*, which was situated less than thirty
kilometres south of Boga but in the province of Nord-Kivu. This parish also encompassed the sub-parishes of Nyali, Talinga and Mbuti.
The dominance of the Hema people and the Hema language as the
EAC developed its internal structures and its local understanding of a
western church model would have repercussions as the church spread
beyond the escarpment. Vernacularisation has been regarded among
scholars of the African Church as significant in providing a contextual
Christianity and a tool for self-determination.[60] However, the partial

---

[57] Interview, Isingoma Kahwa, Edinburgh, French, 07 June 2000.
[58] Ali Mazrui and Alamin Mazrui, *Swahili State and Society: The Political Economy of an African language* (Nairobi, East African Educational Publishers, 1995), 55.
[59] Interview, Tabu Abembe, Bwakadi, French, 06 October 2000.
[60] Sanneh, *Translating the Message*, 125.

vernacularisation on the Semeliki escarpment favoured the influence of some peoples over others and maintained the inequality of power.

The EAC had the outward trappings of a western church: a Prayer Book and hymn book translated from their English setting, a church structure borrowed from the Church of England, even clergy vestments more suitable for a colder climate. The escarpment peoples, isolated at the edge of a vast state, were proud of their international connections and wished to maintain the Church of England traditions. This acceptance, which was part of the conversion process, was facilitated by two factors; the Anglicanism which reached Boga had already gone through a process of Ugandan interpretation, and thus, partly as a result of this, the Hema felt that Anglican structures fitted neatly with their own local traditions. The meaning and significance of outward forms had been adapted to enable their adoption in a new location. Rev. Tito Balinda explained his understanding of this relationship:

> The Anglican Church, in the place where it started, was led by the traditional ruler or King. Here in Boga we are led by the traditional ruler or *Omukama*. This is the thing which binds us together. And so the Anglican tradition is a tradition of calm and order like the tradition of the Hema. And in the Anglican Church [there are] important leaders from the lowest to the highest [level] and even so with our tradition there are leaders for house [level] to section [level] and even to the leader, *Omukama*, who leads all the sections together. Such is the traditional way, so there is no difference for us Hema, we see the Anglican [Church] has a good tradition like our indigenous one.[61]

This was a kind of vernacularisation of church structures and rituals. If the newness of the Christian belief and its correlative skills were part of the appeal of conversion the parallelism of Anglican polity with a familiar socio-religious order was another part. 'Calm' and 'order,' *upole* and *utaratibu*, are words frequently used by Congolese Anglicans to describe their church. According to Tito these attributes are also found in Hema culture. The *omukama* and heads of clans (*abanyoro*) and families were responsible for maintaining political harmony through upholding their stratified social order (an *utaratibu*), handing down from generation to generation the religious rites of the Hema (also an *utaratibu*) and carrying them out with solemnity and dignity (*upole*).[62] The leaders of

---

[61] Interview, Tito Balinda, Boga, Swahili, 02 October 2000.
[62] Isingoma Kahwa, "La Notion traditionelle de la Communauté en Afrique noire et son Integration dans la Vie ecclesiale," 25–26.

Hema society who performed ritual sacrifices maintained an air of *utaratibu* and *upole*, distancing themselves from the lively dancing which accompanied the celebration of major community events.

Apolo targeted heads of families in his evangelism and schooling. When they became Christians, they owned the Anglican Church as theirs through identification with Hema structure and order. When they took on the roles of church workers, they carried out the ecclesiastical rites with the same solemnity.[63] The hierarchical and ritual *utaratibu* already known to the Hema[64] was seen to 'bind together' Hema society and the Church of England. This is unsurprising. The decision to convert to Christianity arises from judgements made in the pre-Christian situation and, as J. D. Y. Peel states, since these judgements, "...undergird the decision to convert, they are likely to continue as a substrate of the new beliefs and practices...".[65] Inculturation on the escarpment included the re-coding of the significance of Anglican structures. Far from the awkward imposition of western religious structures on a helpless people, Hema leaders saw the structure as supportive of their own authority. That said, however, Anglican structure and liturgy *were* a novelty on the escarpment. The association of Anglican structure with Hema society was never complete. The *omukama* and his descendants, for example, became Christians and had significant roles in church ceremonies and decisions, but they continued to observe traditional Hema rites and, therefore, could not become Anglican priests. Nevertheless, the meaning of the Anglican hierarchy of church leaders and the rites they performed was now clothed in Hema concepts instead of English ones. Likewise, Hema culture had taken on a particular Christian aspect that, through migration, would influence the entire Anglican Church in Congo.

The Anglican liturgy fitted well with the mood of the chiefly rites of Hema society. During the seventy years when the Anglican Church remained solely in the escarpment area, respect, solemnity and orderliness were the dominant expression of Christianity. The words most often used in Swahili to describe worship are *utaratibu, upole* and *heshima*, (respect, honour, politeness, dignity). Musubaho makes clear the connection between structure and worship when he looks back nostalgically on the Kainama church when he was young:

---

[63] Personal communication, Titre Ande, 2 April 2002.
[64] Bénézet Bujo, *African Theology* (Nairobi, St. Paul Publications, 1992), 20–21.
[65] J. D. Y. Peel, *Religious Encounter and the Making of the Yoruba* (Indiana, Indiana University Press, 2000), 216.

People were quiet in church. People were taught to shut [their] eyes and to kneel, you could not pray without kneeling or shutting eyes, we were used to this. At this time in the church there was much respect, people very much feared the Lord. [There was] no chatting in church.[66]

Heshima, was an important virtue in escarpment society. Proper *heshima* was given according to the status of a person in society. *Heshima* was also given to God. Decorous order and deferential conduct during the Sunday service was believed to portray appropriate respect for the divine. The conduct appropriate for God was also extended to the preacher as the one proclaiming the Word of God and the congregation remained quiet and attentive throughout the sermon. Lukumbula Kihandasikiri explains how he felt about church workers, 'servants of God', when he was growing up:

The servants [of God] were greatly feared, greatly respected. From their faces they really seemed to present God in God's visible state. A person would not be able to hastily approach the servant, except if that person was also spiritual. And even if the servant called you over you were surprised to see him coming near to you. So we grew up really in fear of the Word of God.[67]

The *heshima* bestowed on church workers arose from the belief that they had a special relationship with God of which people were in awe. For Lukumbula, it is this respect for the servant of God that conferred reverence for the Word of God. This *heshima* was further personalised in respect for the memory of Apolo who introduced the new religious order. As Anglican connections with local structures had enabled local ownership of the EAC so did respect for Apolo:

For the people of Boga the Anglican Church is their own church. That's to say they know well the history of the first evangelist, how he came, how he settled in…[68]

Recognised as a saint, action seen to be in keeping with Apolo's teaching was approved within the EAC. His memory was also called upon to veto innovation. Things were expected to remain as Kivebulaya had left them. There was great appeal in following Apolo into the same work. Nasanairi Mukasa is the prime example. A Ganda, he offered his services when he heard the call for evangelists to go to Boga following

---

[66] Interview, Musubaho Ndaghaliwa, Kainama, Swahili, 05 October 2000.
[67] Interview, Lukumbula Kihandasikiri, Kampala, Swahili, 23 July 2000.
[68] Interview, Isingoma Kahwa.

Apolo's death in 1933 and was to spend almost fifty years connected to the EAC.[69] Those who had known Apolo were held in high esteem as Bitanihirwa Kamakama makes clear when he speaks of Samson Katara of Kainama parish:

> We found that the...pastor there was the first student of Apolo Kivebulaya... So it was imperative to follow [his teaching] with much interest because he himself spent much time with Apolo.[70]

Apolo had preached respect for the written word and its content; the Bible was a guide to a new lifestyle, books were more effective than spears. The escarpment peoples accepted this, but they did so through intermediaries. Apolo had earned their *heshima*. It was inherited by those who followed him to become church leaders. Many of these leaders had a stake in traditional socio-political power structures.

Inculturation

Orderliness in religious rites and respect for those who retained social order were the cement which bonded the new religion with the old culture. The increasing embodiment of Anglicanism in this particular local culture changed it from a religious movement to a church institution. As the new religion took hold of the establishment, however, three significant changes took place. Firstly, the moral code propounded by Apolo and CMS missionaries became an ideal for the most committed rather than a necessity for all Christians. The smoking, drinking and, to some extent, polygamy expected in traditional culture continued even among baptised members of the congregation. The novelty and difference of Christianity that may have attracted the first converts, like the family of Basimasi, became less striking. The indigenous church began making its own decisions in these areas displaying a desire to maintain continuity with its dominant culture. Secondly, people already prominent in society became leaders of the new religion, a situation entirely natural in Hema culture. These people were almost always senior men; some of them had been 'Apolo's boys' who were now heads of families. Although the *omukama* could not become a church leader and still carry out traditional religious rites on behalf of the Hema, family heads did

---

[69] Nasanari Mukasa, Kampala, notes from interview 1998 with Bahemuka Mugeni.
[70] Interview, Bitanihirwa Kamakama, Bunia, French, 10 September 2000.

not have the same dilemma. These men were often, but not always, senior in age as well as position. Ecclesiastical roles were increasingly defined according to locally configured expectations of generation. Thirdly, women stopped taking leadership roles. 'Apolo's girls' did not take official positions as the EAC developed and younger women did not replace them. Ecclesiastical roles had also become gendered.

Female *walimu* working alongside men had been a feature of the rapid expansion of the early COU. Forty-six women were licensed as catechists in Toro between 1902 and 1909. At least two, Damari Ngaju and Erisabeti Duhabya, were from Boga and had been among the first to welcome Apolo and become Christians. Unfortunately, the numbers of women being trained dwindled from 1914.[71] A similar pattern was apparent on the Semeliki escarpment. Before Apolo Kivebulaya's death a number of women appear to have led chapels in the same way as young male *walimu*. After the 1930s there were no other women *walimu* until the 1970s. Conservative European gender expectations were present in the Anglican institution of which the church in Boga was now a part. The Church of England had an entirely male leadership that was replicated by Anglican missionaries throughout the world. Thus the most senior leadership positions in the EAC were available only to men. The ordination of escarpment clergymen in 1937, both significant members of their communities, was regarded as a positive point of self-governance. However, it served to enforce the gender imbalance in religious and social leadership. European gender bias reinforced gendered roles in escarpment society. Although roles were not gendered in the same way as in Europe, men held most of the leadership and decision-making roles.

The cultures on the escarpment were patriarchial and partrilineal. Women were not expected to take a public role in society without permission from their fathers or husbands although post-menopausal women sometimes participated in councils and generally had seniority over younger women. Women had participated in religious events like healing, exorcism, and the promoting of fertility but these things played little part in escarpment Anglicanism.[72] The EAC had associated itself with the social, political and religious hierarchies of the escarpment,

---

[71] Louise Pirouet, *Black Evangelists*, 73–75.
[72] Muhindo Tsongo, "The Role of Women in the Anglican Church in Congo: A case of the Diocese of North Kivu" (M.A. diss., Trinity College, 2000), 9–12.

which were largely loci of gerontocratic male authority, rather than with popular religious expressions[73] and thus did not challenge the gender roles of society or tap the spiritual roles of women. Hierarchical *utaratibu* came to be almost exclusively male but it did so in a manner more structured and formalised than had been common in the religious expression of traditional society. Anglican and escarpment traditions colluded in excluding women from leadership positions within the EAC and making them feel inadequate to carry out such roles. The position of early women *walimu* was always fragile and became more so as the new religious movement turned into institutional church.

If women had lost their brief roles as leaders in the church, however, they were not in the same social position as they had been before the introduction of the EAC to the escarpment. Not only were they expected to fall under the *utaratibu* of the church, they were also provided with their own structural *utaratibu*. The Mothers' Union (MU) was introduced as the conduit through which social order was maintained and socio-religious ideas about the role of Christian women were expressed. It began in England in 1876 and was introduced to East Africa by CMS missionaries. Its stated aim was to promote Christian marriage and family life through prayer and service in the community.[74] Only women who had been married in church were permitted to be members. The MU started in Boga in the 1940s and it was into this group that female leadership potential was channelled.[75] By independence the EAC had institutionalised into a gerontocratic, male-dominated organisation with a subordinate female institution. A similar phenomenon has been noted in other African societies. Esther Mombo, in her study of inculturation on Abaluyia women, concludes that dominant Abaluyia men influenced Quaker missionaries—normally associated with a more egalitarian expression of Christianity than Anglicans—to maintain customs in church life which continued to subordinate women.[76] Meredith McKittrick observed this among the Ovambo of Namibia and concluded that the end result for women was simply a

---

[73] See discussion on role and status of women in spirit possession in Grishick Ben-Amos, Paula, "The Promise of Greatness: Women and Power in an Edo Spirit Possession Cult," in *Religion in Africa*, ed. T. D. Blakley, et al. (London, James Currey, 1994), 118.

[74] http://www.themothersunion.org/content.

[75] PR: Unpublished account of life and work as CMS missionaries by Beryl Rendle, 7.

[76] "A History and Cultural Analysis of the Position of Abaluyia Women in Kenyan Quaker Christianity, 1902–1979" (PhD, Edinburgh University, 1999), 302–303.

"...wider choice of relationships of social dependence."[77] In Congo the EAC had become male-led and oriented towards the maintenance of gerontocratic male power structures. Inculturation came, perhaps, at the price of subversive dynamism.

Maendeleo

Another word frequently used to describe the identity of the EAC by its members is *maendeleo*. It can be used for anything that improves the quality of life, alleviates suffering or provides economic advancement. It is often used in the EAC to refer to church-organised social work of education and health care and other modern social services.[78] The aspirations for such novelties introduced by Apolo from Uganda, were sustained through membership of the COU but were not always realised as fully as EAC members hoped. For example, when Protestant missions were permitted to apply for government educational subsidies in 1946 it was such a high priority in the EAC that it became the first Protestant church in North-east Congo to attain the government standards for its three schools.[79] Even so these subsidies were not granted until 1951. One of the standards demanded was that the medium for primary schools be Swahili, the trade language of eastern Congo, rather than Runyoro.[80] This was the first step in levelling the ethno-linguistic play-ing field and associating more clearly with the nation of Congo rather than Uganda, although it was some time before the church followed suit. In 1965 when the Diocese of Rwenzori was formed, there were nine parishes in the Boga deanery, each with one primary school and at least fifteen chapels. A year later a secondary school was opened.[81]

---

[77] Meredith McKittrick, *To Dwell Secure: Generation, Christianity and Colonialism in Ovam-boland* (Portsmouth, Heinemann, 2002), 220.
[78] *Maendeleo*—development, progression, advance, evolution, improvement (*endeleo* is the singular but is not widely used). It is used by Anglicans to refer to both spiritual and material improvement, although more frequently the latter.
[79] Ndahura, "L'Implantation de l'Anglicanisme au Zaïre," 91.
[80] By 1925 the colonial administration had adopted the policy of using four regional trade languages rather than French in communication with the Congolese population. This was replicated in the education policy that aimed to produce a cheap, controllable labour force. Johannes Fabian, *Language and Colonial Power: The Appropriation of Swahili in the Former Belgian Congo* (Cambridge, Cambridge University Press, 1986), 66–67.
[81] Isingoma Kahwa, "La Monographie du Diocese de Boga-Zaïre" (Diplôme de graduat diss., ISThA, 1984), 49 and 84.

Schools were open to boys and girls, yet education was viewed through the prism of differently gendered family allegiance, as Caroline Mwanga points out:

> Our fathers of the past said it was not good to teach a girl child because it wasted money since she would get married and become a member of a different family.[82]

Families often made the decision only to educate their sons, or to educate them for longer than their daughters, because, for the purposes of lineage, girls were not considered permanent members of the family or clan. Boys, were therefore more likely to receive the *maendeleo* which would equip them to be part of the *utaratibu* of the EAC if they so desired.

The Mother's Union provided a gender specific programme of *maendeleo* for women. It insisted on the domesticity of women's roles and their obedience to their husbands but also provided them with new information and skills with which to carry this out.[83] Sewing, child health, sanitation, prayer meetings, literacy, and Bible study were all provided by the MU. Women appreciated a forum in which their own concerns were paramount and so were able to find channels for their own group expression. In Boga the MU mirrored the activities of the EAC by imparting traditional Hema etiquette along with Bible teaching. Traditional ways of showing respect and of providing hospitality were taught by the older women to the younger ones.[84] The MU was seen by men and women alike to bolster the *utaratibu, upole* and *heshima* (order, calm and respect) of the EAC and escarpment society.

In education the EAC was almost keeping abreast of the changing possibilities within the country. In health care this was not the case. From 1948 Boga had a clinic providing basic medical assistance but the desire to create a hospital at Boga remained unfulfilled until the 1980s.[85] In this situation church members continued to rely on traditional medicine. Traditional healing methods had been closely intertwined with traditional beliefs and were distrusted by the EAC. Although a few Christians distanced themselves from them, as Basimasi's family

---

[82] Interview, Caroline Mwanga, Butembo, Swahili, 16 June 1998.
[83] Marie Tabu, Joyce Tsongo, and Emma Wild, "Unity Must Adapt to Diversity: Congolese Women in Dialogue with Christianity and Culture," *Anvil* 15 (1998), 38.
[84] Irene Bahemuka, personal communication, May 1997.
[85] Ndahura, "L'Implantation de l'Anglicanisme au Zaïre," 92.

seemed proud to do, the EAC on the escarpment was too closely linked with traditional ways to abandon such practices completely. Christians often carried them out in secret and with an accompanying sense of shame.[86]

Maendeleo can be understood to indicate those aspects of EAC activity which were novel to escarpment society and which enabled it to adapt to the forces of colonial change and modern influence. *Utaratibu* as interpreted by *upole* and *heshima* provided a way of containing change and difference within a schema of continuity and similarity. By 1960 this appreciation of traditional values and aspirations of modernity provided a framework of religious identity for the majority of Anglicans on the escarpment.

Uhuru

Alongside the majority there developed an alternative, minority identity—Revivalism. Like the EAC itself, the revival within it came from the COU. The dynamic *Balokole*[87] revival which shook the Ugandan, Rwandan, then Kenyan and Tanzanian churches from 1933 challenging their perceived nominalism and complacency, has been well documented.[88] Studies have argued for its relative European and African influences, its force for social change and its similarity to independency. Within the EAC it provided freedom (*uhuru*)[89] from the dominant expression of Anglicanism and called people back to the moral code introduced by Apolo. The characteristics of this revival were threefold; public confession of sin as a sign that one was 'saved', a strict moral code of conduct, and the formation of fellowship groups for further confession, evangelism, and worship. Lukumbula explains the most important elements of Revival for him:

---

[86] Buyana Mulungula, "Conflit entre la Foi Chrétienne et le Ufumu dans le Milieu Urbain: Bukavu et Bunia" (Licence diss., ISTB, 1996), 22.

[87] Balokole means 'saved people' in Luganda.

[88] For example, C. E. Robins, "Tukutendereza: a study of social change and sectarian withdrawal in the Balokole Revival of Uganda" (PhD, Columbia University), 1975; Kevin Ward, '"Obedient Rebels"—the Relationship between the early "Balokole" and the Church of Uganda: the Mukono Crisis of 1941' *Journal of Religion in Africa*, 19 (1989); Derek Peterson, "Wordy Women: Gender trouble and the Oral Politics of the East African Revival in Northern Gikuyuland" *Journal of African* History 42 (2001).

[89] *Uhuru*—freedom, liberty, liberation.

Really it was to witness how God saved a person from sin. And when a person left sin, how a person could be able to feel *uhuru*, to feel they have been saved and to feel *uhuru*. And to walk in this *uhuru* and also to have courage to witness to others in this state.[90]

Uhuru from sin and courage to witness to others was a common expression of the attraction of revival. Revivalists often displayed a lively and informal use of music, dance and traditional instruments, and a tendency to challenge social, ethnic or racial divides. Leadership was shared and participation was expected of all. Women had more prominent roles within Revivalism than in the mainstream church.[91] It gave them opportunities to lead evangelistic and fellowship meetings in ways that challenged the collusion of Anglican and escarpment hierarchy on the role of women. Susanne Japhara,[92] for example, had been saved in Boga in the 1940s. Her official role remained within the leadership of the MU but her revival commitment gave her freedom and confidence to participate in evangelism alongside church leaders and eventually to study at Bible School in the 1970s with three other women.

When Ganda evangelist, Mukasa Nasanairi, left Boga to train for the priesthood at Mukono he was 'saved' as a result of contact with *Balokole* at the college. He and twenty-five other COU students were expelled in 1941 for refusing to compromise their *Balokole* practices of early morning prayer, preaching and denouncing the sins of fellow students. He was sent back to Congo without being ordained and began a revival ministry among the Lese of Zunguluka.[93] He was relatively successful here among a people who felt distant from the Boga centre of Anglican influence, but although Revival did spread throughout the EAC on the escarpment, among the Hema its influence remained limited. Mukasa organised evangelistic campaigns but only managed to influence a small number of people to a sustained revival lifestyle. Some of those, however, who were 'saved' as young men in the 1950s were to play key roles as the church developed in urban areas in the 1970s and 1980s. Beni Bataaga, for example, connects his revival experience with his ministerial vocation:

---

[90] Lukumbula Kihandasikiri.

[91] Emma Wild, "'Walking in the Light': The Liturgy of Fellowship in the Early Years of the East African Revival," in *Continuity and Change in Christian Worship*, ed. R. N. Swanson (Suffolk, Boydell and Brewer, 1999), 420–423.

[92] Personal communication, Susanne Japhara, 07 October 2000.

[93] Ward, 'Obedient Rebels', 206.

Through [Mukasa] I knew the Lord, I received Jesus Christ as my personal saviour...There was a group of about 12 people. They used to read their Bible once in a week, every Wednesday...Even to feel a call to the ministry, it was through that.[94]

For most escarpment Anglicans, Revival threatened the *utaratibu* and *heshima* of the religious heads of families and the *upole* of rites properly observed because it demanded a more radical rejection of traditional stratified social relations than the mainstream EAC. Revival did not fit with the ecclesiastical myths that were emerging around Apolo's model of church. However, Revival was to appear in more persistent forms as the EAC grew through migration and, as chapter six will show, it provided another identity for those who wished to call themselves Anglican.

"I am still going towards the forest"

Through this history of indigenisation walks Apolo Kivebulaya. Living and dead he inspired a loyalty and respect that made of him a symbol of EAC identity. But what did he symbolise on the escarpment in 1960? Burial narratives written at about this time suggest an alternative to that of the 1996 narrative mentioned in the first chapter. One memoir says Apolo's insistence on being buried in Boga was "so my children of the forest could remain looking at my grave."[95] These words suggest a reverence for Apolo akin to that of a family ancestor, at whose grave veneration would be carried out. It encourages the preservation of his memory and a respect for his contribution to society. Another account plots a more missiological slant on Apolo's request for a westward burial: "I am still going towards the forest to preach the Gospel."[96] Yet even here the emphasis is personal. There is no explicit call for others to follow although one might be expected to infer that Apolo's was an example to be followed. In the 1960s the interpretation of Apolo's burial request probably supported on-going local evangelism. More significantly, Apolo's story is recounted as that of a church founder rather than a mere Christian evangelist. It suggests a belief that his memory would be honoured by the maintenance of the Anglican tradition that

---

[94] Inteview, Bataaga Beni, Bunia, English, 15 September 2000.
[95] Aberi Balya, 'Bishop Balya's Account of Apolo Kivebulaya' (unpublished, n.d.), 11.
[96] Anne Luck, *African Saint: The Story of Apolo Kivebulaya* (London, SCM, 1963), 147.

had developed as a result of his ministry. Thus the ecclesiastical model localised on the escarpment was given legitimacy by a particular narration of Apolo's life and death.

Conclusion

In setting the historical scene for Anglican migration this chapter has analysed the early identity of the EAC. Introduced by Ugandans the EAC was similar to the COU and yet not the same. Christian belief, Anglican structure, liturgy, schools and clinics may once have been foreign to the inhabitants of these villages but over two generations they had begun to own them as theirs. They had fitted the Anglican system with their own chiefly system and accepted the formal worship style as fitting reverence for the Almighty. Unable to spread further before independence because of Protestant missionary comity and Catholic colonial influence, the EAC focused on its internal ecclesiastical structure and rites, moulding them to conform to the rural values that were, symbiotically, shaped by EAC influence. If home is the place where one's meaning is grounded, as suggested in chapter one, then the meshing of Hema culture with Anglican rites engendered an altered expression of home. The result was a small but confident church. By the 1950s the EAC had developed a *modus operandi* on the escarpment which it could sustain for sometime.

Viewed in Congo as a whole, however, EAC identity must be regarded as precarious: it had British connections in a Belgian colony; it was largely African-led in an era of white control; it was small and rural in a huge country with growing industrial towns, Protestant in a state where Catholics were wealthy and influential, Anglican in an area of conservative, anti-establishment American missions. On the cusp of independence the EAC had little power or influence in Congo. It was often ignored and occasionally regarded with suspicion as not quite legitimate. Yet as Anglicans migrated beyond the escarpment area they were to find elements in this marginal religious identity of *utaratibu, upole, heshima* and *maendeleo* that were to sustain them and allow them to feel at home in their new situations.

CHAPTER THREE

BEING AT HOME IN A NEW PLACE:
EAC GROWTH THROUGH RURAL-URBAN MIGRATION

Introduction

By 1975 the *Eglise Anglicane du Congo* (EAC) was present in most of the towns in Nord-Kivu and Irumu. This chapter studies the growth and the change of the EAC as a result of the migration of its members to urban areas in North-east Congo. It scrutinises the way in which the rural Anglican identity studied in chapter two was both affirmed and contested in the urban milieu. The chapter argues that a propitious politico-economic situation encouraged people to migrate from village to town where they established their village church. The prime movers were influential lay members and enterprising evangelists of the EAC.

Helen Rose Ebaugh and Janet Salzman Chafetz in their study of immigrant religion in Houston, USA, conclude that immigrant religious institutions "...are structured to both ensure continuity of practice and to assume adaptive strategies of change. Because these two processes are often contradictory, immigrant religious institutions typically experience real or potential conflicts among groups of members."[1] The tensions caused by the need for both continuity and change within the EAC form a large part of this study. The future of the EAC depended, to quote Ebaugh and Chafetz again, on how members "...respond[ed] to divisive issues rooted in ethnic/linguistic, generational, gender...differences."[2] This chapter analyses how the EAC enabled its members to take advantage of migrant opportunities whilst maintaining continuity with their tradition. Migrants wanted to perpetuate opportunities for social *maendeleo* (development) but their religious identity was expressed in a desire to maintain village values of *utaratibu, upole* and *heshima* (order, calm and respect); an identity often articulated as 'being at home'. The chapter also examines in what ways the position they took began to

---

[1] Helen Rose Ebaugh and Janet Saltzman Chafetz, *Religion and the New Immigrants: Continuities and Adaptations in Immigrant Congregations* (Waltnut Creek, AltaMira, 2000), 134.
[2] Ibid., 134.

be contested by their children. Second generation migrants criticised their parents' conservative religious ethos, desiring a Christian identity that reflected their national and urban identity. The chapter begins with an analysis of the general patterns of rural-urban migration in the area demonstrating where Anglican aspirations intersected with urban ambitions.

Migration

> Many moved because of work. If one had done primary school at Boga one wanted work here in Kainama. But there is no work. One had to go to Oicha or Bunia... Others moved because of *maendeleo*. They saw that to stay here, there is no road, no hospital, no market, so one moves to where the road is,... [in order] to develop. Others moved because of illness. When one is ill one goes to hospital in Oicha or Nyankunde. When one recovers one decides to stay there because to fall ill again and to return again is difficult.[3]

Thus Musubaho Ndahalirwa, who left his village for education and work as a teacher and pastor until he returned on retirement, explained the migration of members of the EAC from the Semeliki escarpment to the towns. The reasons were not unusual: inequalities between rural and urban areas in economic prospects, educational advancement and health care provision encouraged people to move to the towns. The migratory path was not dramatic; some crossed the country to Kisangani and Kinshasa, but most remained within 150 km of their village of origin. They inhabited commercial towns like Bunia, Beni and Butembo, mining towns like Mongwalo and Makiki, and the towns of Nyankunde and Oicha built around mission hospitals. It was a gradual migration, which slowly depopulated villages changing the demographics of the area. Congolese Anglicans were attracted to the perceived opportunities because they had acquired skills taught in the church school for which there were greater employment opportunities outside the rural areas, and in secular rather than church work, a theme that appears throughout African Christianity.[4] The gospel in Anglican form had been presented as part of a modernising package that included healthcare, education and employment, based on literacy and numeracy skills. The

---

[3] Interview, Musubaho Ndaghalirwa, Kainama, Swahili, 5 October 2000.
[4] John Baur, *2000 Years of Christianity in Africa: An African History 62–1992* (Nairobi, Paulines Publications, 1994), 274–275.

isolation of the villages and the marginal position of the EAC meant that relocation to a nearby town where modernity was more apparent was an attractive option for Christians. In encouraging an aspiration for *maendeleo* the EAC had unintentionally provided an impetus for its members to migrate.

Migration to town began during the colonial era when urban settlements were established in greater numbers. It exposed a greater number of people to a monetary economy and European influence and thus altered ethnic relations and gender and generational dynamics. The Belgians controlled the settlement of Congolese in the *centres extra-coutumiers*,[5] the areas of town reserved for those African workers approved by the colonial state. Small numbers migrated in the 1920s and 1930s when colonial officials employed those who had literacy skills learnt in mission schools. For example, Geresomu Kyamulesere, from Boga, was encouraged into government service in Irumu after finishing school in 1944. From 1950 he was a salesman in Butembo and Beni. In 1955 he set up his own transport business between Bunia and Kisangani.[6] Colonial relocation for labour, or as a means of managing the population, was another reason for migration. In the 1940s the Belgians forced thirty men and their families to move to from Kainama, the second EAC parish on the escarpment, to Eringeti in order to work on a road that was to be constructed north through the forest to Bunia and Kisangani. This forced migration meant that Eringeti was the first town with a sizeable proportion of Anglicans in its population. Colonial policy also dictated which ethnic groups were more prevalent in the towns and influenced the relations between them. Hema, Nande and Alur were considered by the Belgians to be more intelligent than the other peoples of the region and were therefore targeted for colonial employment.[7] Hierarchies of superiority developed between groups, some of whom had had little previous contact with one another. The colonial administration favoured the employment of men in urban areas.[8] About 1939 Basimasi Kyakuhaire, who was introduced in chapter two, moved with her husband to Nord-Kivu. He had found a

---

[5] Valdo Pons, *Stanleyville: An African Urban Community under Belgian Administration* (Oxford, Oxford University Press, 1969), 35.

[6] Interview, Geresomu Kyamulesere, Komanda, Swahili, 21 September 2000.

[7] Samba Kaputo, *Phenomène d'Ethnicitie et Conflits ethno-politiques en Afrique post-coloniale* (Kinshasa, Presse Universitaires du Zaïre, 1982), 289–290.

[8] Pons, *Stanleyville*, 44.

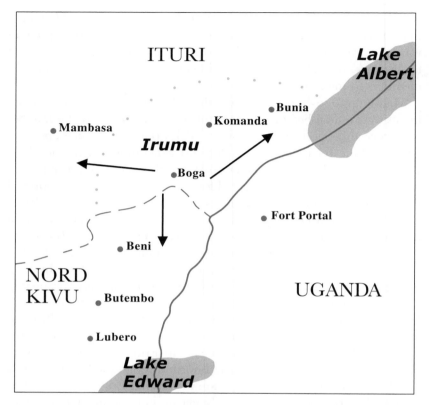

ITURI

Lake Albert

● Bunia

● Komanda

● Mambasa

Irumu

● Boga

● Fort Portal

● Beni

NORD KIVU

UGANDA

● Butembo

● Lubero

Lake Edward

Illustration 3   Diagram of Rural-urban Migration

job as a clerk in a mining area and they both left their posts as *walimu*. The administration did not consider employing Basimasi, whose skills were identical, because she was a woman. Basimasi's public role was lost as a result of economic migration. Colonial bureaucracy adhered to conservative European gender roles and influenced relationships between men and women in Congo.

Four years after independence, the *Simba* rebellion of 1964 destablised the region. The brutality of this military faction of the violent second independence movement[9] resulted in the displacement of rural people in North-east Congo to nearby towns in search of security.[10] These inter-

---

[9] For more details see, Georges Nzongola-Ntalaga, *The Congo from Leopold to Kabila* (Zed Books, London, 2002), 131–135.

[10] Mawa Lekeni, "L'Exode des Lugbara vers Bunia de 1960 à nos Jours: les Facteurs determinants" (Licence diss., ISP, Bunia, 1990), 45.

nal migrants found employment in trade, cash crops, gold-mining and public services. Between 1965 and 1975 opportunities for employment increased in the towns, and rural-urban migration continued as a result. This was the period between the end of civil wars in Congo and the start of economic regression. President Mobutu developed his *authenticité* policy that called for self-determination and a pride in African culture. It included the nationalisation of private companies and the take-over of erstwhile European enterprises by Congolese.[11] The Nande of Nord-Kivu, in particular became well known for their trading abilities.[12] Butembo, Beni and Bunia became significant trading towns bringing goods from East Africa and the Middle East. Statistics from Butembo, the most important commercial centre in North-east Congo, illustrate the economic growth of the first two decades of independence which encouraged migration from village to town. In 1961 the Congolese owned twelve shops in the town. Europeans or Asians owned the rest. Nineteen years later Congolese owned forty-eight of the fifty shops. In 1982 the population of Butembo was estimated at 100,000, three times its size in 1960.[13] Bunia's growth was comparable: in 1965 there were 22, 919 inhabitants, in 1980 the population was 54,166.[14]

During this time of urban growth the EAC was established in towns. Few Anglicans became large-scale business people but several established themselves as petty traders, often maintaining commercial links with their home area. Others became teachers, administrators and politicians through the Christian education they had received in Boga and Kainama. As educational opportunities became greater after independence, village schools could not always keep pace. Many young people migrated from the village in order to further their education. The educational and economic incentives to migrate were mixed with other aspirations. For example, Muhindo Tsongo explains the benefits of urban relocation that she experienced not simply in terms of advancing knowledge but also of 'broadening' behaviour and worldview: "One accepts other tribes, one changes behaviour, one understands what's

---

[11] *Authenticité* later became *zaïreanisation.* It included changing the name of the country, river and money to Zaire. Nzongola-Ntalaja, *The Congo,* 172.

[12] Janet MacGaffey, "Long-distance Trade, Smuggling and the New Commercial Class: the Nande of North Kivu," in *Entrepreneurs and Parasites: The struggle for indigenous capitalism in Zaire,* Janet MacGraffey (Cambridge, Cambridge University Press, 1987), 143–164.

[13] Ibid., 144 & 159.

[14] Muzuro Kana Wai, "Croissance de l'Eglise locale de la Communauté évangelique an Centre de L'Afrique, Section de Bunia" (Diplôme de Graduat diss., ISTB, 1982), 14.

going on."[15] Towns were perceived to be places where assumptions were challenged, status elevated, and liberty gained beyond what one could expect in the socially stratified and culturally conservative village. As Mawa Lekeni puts it, "... the urban centre became a symbol of individual advancement and freedom.... from ignorance poverty and disease."[16] The perceived opportunities of rural-urban migration correlated with the Anglican package found in the escarpment villages; church, school and clinic were attempts to tackle "ignorance, poverty and disease" but the opportunities and resources to do so became greater in the towns than the villages.

It is through such mundane migrations that a plethora of Christian denominations became active in the urban areas. It is apparent that the very structures and ideas introduced by the EAC fuelled the aspirations that led to urban migration. Urban life, however, presented many challenges to rural migrants. Although town life was considered advantageous, village life was often remembered with nostalgia.[17] If the EAC had unwittingly made it easier for Anglicans to migrate it was also to provide a structure for urban adaptation, in which, paradoxically, religious identity was articulated in terms of rural tradition rather than modern skills. The patterns of church expansion and the expectations that underpinned them demonstrate that the migrants were reluctant to leave home completely.

Establishing the EAC in towns

> A few Christians from Boga had come here. And these Christians... very much wanted to have their own church. And this pushed the church to begin here. We sat in the archdeaconry council. It decided to say I should come here. Straight away they sent me to begin the church here.[18]

So Munege Kabarole, evangelist, then pastor and archdeacon of Bunia, explained the process by which, in 1970, the church in Bunia came into being. The pattern was a familiar one for the establishment of a new urban congregation of the EAC; the initiative was taken by lay people who migrated to the towns, it was accepted by church authori-

---

[15] Interview, Muhindo Tsongo, French, Bristol, 10 April 2000.
[16] Mawa, "L'Exode des Lugbara," 34.
[17] Pons, *Stanleyville*, 51.
[18] Interview, Munege Kabarole, Bunia, Swahili, 13 September 2000.

ties in Boga, and a trained evangelist was dispatched from Boga to begin work. In the 1960s there were small numbers of migrants from the escarpment living in towns and meeting occasionally together as a group. They urged the authorities in Boga to plant Anglican Churches in their towns but throughout the 1960s plans were stymied until the migrants had gained local government permission, land and a church worker. There was no willingness to launch an Anglican congregation without either support from Boga or governmental approval: to have done so would have signalled a religious independency that they did not desire. Their aim was to maintain ties with the Boga church and the Anglican Communion.

When the first church in Bunia was established there were perhaps thirty members in all. Ten years later over 100 people attended each Sunday with over 300 at Christmas.[19] In 1980 the Archdeaconry of Bunia was inaugurated and Munege, who was now pastor in Bunia, became the Archdeacon. By this time there were parishes in Komanda and Mafifi with churches in other *territoires* as far away as Mahagi, Aru and Mambasa. Bunia parish itself had sub-parishes at Bogoro and Kasenyi, each sub-parish having several chapels. In Butembo, from 1965, the daughter of Basimasi Kyakuhaire, Mahirani Melena, and others were meeting together and preaching in the market. They requested an evangelist from Boga and Lukambula Kihandasikiri went to work in Butembo from 1971.[20] Once the EAC had a foothold in Nord-Kivu there was an explosion of little chapels erupting along the towns on the main road between Eringeti and Butembo and near the Ugandan border. In 1974 the first archdeaconry in Nord-Kivu opened with its centre in Beni.

It has been noted that, as colonial policy favoured the employment of teachers and clerks, the best students of the mission schools engaged in secular employment rather than church work.[21] This is certainly true of the rural EAC. However, as the establishment of urban chapels shows, their loyalty remained with their village church and they wished to see it transplanted in the urban setting. Most first members of Anglican chapels in towns had grown up on the Semeliki escarpment. Those who requested a church worker and supported his work were

---

[19] BP *Chuo Cha Ibada*, Cité church.
[20] DBk, *Bref Aperçu historique de l'Eglise Anglicane, Diocese de Bukavu.*
[21] Elizabeth Isichei, *A History of Christianity in Africa from Antiquity to the Present* (London, SPCK, 1995), 238.

businessmen, traders and professionals, who had been educated in the Boga and Kainama schools. In the absence of the EAC they attended other denominations but retained loyalty to the church in which they were baptised. Most of them also had close personal connections with Apolo Kivebulaya. Some had been his catechists or the children of his catechists. Others remembered being baptised by him. This personal loyalty cemented commitment to the home church.

Kasuna Tingoli is one example. A Nyali from the forest area of Bwakadi, Kasuna's up-bringing in a Christian family made him a migrant from birth and instilled into him aspirations unobtainable in the escarpment villages. He was born at Kamango on the Semeliki plain in 1938 where his father, who had been trained by Apolo Kivebulaya, was working as a catechist among the Talinga. Kasuna went to school in Kainama and Boga. He was sent to Aungba teacher training school run by CECA 20. For three years he taught at an Anglican school north of Boga. His good qualifications, gained as a result of his church connections, made a move from Anglican village school to urban state school almost inevitable at this time. He took teaching posts in Bunia and Djugu but in 1965 he chose a political career with Mobutu's *Mouvement Populaire de la Révolution*, working between Bunia and Kisangani. When Munege arrived in 1970 Kasuna paid his salary for the first year and took the senior lay representative role of "Head of the Christians" in the new chapel until about 1976.[22] His wife, Evasta Kasuna, was for many years the leader of the Mothers' Union. As Kasuna's story demonstrates, a drift into secular occupation did not necessarily entail a loss of commitment to the EAC. Indeed, it was the continuing commitment of such people that facilitated the spread of the EAC beyond its traditional borders. Although in towns they were taking advantage of opportunities unavailable to them in rural settings, they continued to identify strongly with the lifestyle of their home villages. For them the EAC provided a focal point for the transition from the rural milieu to the urban.

African ecclesiastical history has long recognised the vital role of lay workers in the development of the African Church.[23] Their place in the growth of the EAC is no exception. Adrian Hastings' description

---

[22] Interview, Kasuna Tingoli, Bunia, Swahili, 16 September 2000.
[23] Louise Pirouet, *Black Evangelists, the spread of Christianity in Uganda: 1891–1914* (London, Rex Collings, 1978) is one example.

of African catechists in villages up until the 1950s is true of Congolese Anglican *walimu* (catechists) and *wangalizi* (evangelists) in towns in the 1970s:

> The catechists continued to represent in the context of innumerable villages Ecclesia Catholica, the universal fellowship of Christians, as well as literary modernity, the three R's in fact: Reading, Writing and Religion...To us they stand for the local. To their people, and even to themselves, they stood for and were linked with a world of religious and secular power...They visited their diocesan headquarters from time to time, and the way things were there was the way things should be in the village too.[24]

Hasting's appreciation of catechists as the link between different locations is particularly true of the urban lay workers in the EAC. They were all from the escarpment area, and many were from Boga. They were the bridges between town and village, between a small newly-formed chapel, the diocese and, ultimately, the Anglican Communion. They were experts of ritual worship and, as explained in chapter two, were accorded the *heshima* of those who mediated between humanity and the divine. At the request of EAC members in towns, they were appointed by the diocese, and their individual identity was closely associated with the identity of the church in which they worked, as one example will demonstrate.

Sibanza Buleta from Kainama worked in a number of urban and rural settings in Nord-Kivu, eventually being ordained and becoming an Archdeacon. His parents were members of the EAC and he was baptised in the late 1930s.[25] He trained in Boga as *mwalimu* and then in Uganda as *mwangalizi* and, later, as a pastor. As a church worker Sibanza was peregrinatory, working in different locations, moving among the chapels or parishes under his care, and establishing new chapels by responding to requests or by seeking out Anglicans who had moved to new locations. Like other church workers, he worked locally to build up the church, visiting homes, offices and markets, explaining the Christian faith, and establishing chapels. The Anglicanism he introduced to Mumole, Beni and other places was intended to be a replica of what he had learnt in the villages on the escarpment, which was in turn an attempt to copy the Church of Uganda and thus the Church

---

[24] Adrian Hastings, *The Church in Africa, 1450–1950* (Oxford, Clarendon Press, 1994), 581.
[25] Interview, Sibanza Buleta, Kainama, Swahili, 5 October 2000.

of England. In this, for the people he worked amongst, he represented the wider Anglican world. Ironically, in Congo the 'wider Anglican world' was most immediately accessed in the isolated villages of the escarpment. Those who had migrated to the 'wider Congolese world' found themselves distanced from the Anglicanism with which they had grown-up and it was incumbent upon church workers like Sibanza to ensure urban Anglicans retained proper Anglican rites and practices. Centralised appointments were desired by both migrants and church authorities as a way of maintaining Anglican identity, forged on the escarpment, present in towns.

Maendeleo, the main reason for urban migration of Anglican members, came from their commitment to the EAC. It also affected the way in which the EAC was introduced in the towns. In order to pursue *maendeleo* Anglicans needed to be respected in the bureaucratic realm of the towns. They, therefore, required legal recognition from the local government to avoid persecution. Thus legitimacy was a matter of state approval as much as ecclesiastical integrity, these two dimensions being equally highly regarded. Church members who had migrated to take advantage of social *maendeleo* did not wish to jeapodize those opportunities by religious radicalism. After independence, in a deliberate reversal of colonial law, religious freedom was permitted on the condition that religious groups respected public order.[26] This proviso was strictly defined during the Mobutu regime. As in colonial times, the government feared political opinion being expressed in religious movements and so resisted the spread of African Initiated Churches and Pentecostal groups, lumping them together under the dismissive description of 'sectes'.[27] Churches, therefore, had to be recognised by the state, and their orthodoxy in Congo was finally understood not according to doctrinal belief but according to possession of a *personalité civile*, the legal document that allowed a particular denomination to operate inside the country. For Protestants this was only granted if they were a member *communauté* of the umbrella organisation, the *Eglise de Christ au Congo (ECC)*, which was created in 1970 from the Congo

---

[26] Philippe Kabongo-Mbaya, *L'Eglise du Christ au Zaïre: Formation et adaptation d'un protestantisme en situation de dictature* (Paris, Karthala, 1992), 208.

[27] Wyatt MacGaffey, *Religion and Society in Central Africa: The Bakongo of Lower Zaïre* (Chicago, Chicago University Press, 1986), 248.

Protestant Council (CPC).[28] Despite these strictures the State allowed ECC members to work outside the territory allotted to them by missionary policy.

Most EAC chapels were not started until this law had been passed. The EAC, like most Protestant Churches in Congo, was quietist in its political stance, aiming to maintain cordial relations with civic authority so that it would be allowed to operate unhindered in the religious and social sphere. Furthermore, the close association between church and chief learnt in Boga prepared them to respond appropriately to state demand. *Utaratibu*, *upole* and *heshima*, qualities of Anglicanism in the rural areas, were natural complements of legitimacy and bureaucracy. These qualities were encouraged by the Mobutu regime in opposition to the 'sectes' whose perceived lack of order and respect made them appear potentially subversive. This situation engendered the adoption of attitudes to governance similar to those prevalent in the independent nation-state.

The Anglican migrants also wanted to obtain recognition from members of the local Protestant Church and the Catholic Church. This external ecclesiastical legitimacy came slowly and sometimes grudgingly. Newly established Anglican Churches were often viewed with suspicion by other urban dwellers. For outside observers sceptical of the legitimacy of the EAC it was the arrival of a permanent priest that frequently reassured them. He demonstrated that this was no new '*secte*', with dubious credentials, outlawed by the State. Legitimacy, the bureaucratic outworking of *heshima* and *utaratibu*, was ultimately conferred on the urban EAC chapels with the establishment of a parish and the subsequent arrival of an ordained pastor. *Wakristo* and *walimu* were instrumental in the urban spread of the EAC but ultimately the urban EAC was only properly considered legitimate when a priest was in place.

Maendeleo was the aspiration that Anglicans acquired in their village churches. It encouraged them to migrate to the towns. Paradoxically, once they established the urban EAC chapels they articulated most strongly a desire to retain *utaratibu*, *upole* and *heshima* learnt in their rural homes. It is to their articulations of attachment to the EAC that we now turn to understand the importance of belonging to EAC for migrants.

---

[28] Kabongo-Mbaya, *L'Eglise du Christ au Zaïre*, 218.

Returning Home

The EAC had developed a localised Christian expression on the
escarpment because it retained and incorporated into its worship and
leadership structure values already present in society and particularly
in corporate religious acts. The values of *utaratibu, upole* and *heshima* had
become emblematic of Anglican worship: as one person said, "Our parents, the elders, were used to worship in quietness, in meditation, they
liked listening reverently."[29] Migrants believed that respectful adherence
to solemn rites as practised on the escarpment should be replicated in
towns. Alterations for a different context were not considered. Mahirani
Melena, for example, was concerned that correct practice in worship
be maintained in the towns:

> There in Butembo they didn't know how to pray and to kneel, this is
> what I introduced slowly into the Butembo church—our praying, the
> law of the church.[30]

Mahirani and other migrants expected the liturgy of the *Book of Common
Prayer* to be followed in a steady and measured way. The service was
led entirely by the *mwalimu* whose dress set him apart from the congregation and symbolised his position in the hierarchical order. The
congregation participated where stated, reading the Confession, the
Lord's Prayer, the Creed, and perhaps the Gloria, a Psalm and responses.
The hymns, sung slowly with little obvious rhythm, were from *Nyimbo za
Mungu*, a translated collection of British and American hymns used by
Protestant churches in the area.[31] There were no musical instruments,
no actions or movement during singing.[32] They listened to the Old
and New Testament readings, the sermon and the prayers. Morning
Prayer was the norm. Each pastor had several churches to visit and
Holy Communion was infrequent. The Prayer Book was perceived to
express *utaratibu* and *upole*. Congregational participation demonstrated
heshima. Slow, quiet services retained close association with their culture
of origin. This was what they owned. This was part of what made them
feel at home in a new place. Evasta Kasuna, for example, was delighted

---

[29] Interview, Mbusa Bangau, Kampala, French, 28 July 2000.

[30] Interview, Mahirani Melena, Komanda, Swahili, 21 September 2000.

[31] Peter Wood and Emma Wild-Wood, "'One Day we will Sing in God's Home':
Hymns and Songs in the Anglican Church in North-east Congo (DRC)," *Journal of
Religion in Africa* 34 (2004): 147–148.

[32] Interview, Kamayura and Isingoma Chwa, Bunia, Swahili, 23 September 2000.

when the EAC started in Bunia because she had found the CECA 20 services 'confusing,' and was pleased to return to familiar rituals.[33]

The practice of this solemn, respectful worship was reinforced by the memory of the role of Apolo Kivebulaya who had been the conduit through whom the EAC developed its escarpment character. Anglicans were proud of him and referred to his precedence. When Mahirani Melena taught the Anglicans in Butembo how to kneel to pray in accordance with the 'law of the church' she believed she was following Apolo who had baptised her and taught both her parents to be *walimu*. If Apolo was believed to have introduced something, it was considered sacred and not to be altered. Those who established the EAC in urban areas saw themselves as replicating the familiar religious patterns of home and also of carrying forward the ethos of 'Saint Apolo', of doing things according to his rubric. It was assumed that this tradition was a copy of a universal Anglicanism. The EAC in the towns was small and marginal in the 1970s. To be aware that this position belied connection with a much larger organisation gave its members a sense of satisfaction and, at times, a feeling of superiority over other Protestant churches. They found solace in the values and rites from the village and were proud of the wider connections they signalled.

In following Apolo, Congolese Anglicans were claiming that the EAC was both an indigenous church and a global church. They were also adhering to rural Anglican tradition rather than instigating change. In interview the reasons given for this conservative stance were explained by speaking of the EAC as home:

> I was born in this church, so I love this church that I was born in, and when we saw it had come here [to Bunia] we were happy because a person must love the house and the place of [their] father, of [their] parents.[34]

Here is a typical expression of strong attachment to the Anglican Church as a connection with the speaker's origins, an affirmation of the connection between family ties, place of origin and denominational loyalty. It was made by Rwakaikara André, who had left Boga as a teenager but whose attachment to the place and the culture of his birth remained firm. A trader who had worked near Irumu for over twenty years and worshipped at the Immanuel Brethren Church, he moved to Bunia in 1976 and later succeeded Kusuna as Head of the Christians in the

---

[33] Interview, Evasta Kasuna, Bunia, Swahili, 16 September 2000.
[34] Interview, Rwakaikara André, Bunia, Swahili, 23 September 2000.

EAC. His belief that, "there is one Word of God" and "one Jesus"[35] had allowed him to attend another denomination but he was adamant that during his years at Immanuel he had remained faithful to the EAC. Not to do so would have shown disloyalty and flightiness of character. Munege Kabarole also acknowledged the desirable characteristic of constancy, also by speaking of home:

> I was born in this church, I grew up in this church, and now I am in it. So it's my home, I can't leave to go to another house, or keep changing to find another place because there is [only] one faith.[36]

The very fact that all Christian denominations were seen to be preaching the same essential message made a nonsense of permanently joining a different church. Munege added that Anglicans who worshipped in other denominations, "...see themselves a bit like refugees [when] in other places."[37] For Anglicans other denominations did not have the familiarity of home; they felt alien, distant from their parents and the culture in which they were brought up.

It seems that the use of the word 'home' went beyond the metaphorical when migrants referred to church. Instead 'home' should be understood as having a conceptually wide spatial and emotional reach that included kinship ties, land, and ritual worship. It indicated a broad and public sense of belonging. 'Home' had a geographical hub on the escarpment but 'home' could radiate from that hub as long as it remained connected to it. The EAC was a significant means for maintaining a relationship with the home-hub because it was the place in which personal, social and spiritual identity were grounded. Thus it provided a home away from home's epicentre and aided a sense of belonging despite relocation and new circumstances. Membership of the EAC allowed migrants from the escarpment to be at home in the towns.

Confirming the centrality of home in identity is the emphasis on '*our* church,' *kanisa letu*, which appeared frequently in interviews. It speaks of the collective ownership of a way of worship and a structure of faith. Migrants established a church, or joined it once it was established in a particular place, because it was *their* church. Tito Balinda, the first Archdeacon of Beni, says:

---

[35] Ibid.
[36] Munege Kabarole.
[37] Ibid.

...when their church came they went back to their church...they were very happy because they could return to their home.[38]

Such strength of attachment demonstrates the success of indigenisation in Boga and Kainama. For those who had grown up on the Semeliki the EAC was *their* church, the church of their household, their home. All the associations of family ties, comfort, security, familiarity and tradition were found in the Anglican identity of these migrants. The traditions of the escarpment, reinterpreted with the advent of Anglicanism, were understood by migrants to provide security, comfort and belonging; values they did not wish to leave behind. *Maendeleo* may have provided the impetus for urban migration but, for first generation Anglican migrants, home was most nearly expressed through *utaratibu upole*, and *heshima* now enshrined in Anglican practice. These words summed up migrants' description of their corporate religious home and signified their personal identity.

Part of migrants' identity was an ethnic one. The narration of the religious identity of the EAC on the escarpment was plotted with ethnic identity. As a result of missionary agreements and colonial policy the EAC was unable to spread beyond the escarpment until after independence and so its identity was shaped by the Hema as the dominant ethnic group in the area. This identity was reinforced by those who first established EAC chapels in towns as providing 'home' in a new location. The theory that "migration, more than any single phenomenon, brings to the fore aspects of ethnic identity which otherwise may remain relatively latent..."[39] can be seen in the early establishment of the urban EAC. Scholars have noted the heightened awareness of ethnic difference and the provision of kinship support through ethnic associations as the result of migration to towns.[40] Research in the towns of Congo suggests that the alliances formed in the alternative economy from the 1970s onwards became increasingly based on perceptions of ethnic loyalty.[41] For first generation migrants Anglican rites and Hema customs were intertwined in the *utaratibu* they respected in church.

---

[38] Interview, Tito Balinda, Boga, Swahili, 2 October 2000.

[39] Victor Uchendu, "The Dilemma of Ethnicity and Polity Primacy in Black Africa," in *Ethnic Identity: Creation, Conflict and Accommodation* ed. Lola Romanucci-Ross and George De Vos (AltaMira, Walnut Creek, 1995), 131.

[40] For example, Anthony O'Connor, *The African City* (London, Hutchinson & Co., 1983), 101 and 116.

[41] Tshikala Biaya, 'Parallel Society in the Democratic Republic of Congo', in *Shifting African Identities*, ed. Simon Bekker et al. (Human Sciences Research Council, Pretoria, 2001), 52.

To avoid an approach to Christian belief that reduces it only to a social function of belonging it is necessary to comprehend the meaning and place of *utaratibu* in the homely faith of migrants. EAC members regularly pronounced, "God is a God of *utaratibu*". It was often the first, reflexive statement made of God's nature. A God of *utaratibu* expected orderly systems through which to manifest his power. Anglican *utaratibu* of rites properly performed with *upole* and *heshima* was considered one way of responding to this orderliness. Spontaneous, informal worship was suspect because it did not seem to reflect this order and threatened the submission to the hierarchy and the liturgy. Order permitted belonging; one knew one's place and, through belonging to this order, God's power could be accessed. Although, as evangelical Protestants, they believed individuals had access to God through prayer, many EAC members considered that order was effectively a hierarchical transference of power through which God's will could be carried out.[42] Theologian, Benezet Bujo claims this is part of Bantu philosophy:

> God then is the dispenser of life...Life is a participation in God, but is always mediated by one standing above the recipient in the hierarchy of being.[43]

Order, as mediated through a hierarchical structure was found in indigenous socio-religious worldviews and was, therefore, important to many Congolese not just Anglicans. Religious order was particularly important in a social situation of disorder, whether that be disruption as the result of migration, or the fear and unease of living in a disordered state.

Occasionally some EAC members found the *utaratibu* through which power was mediated oppressive and constraining. Most, however, spoke of it in terms of providing meaning, direction, purpose, and belonging to an entity larger and more powerful than oneself or ones' family. They believed that order provided a conduit for power, both social and religious. For migrants this was particularly useful. By belonging to the EAC they were adhering to an *utaratibu* that linked them to power when they felt most powerless. In the dislocation of migration *utaratibu* for Anglican members was also seen as a form of security. *Utaratibu*, both

---

[42] Titre Ande, "Authority in the Anglican Church of Congo: The Influence of Political Models of Authority and the Potential of 'Life-Community Ecclesiology' for Good Governance" (PhD Birmingham University, 2003), 152.

[43] Bénézet Bujo, *African Theology in its Social Context* (Nairobi, St. Paul Publications, 1992), 20.

hierarchical and ritual, offered migrant EAC members continuity with the locations from which they had migrated and security in a strange and disordered present. The institutionalisation of religious movements has been criticised in terms of them losing their popular appeal, becoming bureaucratised and misusing power.[44] Yet the migrant laity involved in planting churches wanted an institution. When faced with migration or with the actions of state organisations that seemed at best arbitrary and at worst cruel, belonging to an ordered, recognised institution provided some sense of safety. Meredith McKittrick, in her book *To Dwell Secure*, has hypothesised that the rapid growth of Christianity in Ovamboland, Namibia, in the early 20th century was a result of the convergence of Christianity with migration and the perceived need of those who responded to both for increased security.[45] The Christian trope of security surrounding the message of a need to be saved from sin, McKittrick argues, made sense to the Ovambo after a history of social, political and economic upheaval, thus an increasing number of people were willing to become Christians. In the Congolese context, however, most of the EAC migrant members had made their initial response to the message of Christ's redemption prior to migration. For them the uncertainty of migration created the need to reproduce the particular religious organisation which they believed offered security in terms of familiarity, order and protection. If these attributes conjured home then migrants were indeed returning home when they joined an urban EAC congregation.

Second generation migrants

The understanding of the EAC as home was the foundation on which migrants from the escarpment constructed their identity and yet the nature of home was soon contested among the urban EAC members. The children of migrants were also members of the emerging chapels but they experienced the urban EAC rather differently from their parents. As second generation migrants, they were more at home in towns than in their parents' village. They had more fully adapted to the urban

---

[44] David Maxwell, *Christians and Chiefs in Zimbabwe: A social history of the Hwesa people, c. 1870s–1990s* (Edinburgh, Edinburgh University Press, 1999), 97–100.

[45] Meredith McKittrick, *To Dwell Secure: Generation, Christianity and Colonialism in Ovamboland* (Portsmouth, NH, Heinemann, 2002), 275–276.

milieu and assimilated an urban identity than their parents had done. Three identity features of towns in North-east Congo are particularly pertinent to the development of an urban EAC, and merit discussion; nationalism, multi-ethnicity and generation difference.

From the 1960s onwards a nationalist discourse was prominent in the political sphere. Initially articulated by the independence movement it was then adopted by the Mobutu regime. Mobutu's centralised government was based on a narrative of cultural pride aimed to inculcate national unity through a return to 'authentic' African ideas centred around the cult of the leader.[46] Its aim was to rid the country of Eurocentric ideas and to plumb the past to access a genuine African identity.[47] The past was then given a contemporary gloss and nationalism was perceived as an indication of improvement and an African expression of modernity. Time demonstrated the corruption of Mobutu's regime, the instability of its economic policies, and the difficulty of manufacturing 'African culture'.[48] The sense of belonging to a proudly independent nation, rich in resources and culture, endured, summed up in one of Mobutu's oft chanted slogans, "Notre beau pays—le Zaïre". Those dislocated from traditional communities found nationalism persuasive as they adapted to new situations and formed new identities.[49] Mbusa Bangau explains how those living on the Semeliki escarpment close to the border with Uganda changed their "outlook" in one generation, increasingly looking westwards to the Congo nation for their wider orientation and identity:

> I would say that during our parents' era they felt closer to the Ugandan people than to the people of Congo. That's the period before independence...At present we feel more at ease with other Congolese than foreigners. President Mobutu actually left positive elements. The element in which he was successful was the unification of all peoples, all these tribes which are found in the country.[50]

In Mbusa's assessment, Mobutu's centralist, nationalist policy provided an alternative identity in which Congolese peoples felt united in a com-

---

[46] Kevin Dunn, *Imagining the Congo: the International Relations of Identity* (New York, Palgrave Macmillan, 2003), 76 and 112–113.
[47] Isidore Ndaywel é Nziem, *Histoire Générale du Congo: De l'héritage ancien à la République Démocratique* (Paris, De Boeck & Larcier, 1998), 706.
[48] Winsome Leslie, *Zaire: Continuity and Political Change in an Oppressive State* (Colorado, Westview, 1993), 104–105.
[49] Ndaywel é Nziem, *Histoire Générale*, 718.
[50] Mbusa Bangau.

mon nation state. It was particularly attractive to the rapidly growing towns where there was a mix of ethnicities, languages and cultures. Thus the post-independence years saw a shift in the understanding of corporate identity. Ethnic identity was only one element in establishing oneself in the growing town. Samba Kaputo, in his detailed study of the Ituri province,[51] argues that urban identity was being constructed along social and economic lines according to the employment offered by the towns. North-east Congo is an ethnically heterogeneous area. Migrants came from most of the ethnic groups represented in the region, with no single ethnic group having numerical dominance. The towns of Irumu *territoire* and Nord-Kivu became multi-ethnic[52] and created a new society in the process. Nationalism and ethnicity are sometimes perceived as opposites, in which the dominance of one annuls the influence of the other. In Congo ethnic and national sentiments were held together, but, as demonstrated below, they were influenced by circumstances and altered one another. This was apparent in different perceptions of nationality and ethnicity articulated by different generations.

A third characteristic of urban society was an increase in the 'generation gap'. There has always been tension between the young, desirous of influence, and their seniors who enjoyed traditional status.[53] In towns these tensions were exacerbated. The first generation migrants negotiated the nationalism and multi-ethnicity of the towns in the workplace but resisted them in the church. They generally retained their rural language and culture, and their primary identification was with their society of origin. Worshipping in the EAC was a return to the rural, ethnic and familial. Most of them could be described as maintaining "the rural-urban continuum" and continuing "spiritual and economic communion with their villages."[54] Their children, on the other hand, had generally undergone a process of urbanisation and were emotionally removed from their ancestral escarpment tradition. Ethnic identity had an altered meaning for them. In certain circumstances they emphasised their ethnic loyalty but they were less observant of its customs and rules than their parents. They were likely to be more fluent in Swahili than the language of their parents, to enjoy the music from Kinshasa and

---

[51] Samba, *Phenomène d'Ethnicitie et Conflits ethno-politiques*, 408.
[52] Butembo, having a large Nande majority, is an exception to this.
[53] McKittrick, *To Dwell Secure*, 5–7.
[54] Ali Mazrui and Alamin Mazrui, *Swahili State and Society: The Political Economy of an African Language* (Nairobi, East African Educational Publishers, 1995), 66.

to appreciate the faster, more cosmopolitan pace of urban life. Their culture was in many ways a national one and they wished to see it acknowledged in church. They were more 'at home' in the towns and found Anglican services dull and uninspiring. As the EAC established itself in the urban areas during the 1970s these urban identity issues of nationalism, multi-ethnicity and generational difference were played out within the church. Their influence is mentioned here and will be studied further in later chapters.

Irene Bahemuka, the daughter of Rwakaikara, was twelve when she moved to Bunia in 1976. Prior to this she too had worshipped in the Brethren Church near Irumu. She remembers her disquiet when her father sent her to the EAC. She found it cold, formal, unfriendly, dominated by Hema, and, in liturgy and structure, rather too close to the Roman Catholic Church for her Brethren sensibilities.[55] Although the EAC claimed it was Protestant, the dress of its clergy and evangelists looked Catholic to most people in the towns, and the Prayer Book resembled the Catholic Missal. This liturgical formality which other Protestant denominations and second generation migrants found so alien was precisely part of the order of which first generation Anglican migrants were so fond. In Irene's remembered assessment of the EAC identity in the 1970s she perceived the village values differently to her father. Irene understood her parents' connection between home and the EAC as a conservative expression of culture and tradition that gave prominence to Hema customs. She was uncomfortable with the close association between ethnicity and denomination and did not associate any expression of Christian faith with ethnic loyalty.

In Irumu *territoire* the EAC's identity was closely associated with the ethnic group that had maintained its presence in Congo for 80 years. The traditional understanding of the solemn performance of religious rites by family heads in Boga affected urban worship and did not encourage non-Hema to participate. To those unfamiliar with the service it seemed "cold" and uninspiring. It was known as the "Hema church"—an appellation which, whilst never entirely true, alienated many, including younger Hema. How could the place of Hema fathers also be the place of non-Hema fathers? The success of the inculturation of the EAC on the escarpment presented problems in a different social setting. The predisposition of an ethnic group or clan to a particular

---

[55] Interview, Irene Bahemuka, Boga, French, 30 September 2000.

denomination had been a consequence of the division of territory between different missionary societies. Nevertheless, Protestant urban migrants from throughout the country were expected to attend the local Protestant church rather than establish their own denomination.[56] The rise of the urban EAC in the 1970s did not fit with the nationalist multi-ethnic ethos that was emerging in the towns. Moreover, despite the potentially divisive results of missionary comity, Christianity was expected by Congolese Christians to break down barriers of ethnicity, bringing an end to distrust among ethnic groups. "There is neither Jew nor Greek...all are one in Christ" (Gal. 3:28), was often quoted as the appropriate Christian response to the issues of ethnic tensions. Younger EAC members considered that a largely ethnocentric church was problematic in an urban setting. However, there was little awareness among the first generation Anglican migrants of the extent to which the EAC worship reflected escarpment village culture and there was also an unwillingness to sever entirely that connection. They were caught between the reality of the familiar and comfortable of the EAC which was effectively exclusive and the ideal of inclusive Christianity which threatened to be alien and 'un-anglican'.

Language use can exacerbate or deflect ethnic tensions. Studies of the African Church have recognised the importance of the vernacular in the indigenisation of Christianity.[57] Here the issue is turned on its head. Within the EAC, the vernacular was limited to one people and, therefore, effectively excluded others. The EAC, now spreading over a large and linguistically diverse area, needed a language in which all its members could participate equally. Swahili, the language of trade, towns and schools, fitted that role. Copies of the 1662 Prayer Book in Kenyan Swahili had been available to the EAC from about 1971.[58] In 1973 the EAC produced its own simplified Congolese Swahili Prayer Book. It was both comprehensible and affordable for most Congolese. Tabu Abembe considered that the Swahili Prayer Book gave the impetus necessary for the EAC to follow Apolo Kivebulaya's dying commission to take the Gospel further west into Congo:

---

[56] There were also a small number of Muslims and Kimbanguists in Bunia at this time.

[57] Lamin Sanneh, *Translating the Message: The Missionary Impact on Culture* (Maryknoll: Orbis, 1989), 124–125.

[58] Bakengana Lukando, "Histoire de la Paroisse Anglicane de Kainama: Vue panoramique des origines à 1995" (Diplôme de Graduat diss., ISThA, 1997), 11.

Once the Prayer Book was changed from Runyoro to Swahili people began to say, 'That's right, it's the Word of God.' So we could continue westwards as Apolo had said.[59]

The EAC could not have expected to operate any distance from Boga until its services and its administration were conducted in the *lingua franca* of the wider area. Re-plotting the narration of Apolo's burial wishes provided justification for a change in language that, in turn, gave an impetus for the EAC to spread beyond its traditional rural areas and to be accepted in the towns. It also undermined the intimate relationship between the Hema and the EAC. If some of the first migrants were uneasy about it many of their children welcomed the change. Their urbanisation was intimately connected with their fluency in Swahili.

Contested loyalty

Second generation migrants could not entirely understand their parents' attachment to the formal, slow, quiet Anglican ways but they did not desert completely the family church into which they had been baptised and confirmed. Open contestation was often difficult for junior members of society but negotiations around religious practice were possible. As a teenager Irene Bahemuka attended the CECA 20 youth Bible study on Sunday evenings for her own spiritual edification, in spite of her parents' disapproval. Where there was an EAC they wanted her to attend it as the church of her family and were suspicious of anything which might draw her away from it. So, on the insistence of her parents, she continued to attend Sunday morning Anglican services. Perpetuating village church structures and rites that maintained a sense of home was understood as the only way of being Anglican by those who established the churches. They did not want to lose this expression of religious identity and yet their own children were uncomfortable with it. If these elements made the migrants' own children uneasy they were unlikely to ensure the survival of the EAC as it moved from close-knit, mono-ethnic, remote village communities to rapidly growing, multi-ethnic, urban centres. These contested elements of identity were to become more acute as the children became adults. Second generation migrants challenged the relationship between 'home' and 'church'. The rural

---

[59] Interview, Tabu Abembe, Bwakadi, French, 6 October 2000.

home of their parents did not stretch psychologically into their own location. If church was to be included in their definition of 'home' it needed to develop a more national, urban identity. However, as well as the values of *utaratibu, upole* and *heshima* mentioned above, there was another value from their home villages which second generation migrants appreciated as integral to EAC's identity more than their parents did; the *maendeleo* introduced by the church.

Maendeleo was another village value that indicated the identity of the EAC. It was also appreciated in the towns by the younger generation. Indeed, where first generation migrants expected to see schools and clinics attached to urban chapels but were emotionally and spiritually sustained by *utaratibu, upole* and *heshima*, their children saw *maendeleo* as a vital part of the EAC without which the church held little attraction. A study of the development of Butembo chapel, which was to become the Nord-Kivu diocesan headquarters in 1992, illustrates the aspirations of progress generated by these urban chapels. The description is given by Estella, daughter of Mahirani Melena:

> When the Anglican Church came to us they read in our house.... They started to read in our living room every Sunday with our family, the family of Zakayo [Kyuma] and Lukambula's family. And Mukasa came every so often. And other people round about wanted to come in and read. Later we gave a very small offering to get the place there. It was completely bush... The fathers took their scythes, the mothers dug. Finally they managed to build a house with straw [roof]... Later they thought to build the house of the evangelist... the work went on. When there were many people, many Nande, when the straw house was there and Lukambula's house, they built the pastor's house... We destroyed the straw [house]. We cut iron sheets. And we also read there and we were choristers there. And Mother taught the women to read and to write, and Sunday School, these things, work, little *maendeleo*... to know cooking. Now *maendeleo* has really progressed. There are many Christians. Later we built with iron sheets for the school, the primary school. We children made... the school with [our] hands... Later we began work on that big church.[60]

Estella's remembrances of the development of the church in Butembo were ones of transforming bush into buildings and of the community work of construction and education. They provide a striking contrast to her mother's memories of teaching Anglican rites to the new

---

[60] Estella in Mahirani Melena.

congregation. The different emphases of recollections over thirty years reflect the varying priorities between generations.

Estella's description relates the move of the young community from the private sphere of her parents' home to a simple, purpose built public chapel. The outward sign of church growth was apparent in the necessity and ability to provide larger, more solid, and more numerous constructions, in which to meet and worship, to house church workers and to teach. Progress was marked in the change from evangelist to pastor, sub-parish to parish and in the move from occasional or short educational groups like Sunday School and women's groups to the provision of an entire permanent primary school. A secondary school and large dispensary would follow. *Maendeleo* encompassed a variety of social activities surrounding the establishment of the chapel. The relationship in the EAC between formal education and Christianity is apparent in Estella's words. *Kusoma*, literally 'to read', is the word she used for the activities of the Sunday morning service and the purpose of her mother's literacy class. She used the related noun, *masomo*, for 'school'. Both Lukambula in Butembo and Munege in Bunia were headmasters of the first primary schools as well as catechists. They were *walimu* in the dual sense of being both schoolteachers and church leaders. As in other African languages, education and Christian worship are linguistically synonymous, rites of adoration and modern educational skills fall within the same vocabulary network and the same socio-religious continuum.[61] The chapel was not there simply for the performance of religious rites but to provide services for the wider community.

This was the way it had been on the escarpment but first generation migrants found it problematic when they moved. The establishment of the EAC in urban areas coincided with the need for more schools in the growing towns. The colonial government had been slow to provide education. Other Protestant Churches had disassociated themselves from this intimate relationship between Christianity and social services.[62] However, the skills and standards of EAC *walimu* were rarely sufficient to meet the more rigorous requirements for schools in the 1970s. The Anglicans' resources were meagre and their achievements patchy. The EAC had to employ professionals to do many jobs most closely associated with *maendeleo* and church members were less intimately involved.

---

[61] W. A. Anderson, *The Church in East Africa, 1940–1974* (Dodoma, Central Tanganika Press, 1988), 111.

[62] J. E. Nelson, *Christian Missionizing and Social Transformation: A History of Conflict and Change in Eastern Zaire* (New York, Praeger, 1992), 5–7.

Nevertheless, they took advantage of the shortage of government accredited schools and presented the EAC as a forward-looking church desirous of serving the community in its modernist aspirations. In doing so they gained new members, particularly from the Baptist Churches in Nord-Kivu that had split acrimoniously.[63] The EAC also established clinics to further health care. They expressed concern that *maendeleo* was not happening fast enough, that they were not achieving the rate of success they wanted.[64]

A second problem for migrants was that they did not want 'development' to alter the worship or church structure which that their emotional ties with 'home'. Some, indeed, saw it as a distraction from worship.[65] They wanted the social development projects to remain discreet entities without impinging on *utaratibu, upole* and *heshima* of other areas of church life. They had moved from the escarpment because of *maendeleo* aspirations they learnt in the EAC but they did not want these aspirations to touch the urban church. In trying to form home in a new place they fully integrated only part of the home identity. That said, however, the fact that they appreciated *maendeleo* as part of the Christianity of the rural Semeliki escarpment villages meant that Anglicanism, as accepted and adapted by the villagers of the escarpment, was open to further change. If the chapels provided a haven in the town for the expression of traditional village values, they had been, in those villages, instruments of the modernising processes centred upon education and health care that had begun with the introduction of Christianity. Migrants' children, on the other hand, were grateful for the institutions but wished to see *maendeleo* penetrating all aspects of life, including worship, in ways that would reflect the ideals of nationalism and youth. *Maendeleo* is a word with a wide breadth of meaning and the second generation shifted its application to express a desire for change within the structures and worship of the EAC. As later chapters will demonstrate, this aspect of EAC identity would stimulate further shifts in ecclesiastical identity that would prevent the urban chapels from a retreat into a ghetto of rural conservatism or from a haemorrhaging of their young people to other denominations. In the 1970s and 1980s, however, it was the continuation of *maendeleo* in the church, however narrowly defined, which retained the loyalty of the second generation to the EAC.

---

[63] Ibid.

[64] Beatrice Kalumbi, Butembo, Swahili, 16 June 1998.

[65] Bampiga Bailensi, "Etude sur le Développement économique dans la Paroisse anglicane de Bunia" (Diplôme de Graduat diss., ISThA, 1994), 9–10.

A national, urban church

The identification of the EAC with 'home' was so strong for the first generation migrants that the importance of nationalism and urbanism was grasped by senior EAC leaders rather than the grassroots. This chapter has demonstrated that Anglican migration was fuelled by expectations of *maendeleo* and that the subsequent establishment of the EAC into urban areas was a grassroots initiative, motivated by migrants' desire to worship at home. This initiative was, however, encouraged and steered by church authorities and became, under the Bishops, a central policy of the EAC. Their interest gave greater impetus to migrant members and lay church workers.

Significant administrative changes in the EAC were taking place as members migrated. In 1972 impetus was given to the spread of the church by the inauguration of the first Anglican diocese in Congo. It is estimated that the EAC had 30,000 members in 14 parishes in this year. Having its own diocese gave the EAC greater national autonomy and chimed with the nationalism of the 1970s. Its headquarters were in Boga and its Bishop was CMS missionary, Philip Ridsdale. In 1976 the churches in Nord-Kivu came under the jurisdiction of a new diocese based in Bukavu.[66] Their Bishop was Bezaleri Ndahura, a well-travelled, well-educated schools' inspector with a strong nationalist bent. Originally from Boga, he had already influenced introduction of the EAC in Kisangani and in Maniema. His work had contributed to the rapid growth of the church. Bezaleri and Ridsdale wanted to see the EAC spread throughout Congo. They saw the strategic importance of having an Anglican presence in urban centres so they responded to the urban migration which had taken place and gave support to local initiatives. In 1975 in a report outlining their missionary strategy for the EAC they wrote:

> Many of our people are amongst those who gravitate to towns, and are lost. We are commencing work in many towns, as this is where the demand is, the need is, and the necessity is.[67]

Both men were convinced that the Anglican system was an appropriate one for Congo, and both saw evidence that it was appreciated by

---

[66] PRP "Report on Visit of Miss Diana Witts to the Dioceses of Boga and Bukavu, Zaïre, October 1979–May 1980," 7.

[67] DBk, "New Diocese in Zaïre" by Philip Ridsdale and Ndahura Bezaleri.

Anglicans and non-Anglicans alike.[68] Their expansionist aims at times smacked of arrogance and ecclesiastical imperialism but the result was that they worked to make the EAC a national and urban church. On one hand, they were simply catching up with what was already happening. On the other hand, they were providing an ideology and a plan of action to maintain the growth of the EAC. Bezaleri in particular understood the implications of the political ideology of nationalism as expressed in *authenticité*. He considered that the EAC needed to adapt to this idea if it was to expand. As an option for self-definition, however, it sat uneasily with loyalty to the values of a particular, local ancestral home. Nationalism challenged both loyalty to a particular ethnic group, and the appropriateness of transnational ties.

Ultimately, EAC members came to accept change wrought by others that diminished ethnicity as interpretative of the EAC. Firstly, they wanted growth in an ethnically plural region, a desire legitimised by their interpretation of Apolo's burial request. Secondly, no matter how dominant the Hema were in the EAC, the church had never been an entirely mono-ethnic institution on the escarpment. Hema dominance came to be seen—even by many Hema—as undesirable in a national denomination. Thirdly, their political and economic acceptance of nationalism in the 1970s made it more feasible for them to accept a national rhetoric in religious life. Migration did initially bring to the fore latent ethnic loyalties within the EAC but the dominant universalising discourse of leaders and members diminished the emphasis on those things held to be exclusively Hema. In the long term urban EAC migrants believed that particular expressions of ethnic belonging were inappropriate in church.

The establishment of dioceses signalled that the EAC was loosening its administrative ties to a church in another nation, and recognised that internal migration from the escarpment to the towns was transforming it into a Congolese institution. The self-understanding of the Church evolved in a national direction. Beni Bataaga, a senior clergyman at the time, explained:

---

[68] In Maniema and Shaba from 1973 a number of independent churches, unable to obtain a *personalité civile*, decided to become Anglicans rather than affiliate with another member-denomination of the ECC. In 1976 there were approximately 180,000 EAC members as a result of this.

We were no longer waiting for a programme from Uganda for ordination, for confirmation and other things. Our programme was here. Our
synod and other executive reunions were here. So we felt we were deeply
concerned with our own affairs in our country...So this started changing
the life of the church.[69]

Bataaga felt that the church had greater freedom and authority and
became more concerned with the situation in Congo. It began to face
west, toward the centre of the country, rather than east towards Uganda.
It began to share in the spirit of optimism about Congo that marked
the 1970s, with the promise of self-determination for the country. The
recognition by church authorities of the advantages of nationalism and
urbanism meant that the EAC, although small and marginal, was able
to engage the new nationalism and involve itself in working for *maendeleo*
in Congo. The EAC developed a greater interest in events in the rest of
country and took on an increased Congolese identity; a welcome move
for second generation migrants. If some senior members of individual
EAC chapels still clung consciously to their village values others were
beginning to accept the new national order. Their desire for *maendeleo*
and legitimacy made modernisation acceptable, their deeply held affection for the 'place of their fathers' made it gradual.

'...so that the work of the Lord will continue.'[70]

One photograph,[71] shown below, indicates this conscious change in orientation of the EAC from local and rural to national and urban. It was
taken on the 27th May 1979, the Sunday closest to the anniversary of
Apolo Kivebulaya's death on the 30th May. There was a large ordination service in Boga cathedral on that day, and the picture was taken in
the grounds. There are four clergymen, dressed in black cassocks, white
surplices and black preaching scarves grouped around Apolo's grave.
Two have their hands resting on the grave's cross. All of them hold two
or three books; the large black Bible, the slim blue Prayer Book and the
yellow hymnbook, *Nyimbo za Mungu*. All are archdeacons; from left to
right, Tito Balinda, Archdeacon of Beni, Tibafa Sylvestre, Archdeacon
of Kisangani, Festo Byakisaka, the Archdeacon of Boga and one of

---

[69] Interview, Beni Bataaga, Bunia, English, 15 September 2000.
[70] The reported words of Apolo Kivebulaya.
[71] DBg *Journal de Bord: Diocese de Boga-Zaïre*, Philip Ridsdale.

Illustration 4   Photograph of Four Archdeacons at Apolo's grave

'Apolo's boys', and Kabonabe Tibafa, Archdeacon of Butembo. All
of them would have known that Apolo, above whose body they were
standing, was buried with his head pointing westwards. How did they
interpret Apolo's request in 1979? Were they rooting themselves in the
tradition of a revered leader? Undoubtedly. Were they acknowledging
Apolo's work among the Mbuti in the forest? Possibly. Is this photograph
a conscious attempt to root the EAC expansion in the missiological myth
surrounding Apolo Kivebulaya's burial commission? Very probably.
All were responsible for a network of small chapels. All but Byakisaka
were working beyond the limits of missionary comity for the EAC. A
photograph round Apolo's grave linked them to a respected tradition: if
Boga was home, then Apolo's grave symbolised the centre of home. The
photograph also presented them as missionaries like Apolo, taking their
home with them. By 1979 Apolo's burial request was interpreted not

simply as taking the gospel, with its accompanying reading and healing, further into the forest, or maintaining Anglicanism on the escarpment. It legitimised the process by which clergy established parishes among Anglican migrants throughout modern Congo and provided for them a reproduction of escarpment Anglicanism as religious identity. The four men who stand so proudly round Kivebulaya's grave had a very different concept of the land that lay ahead than did Apolo but they believed they were carrying out his commission.[72]

Conclusion

This chapter has argued that the urban EAC of the 1970s consciously attempted to replicate the escarpment church, but that the process of migration and subsequent urbanisation germinated seeds of change dormant in the rural EAC. In ensuring the "continuity of practice," mentioned by Ebaugh and Chafetz, migrants maintained as the locus of personal identity within the EAC the corporate entity of their ancestral home. They determined to remain loyal to the qualities of *utaratibu*, *upole* and *heshima* learnt in Boga worship. Its formal, liturgical style kept migrants in touch with home and with the familiar aspects of Christian worship with which they had grown up. This religious identity allowed members to maintain continuity between village and town and provided a conservative force in terms of worship and ecclesiastical governance. In developing "adaptive strategies for change," *maendeleo*, which led many to migrate in the first place, was used to help members assimilate new social realities. Yet for many first generation migrants *maendeleo* seemed to threaten the values of *utaratibu*, *upole* and *heshima*. As a result of this contradiction *maendeleo*, as identity signifier, was permitted to operate within the social but not the spiritual sphere of church life. It did not sufficiently describe, for first generation migrants, their emotional attachment to the EAC. The on-going commitment to *maendeleo*, however, prevented the EAC from losing its young people who, removed from rural culture, did not find a home in the slow, orderly, respectful ways of the escarpment and contested the identity of the church they attended. *Maendeleo* paved the way for a more contemporary national and urban identity for the EAC by allowing a room for discourse on

---

[72] Muhindo Tsongo.

potentially divisive issues. Within the EAC at the beginning of the 1980s the tensions between tradition and change—staked-out in terms of *utaratibu, upole* and *heshima* versus *maendeleo*—provided sufficient openness to prevent ghettoisation while at the same time causing pain and resentment for some.

CHAPTER FOUR

RETURNING HOME TO A STRANGE LAND: EAC GROWTH THROUGH TRANS-BORDER MIGRATION

Introduction

In 1979 the fall of President Idi Amin precipitated an exodus from Uganda into the most north-easterly corner of Congo of ethnic groups closely associated with his regime. The refugees began to form Anglican congregations in communion with the diocese of Boga. In contrast to the urban spread of the church in Irumu and Nord-Kivu, the EAC in the *territoires* of Aru and Mahagi was established through sudden migration resulting from civil conflict. The Eastern border of Congo is often troubled and refugees have both fled *from* and *into* Congo using the boundary to their advantage during times of unrest. This chapter demonstrates that international borders in Africa are as much conduits as they are barriers in the spread of Christianity.

Dislocated from their life in Uganda in 1979 migrants re-configured their identity. Anglicanism was seen as an appropriate vehicle for identity adaptation in the socio-religious sphere, providing a framework in which they could apply their aspirations for order, development and freedom. The establishment of the EAC in these areas operated with different dynamics to that of the EAC in Irumu and Nord-Kivu; the chapel planting initiative was less centralised, more informal and lay-led. Thus it acts as a contrast to the story of the previous chapter, demonstrating that groups within the EAC developed varying identities. *Utaratibu* (liturgical and hierarchical order) and *maendeleo* (development) remained important needs for those identifying themselves as Anglicans as the EAC expanded through trans-border migration. As a result of different historical circumstances, however, these identity signifiers were differently interpreted through the use of *uhuru* (freedom). The previous chapter acknowledged that migrants wish to ensure continuity of religious practice whilst developing strategies for adaptation. This chapter demonstrates the complexities and tensions behind this assertion. In studying the identity of the northern EAC members through the development of chapels and the work of evangelists, it is clear that the continuities are carefully chosen and may not reach far into the past.

Migration

In May 1979 President Idi Amin fled from power following a coup which toppled his unpopular regime. From then until the end of 1983 about 125,000 people took refuge in Aru and Mahagi zones in Congo.[1] Amin's ethnic group, Kakwa, and neighbouring Lugbara and Alur had benefited disproportionately from his time as president. Many had participated in the violence of the regime and they feared reprisals from the Acholi who had regained influence in Uganda. Many who fled into Congo considered themselves Congolese, even though some of them had spent a lifetime away from their home villages. By the time it was thought safe to return to Uganda, they had re-established themselves in Congo and some had lost their land in Uganda. In 1987 perhaps 20% of the 300,000 people inhabiting Aru zone were refugees from Uganda.[2] Amongst them were those who established Anglican chapels.

Migration among the peoples of this area had been part of life for centuries. Prior to colonisation boundaries between groups were fluid: expansion or retreat could lead to migration into the area of another group. Customs and systems of governance might shift as a result and group membership was often flexible. The Alur, a Nilotic speaking group related to the Lwo of East Africa, migrated into the present area north of Lake Albert during the seventeenth century. The Alur were members of several politically independent chiefdoms, or 'segmentary states,' whose membership, geography, and relative power were fluid and assimilative of neighbouring groups like the Lendu and Ndo.[3] Alur chiefdoms had a sense of common ancestry but did not form one large cohesive group. Thus the colonial boundary established on the Nile-Congo watershed through Alur territory did not divide a single political entity but did cut similar cultures in two. The Nilotic Kakwa migrated in eighteenth century to the area they now occupy which is situated in the nation-states of Congo, Sudan and Uganda. The Kakwa have close relations with Lugbara[4] and intermarriage is

---

[1] Jeff Crisp, "Ugandan Refugees in Sudan and Zaire: the Problem of Repatriation," *African Affairs*, 85 (1986): 164–5.

[2] Oliver Jardin, "The 'Mama Bakita' centre for the disabled at Aru," *Refugee* (November 1987), 40.

[3] Aidan Southall, "Partitioned Alur," in *Partitioned Africans: Ethnic Relations Across Africa's International Boundaries, 1884–1984*, ed. A. I. Asiwaju (London, C. Hurst, 1985), 87–88.

[4] Boliba Baba, "Adiyo: The coming of the Kakwa and the Development of their Institutions" (B.A. diss., Makerere University, 1971), 10.

common. The Lugbara migrated from the Sudan area during the seventeenth and eighteenth centuries into what are now Uganda and Congo. The acephalous, virilocal systems of the Lugbara and Kakwa had more pronounced segmentation than the Alur. Clans were made up of sub-clans and family clusters under the authority of an elder who was usually the custodian of the ancestral shrines.[5] Clans possessed a sense of unity through genealogy but in daily life family clusters provided social cohesion. In 1912 the Belgian administration introduced an indirect rule system of *chefferies* in larger *collectivités* which co-opted or imposed *grands chefs* on peoples and thus consolidated what had been fluid systems of alliance-building. Among the Lugbara and Kakwa, particularly, this imposed a social stratification previously unknown in their cultures and divided clan structures.[6] The Belgians took social engineering further. For example, they considered Alur influence over non-Alur to be a form of slavery and set about disentangling non-Alur by resettling them in distinct geographical areas, an intervention that the people themselves did not always appreciate.[7]

Cross border migration started in 1910 when West Nile came under British colonial jurisdiction having previously been part of the Belgian Congo. Its study demonstrates the economic fallout of differing colonial policies and the subsequent social implications. British rule in Uganda was considered less severe and offered preferable labour options to those provided by Belgian rule in Congo where taxes were high and conscription frequent.[8] The fact that the same ethnic groups straddled the arbitrary borders provided opportunities for those on the Congolese side. The Congolese Alur, Kakwa and Lugbara left Congo to become soldiers, to work on plantations like those in Bunyoro, or in the Lugazi sugar industry near Jinja.[9] Others settled with their cattle just over the border in Uganda. Attempts by the Belgians to prevent this cross border

---

[5] John Middleton, *The Lugbara of Uganda* (New York, Holt, Rinehart & Winston, 1966), 26–30.

[6] John Middleton, "The Roles of Chiefs and Headmen Among the Lugbara," *Journal of African Administration* 8 (1956): 127–128.

[7] Aidan Southall, "Ethnic Incorporation among the Alur," In *From Tribe to Nation in Africa*, ed. Ronald Cohen and John Middleton (Scranton, Chandler, 1970), 72–74.

[8] Kamba-Opima, "Evolution politique et économique separée des Lugbara au Congo belge et en Uganda sous le Regime colonial, 1914–1956" (Licence diss., ISP, Bunia, 1991), 76.

[9] Samson Embaga-Ujiga, "The Mission of the Church to the Lugbara Community of Lugazi Sugar Factory" (Diploma of Theology diss., Bishop Tucker Theological College, 1981), 7.

movement had limited success and it continued throughout the colonial era.[10] Migration to Uganda increased after independence when *Simba* rebels threatened the stability of villages in Congo in 1964. Many fled into Uganda making the most of family connections with those already working there. In the 1970s some took advantage of their ethnic or clan connection with Idi Amin and found good jobs in Kampala.

John Middleton[11] explains the results of these migrations: the Alur, Lugbara and Kakwa became rapidly aware of the outside world and accustomed to mobility. Young men who led the migratory trend gained life experiences different to those of their elders and on their return they challenged the traditional order of their communities. As migrants returned with knowledge of the hierarchical social systems of southern and central Uganda, social stratification was introduced to a greater degree than had been common in their Nilotic and Sudanic acephelous social structures, continuing a trend set by the Belgian administration.

Migrants often saw themselves as more progressive and successful than those who had never migrated. They regarded Uganda as the country of development and admired the workings of different sectors of its modern society. Such was the influence of this migratory pull that there were few families who did not have some members who had spent time in Uganda. They had made their home in Uganda and may never have returned to Congo had not Amin's regime been so decisively overthrown.

When refugees returned they preferred to go to their fathers' home villages, rather than live in refugee camps that were populated with those who had little previous connection with Congo. Identification with paternal villages allowed them to settle in what was often an unfamiliar place, to call it home, and to identify themselves as Congolese. Otuwa Simeon, a Lugbara, succinctly sums up the situation:

> Here is home. I came back to come home. Our parents birthed us there [in Uganda], we married there, and we've returned home to Congo.[12]

---

[10] Aidan Southall, *Alur Society: A Study in Processes and Types of Domination* (Cambridge, W. Heffer & Sons, 1953), 318–321.

[11] J. Middleton, "Political Incorporation Among the Lugbara of Uganda," in *From Tribe to Nation in Africa*, ed. R. Cohen and J. Middleton (USA, Chandler, 1970), 67.

[12] Interview, Otuwa Simeon, Aru, Lugbara, 11 August 2000.

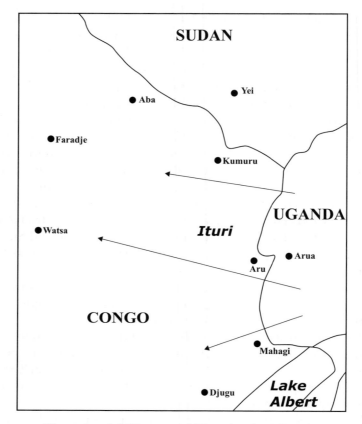

Illustration 5　　Diagram of Trans-border Migration

Home was the place of one's father's ancestors. One may have never visited it before but as a location for belonging it held a paramount position. Ozua Samson plotted his migration with the biblical Exodus and spoke of his family's traumatic escape from Uganda as leaving Egypt for the Promised Land,[13] the place where they truly belonged. The strong attachment to the village of one's father, nurtured during absence from it, did not negate the fact that life experiences in Uganda left the returned migrant with aspirations for self-improvement and expectations of a higher standard of modern living which, along side the sudden dislocation from all that seemed familiar, caused a sense

---

[13] Interview, Ozua Samson, Aru, Swahili, 10 August 2000.

of isolation for returned-migrants. Yuma Ajule, settled in his father's village, felt differently from Otuwa and Ozua:

Here [in Congo] I'm in exile. In my spirit, I'm in exile.[14]

His sense of dislocation remained over twenty years later. Often this arose in those who felt a sense of lost opportunities. The media of schools was French and Lingala[15] rather than English. Children who fled Uganda often failed to integrate into the Congolese system. Congolese migrants had returned to the place they called home and found it strange.

The social effects of migration were mirrored in the churches. During their time in Uganda Congolese migrant workers had joined churches. For some this was their first significant Christian experience. Others joined a church affiliated to the one with which they had been familiar in Congo. Those from Communauté Evangélique au Centre de l'Afrique (CECA 20), the only Protestant Church in Aru and Mahagi zones, joined the Anglican Church of Uganda (COU), the only Protestant church in Uganda. Congolese working in large plantations and factories in Uganda could usually find a congregation that spoke their mother tongue. In Lugazi for example, between 1936 and 1974 five Protestant Lugbara congregations, three Bangala congregations, and another for Logo from Congo were formed to serve the sugar factory workers.[16] They were usually started by workers who did not want to worship in Luganda and felt that there was discrimination against them as northerners. The tendency to form congregations of small units, serving specific groups would be replicated on the return to Congo. The confidence to challenge official uniformity that, in Congo would result in conflict with CECA 20, began as migrant workers. These challenges remained a localisation of western mission Christianity rather than the development of independency.

Not only was the formation of small chapels along socio-linguistic lines learnt in Uganda, a specific spirituality was adopted by many. Among the returnee refugees were those who had a dramatic conversion experience through association with the Balokole Revivalists whose hallmarks were open-air evangelism, public confession of sin, fellowship groups and critical membership of the Anglican Church. They challenged the perceived nominalism of orthodoxy, demanding strict

---

[14] Interview, Yuma Ajule, Kumuru, Swahili, 18 August 2000.
[15] Or Bangala, a dialect of Lingala.
[16] Embaga-Ujiga, "The Mission of the Church to the Lugbara", 34–35.

discipline and commitment to fellowship and evangelism. From 1960
a few Balokole began to return to Congo, where they were known
as Wokovu ('salvation' in Swahili), and called their own people to
repentance and revival. Their contribution to the EAC will be studied
in chapter six. It must be noted here, however, that revivalism contributed to the expectation by the migrants of religious freedom and
evangelism.

As has been observed elsewhere on the continent, affiliation of a religious group can enable members to become 'social agents' for change in
a refugee situation.[17] In a particular set of historical circumstances, the
EAC was to become the, perhaps unlikely, instrument for the realisation
of returned refugees' aspirations that they had developed in Uganda. It
was praised and criticised by its members as they measured it against
these aspirations. And it gained non-migrant members, in part, as they
assimilated the aspirations brought to them by their migrated friends
and relations.

Implanting an Anglican Church

A brief survey of events surrounding the establishment of the EAC
in the northern area is presented below. A Wokovu group in Mahagi
made the first move to contact the EAC in Boga in 1979. Wokovu had
been operating in Congo since the 1960s but they were banned from
CECA 20 and imprisoned for their activities. They wanted to worship
and evangelise freely but needed to belong to a state-recognised church
in order to do so. A well-educated Ugandan refugee told them about
the church of 'Boga-Zaire' and helped them make contact. They were
accepted into the EAC in December 1979 by Munege Kabarole with
Wokovu leader, Thumbe Ferdinand, as local EAC leader. Their first
pastor, Bahemuka Ndahura from Boga, arrived in December 1980.[18]
After inaugurating the church Munege stayed on for a Wokovu convention. Here he met thirty Wokovu men and women from Aru who
were intrigued to see a clergyman dressed in the same robes as those
of the COU. They spoke with him and decided to introduce the EAC
to Aru zone. Sila Bileti, the Aru area W*okovu* leader became the Aru

---

[17] K. B. Wilson, "Refugees and Returnees as Social Agents," in *When Refugees Go Home*,
ed. T. Allen and H. Morsink, 237–250 (New Jersey, Africa World Press, 1994), 237.
[18] ArchA, *Hadizi ya Archidiacone ya Aru* 1996, 2.

EAC leader of several small chapels. The EAC in Aru was officially opened by Munege in May 1981.[19] The first pastor, Kabarole Baguma from Boga, arrived in 1982 to discover fifteen chapels already formed by *Wokovu* using their regional networks. Whilst this was happening, Anglicans who had initially tried to join CECA 20 after their forced migration into Congo were told that their baptism was not recognised and they needed to be rebaptised. This they could not accept and so joined the EAC, establishing more chapels in their home villages. The news of the introduction of an Anglican Church in the Aru area reached the Kakwa in 1983 via the *Wokovu* network. Adoroti Ombhabua, a Ugandan *mwangalizi* (evangelist), who had been working in Aru, went to the Kakwa and encouraged the establishment of small chapels wherever there were Anglicans who had been in Uganda.[20] Sudanese refugees from the protracted conflict in Sudan also swelled the numbers in these early Anglican chapels. Within 20 years the EAC reached west to Faradje and Watsa and south to Djugu. There were 14,000 communicants and a large affiliated membership of up to 30,000.[21] Most refugees had been unaware of the continuing presence of an Anglican Church in Congo. However, most of them knew of Apolo Kivebulaya as a great missionary. The realisation that they were entering relations with the church that Apolo started gave it added legitimacy in their eyes.[22]

Unlike the urban EAC further south, the presence of centrally trained *walimu* was not considered a prerequisite for internal ecclesiastical legitimacy of a local chapel. As David Maxwell notes in his study of Christianity among the Hwesa of Zimbabwe, migrants returning home possessed an independence and a self-confidence that challenged the present *status quo*.[23] As refugees fleeing war the returned-migrants in Aru and Mahagi zones may not have had the same wealth or status as the Hwesa mine workers, but they felt the constraints of the traditional ways of their fathers' village and were keen to negotiate change within it. In both cases the alternative lifestyle they offered was expressed in

---

[19] ArchA, Sila Bileti, "Historical Background of Anglican Church in Leri," 1988, 1.

[20] *Hadizi ya Archdiaconé de Kumuru*, 1996, 2.

[21] Kumuru and Aru Archdeaconry *Statistiques*, 2000. This is over 15% of the Alur, Kakwa and Lubara populations. Grimes, Babara F. "Ethnologue." http://www.sil .org/ethnologue/countries/Zair.html: SIL, 2000.

[22] Interview, Oloni Seth, Aru, English, 11 August 2000.

[23] David Maxwell, *Christians and Chiefs in Zimbabwe: A Social History of the Hwesa People, c. 1870s–1990s* (Edinburgh, Edinburgh University Press, 1999), 66–69.

religious terms. For the Hwesa miners in the 1950s it was Pentecostal
Christianity that challenged traditional Hwesa beliefs. In the northern
corner of Congo two decades later it was Anglicanism which provided
more choice in the religious market. In both cases it was a localised
form of a global church that grew quickly as it was perceived to meet
a wide spectrum of needs in the community.

Chapels

During interviews, Anglican Christians in the north articulated the
reasons they established the EAC in a similar way to urban Anglican
migrants further south. The primary reason given for wanting a chapel
was a sense of belonging to *kanisa letu*, 'our church' through baptism and
salvation as a result of time spent in Uganda. This sense of ownership
came across in Samson Ozua's repetition of these words:

> ...it was my father who started it....He saw that this church was *kanisa
> letu*. We hadn't gone to CECA. CECA wasn't *kanisa letu*. Now this was
> *kanisa letu* so we must start it.[24]

Migrants knew from Uganda that chapels and the catechists who
ran them could be swiftly organised but they were the first rung on a
ladder of church structure which they hoped would follow. *Kanisa letu*
connected migrants to a familiar order, *utaratibu*. Northern Anglicans
were familiar with Anglican 'tradition', 'the way of living', and wanted
to replicate it. Anguzu Alfred explained it thus:

> ...the thing which I really like about this church is the *utaratibu*...of the
> service. And also the rank of every person. Yes, this really pleases me.[25]

Utaratibu as liturgical and hierarchical order was for these northern
Anglicans, as for their urban counterparts further south, an integral
part of Anglicanism. The *utaratibu* of the EAC offered familiarity in
situation of dislocation. It was important to people that they were part
of a church similar to the one they left in Uganda, possessing the same
liturgy, the same clerical hierarchy, immediately visible by the same
vestments, and having the same groups operating within it. Worship
style and church structure united migrants to a larger organisation that

---

[24] Ozua Samson.
[25] Interview, Anguzu Alfred, Aru, Swahili, 10 August 2000.

gave a sense of security; one may have arrived in haste during war, the congregation may meet under a tree but that belied the opportunities of belonging to an organisation with global connections. *Utaratibu* filled a socio-religious need for belonging, security and order and reflected the nature of the God of order whom they worshipped. Joining the EAC was not simply an ideological decision, it also showed religious pragmatism. To operate openly as a church community returned-migrants needed to be part of the Congolese Protestant administrative order, the *Eglise du Christ au Congo* (ECC). The establishment of an independent church was unattractive because it was viewed as subversive to the order of the state and would lead to persecution as well as a sense of isolation. For trans-border migrants as well as urban ones, the EAC, as both member of the ECC and the Anglican Communion, provided a sense of external legitimacy.

The *utaratibu* of *kanisa letu* was a common identifying factor amongst mainstream Anglicans throughout North-east Congo. However, other identity features affected the way each group considered what *utaratibu* meant in practice. Variations in their understandings of Anglicanism were influenced by different migratory experiences. For the northerners *kanisa letu* did not entail the *upole* and *heshima* of escarpment village values but rather the antithesis of these, the modern values of well-travelled migrant labourers. Among northerners, aspirations of *uhuru* (freedom) and a stronger sense of *maendeleo* influenced their interpretation of *utaratibu*. *Maendeleo* was used by urban and trans-border migrant members of the EAC as an identity signifier. Superficially, the two groups used *maendeleo* in a similar way. The emphasis in common parlance was usually on material *maendeleo*, although material benefit was often closely associated with spiritual improvement.[26] Trans-border migrants, however, possessed none of the ambiguity about *maendeleo* articulated by urban migrants, desirous of preserving a conservative form of *utaratibu*. For northerners labour migration to Uganda had been seen in terms of an improved standard of living. Membership of the COU was linked to this improvement because the COU promoted social development. Their hasty return to Congo was considered a backward step of economic regression, so northerners saw *maendeleo* as an opportunity to reverse the downward mobility caused by their latest migration. Thus church workers who preached a message of *maendeleo* had a ready audience.

---

[26] Interview Arie Rose, Kumuru, Kakwa, 17 August 2000.

The *maendeleo* message centred round small-scale familial development
that was expected to improve the church community, as Atuku Abe
asserts:

> ...particularly on the corporal side, the church gave itself completely to
> educate people about poverty...to say, 'Life is like this now, we will make
> plans now, we will have projects to improve people at home and so we can
> share until it affects the church.' Thus it can carry the church forward.[27]

Northerners desired schools and clinics but their priority was the alle-
viation of immediate poverty. Communal fields and animals, basket
weaving, sewing, *inter alia* were part of *maendeleo* in which the whole
community could engage.

The village of Giyawa, in the parish of Azangani, for example,
wanted *maendeleo* for their community. Giyawa EAC chapel was started
by CECA 20 members who appreciated the *maendeleo* discourse of
the EAC and so became Anglicans as a group.[28] It is likely that some
Giyawa villagers had stayed in Uganda and so believed that this small
denomination in Congo could deliver its promises. It was a link with
the old life and a sign that the new life might improve beyond the
daily struggle for survival. Although a denomination swap by a whole
congregation was less common than the founding of chapels by marginalised individuals, it happened elsewhere and indicates that the
aspirations for personal and communal advancement could be stronger
than denominational loyalty. *Maendeleo* was prominent in the northern
discourse of EAC identity because members wished to chose from the
Christianities available to them one that was most conducive to their
socio-religious needs as disadvantaged returned-migrants with useful
life-experience. This differed from the priority of urban migrants to
conserve one particular tradition in an economically promising situation. Thus northerners were more conscious of the positive possibilities
within the EAC for socio-religious change than were urban migrants
from the escarpment. For trans-border migrants the appeal of *maendeleo*
was a potent one but they required the social space in which to make
it work. This they referred to as *uhuru*.

---

[27] Interview, Atuku Abe, Kumuru, Swahili, 19 August 2000.
[28] OHA, "Histoire de la Paroisse Azangani," 1999.

Uhuru

The desire for ecclesiastical *uhuru* arose for many as a result of the religious marginalisation encountered by returned-migrants because they refused to accept re-baptism. Leonora Draru remembers the distress of her rejection by CECA 20:

> ...at the time for Holy Communion, it was refused us. They said that if we wanted to go for Holy Communion we must go for instruction now and we would be put in water a second time. As...in Uganda, I had already received baptism along with confirmation, it was now difficult for me.[29]

Returned-migrants wanted to partake in Holy Communion in order to belong fully to a Christian Church. In the words of Yobo Kupajo, "When we saw that CECA has made life difficult for us we wanted *uhuru* in Jesus,"[30] which meant freedom from CECA 20 and its constraints. Isaac Ageli explains the nature of these constraints:

> Let me say that the CECA church, now that it has existed there for many years, people have now turned it, they have now mixed it really with tradition. Because right now you see most of the CECA church leaders are people who are clan leaders so when they have traditional problems they just mix [them] together with religious problems.[31]

Christianity may have been introduced only sixty years previously but, as in Boga, it had allied itself with the traditional sources of social power. CECA possessed the protestant monopoly, and in some Kakwa areas it was the only Christian church. CECA retained the socio-religious *status quo* through the membership of influential families. There was a belief that if you were not related to prominent members of CECA leadership there was no freedom to advance in education, in jobs within the church, and so on. CECA opportunities had reached saturation point and those who occupied senior positions were not chosen on merit but on family connections. The social contextualisation which had taken place in CECA was unappealing to returned-migrants. They were suspicious of a mixture of 'tradition' and 'religion' that questioned their Christian identity. The development of different Anglican and CECA identities will be analysed in the following chapter. However, northern

---

[29] Interview, Leonora Draru, Aru, Swahili, 12 August 2000.
[30] Interview, Kupajo Yobo, Kumuru, Kakwa, 17 August 2000.
[31] Interview, Ageli Isaac, Kampala, English, 26 July 2000.

migrants believed that there was little *uhuru* in CECA to permit social advancement and allow the utilisation of skills and experiences learnt in Uganda. This concern was expressed in a socio-religious manner by providing an alternative to CECA's church discipline, social influence and style of worship. In establishing the EAC returned-migrants achieved *uhuru* in providing a socio- religious choice previously unavailable. As noted earlier, those returning from Uganda, had, for decades, challenged the *status quo* with new ideas brought from their time away from the village. The returned Anglicans introduced a new religious, moral and social order which, whilst not being radically different from the Christianity already available, was different enough to be perceived as a threat to the Protestant denomination already present.

The *Histoire de la Paroisse Azangani* (1999), a hand-written document on the emergence of the individual chapels that make up the parish,[32] claims that those who started local chapels were native to the village. This is a defence against those who said that the EAC was *dini ya wakimbizi*, refugee religion. A foreign church that disappeared when its members returned to their own country would have been less of a threat to CECA. The members of the EAC were declaring their intent to stay in Congo and insisting that they could both belong to their fathers' village and have the *uhuru* to belong to a church from Uganda. They were proud that their church was local as well as being international. Here is a paradox, of wanting freedom, being prepared to challenge the local *status quo*, but also desiring legitimacy and security in one's own village. Returned-migrants were attracted to independent choice, but after the dislocation of sudden migration many felt some degree of economic and psychological dependence on their father's village. They desired freedom but also required a particular order. Thus the extent of their choices was restricted by their desire for respectability in the village and safety from heavy-handed government authorities. The *uhuru* that informed the *utaratibu* of *kanisa letu* was real but limited. Nevertheless, desire for both *maendeleo* and *uhuru* was a potent force for change. As interpreters of *utaratibu*, northerners were to make Anglican observance less rigid and more applicable to their own social realities.

The reasons for the establishment of chapels shows that identity was constructed partially in terms of aspirations learnt in Uganda and partially in terms of negotiated belonging to home villages. They could be clustered round the Anglican Church because the migrants knew

---

[32] OHA, "Histoire de la Paroisse Azangani," 1999.

it from Uganda and because, as a recognised member of the ECC, it could operate throughout Congo.

Chapel planting methods

The *Histoire de la Paroisse Azangani* also alludes to chapel planting methods. Two main methods were in operation in the 1980s. They differ from the centralised approach studied in the previous chapter in that they replicated the rural identity of the church. In the zones of Aru and Mahagi growth was largely uncontrolled by the diocesan centre and leadership was a local rather than central choice.

In the first method an individual or group organised a chapel in their own village, appointed a leader and contacted a nearby EAC chapel. Worship was carried out in Alur, Kakwa or Lugbara using, where available, Prayer Books with hymnals translated in Uganda. Members of the chapel understood themselves to be the primary initiators, meeting together, making a decision to open an Anglican chapel, visiting or sending a letter to the parish or sub-parish centre and following what they knew of the Anglican order. They saw themselves as making a choice for religious self-determination. Their actions took place, however, with the prior knowledge that other Anglican chapels were being established and that the EAC was a legitimate presence in the Kakwa *collectivité*, recognised by the local administration. Head of families acted to found an EAC chapel when they heard of others already started in the area but they had few ambitions beyond their village.

This method of chapel planting operated from village to village. Neighbouring villagers decided that they would like to attend the EAC and organised a chapel in their own village. Sinziri Onadra gives an example from Mingoro parish in his archdeaconry of Kumuru:

> ...when the church of Mingoro arrived people came from different places, some came from five kilometres away, others came from ten kilometres away, they came to worship in one place...The people from ten kilometres they multiplied there, they saw that they had been a small family and now many had found faith. Now they sat down and said, 'Now brothers, we are far away—to do ten kilometres every Sunday is far. Please, now we've reached ten or twenty people, how would it be to make a branch of the church here?'...Finally we have lots of churches coming from one church.[33]

---

[33] Interview, Sinziri Onadra, Kumuru, Swahili, 18 August 2000.

This segmentation meant that attendance at individual chapels could be as low as twenty to thirty people. As Archdeacon, Sinziri was pleased to see the spread of the church, although he saw a danger implicit in this method of chapel planting in an area of traditionally acephelous and segmented ethnic groups. Geographical distance often corresponded to clan boundaries and he expressed concern that chapels formed, even coincidentally, along clan lines would encourage local divisions rather than being a means of breaching them:

> Because a church like this—if it is one family alone not welcoming other people—in the end it will stay still, there wont be *maendeleo*, it will just decline without becoming a real church which welcomes everyone...There is danger in people saying, "It's my church, it's my church." Really it not the church of a person, it's the church of Christ.[34]

The local village may have been proud to have *kanisa letu* but for Sinziri the purpose of the Christian church was to welcome and unite people outside the boundaries of family, clan and ethnic group and he feared that an emphasis only on local issues might hinder *maendeleo*. The localised character of each village chapel was perceived as a weakness when viewed through the belief in the inclusiveness of Christianity. Church leaders often emphasised the inclusiveness of a global church, appreciating its wider units of belonging, whereas lay members often placed greater emphasis on its local appeal. Anglican members had to work out the relationship between numerous clans and ethnic groups with different languages and customs and larger networks of belonging presented through the EAC and its membership of the Anglican Communion. Furthermore, northern leaders would contest the Congolese expression of, what they considered to be, an inclusive institution with universal values. As will become apparent, they did not equate Anglicanism with the cultural expression it had developed on the Semeliki escarpment and felt that it was, at times, dismissive of the Anglican expression they had learnt from Uganda.

The second method was the itinerant evangelism of certain *walimu* and *wangalizi*. These lay church workers would call upon a family head known to have lived in Uganda and suggest that he gather his wider family into a chapel. Once again a *mwalimu* was appointed from within the small congregation. Operating in the area at this time were two of the most enterprising church planters, Adoroti Ombhabua and Asiki

---

[34] Ibid.

David. They actively tried to raise the profile of the EAC by encouraging the creation of chapels among those returned from Uganda. They influenced family elders who may not have taken the initiative, they promised *maendeleo* in ways in which it would be difficult to fulfil, and they, along with the *Wokovu* network, were responsible for taking the EAC beyond clusters of neighbouring villages to new areas and new ethnic groups. Spontaneous as this approach might seem, ecclesiastical and state recognition was always sought, as Asiki explained:

> And we open them by going to the government. First of all I go and give my record and then I go and establish a church there. After I established a church, when I see people coming there—because you see people coming, thirty or fifty, even a hundred—then straight away I take it to the parish.[35]

After Christianity had been present in Aru and Mahagi zones for sixty years, people began to choose what sort of Christianity they wanted, and to be active in introducing it. Ordinary Christians, who had no official position in the church, were responsible for establishing churches and bringing scattered Anglicans together. In areas of rapid, grassroots growth where centres of ecclesiastical power were distant the demarcation between lay member and church leader was often blurred. As the number of chapels grew, the work of catechists was recognised by making them evangelists and pastors and so the demarcation became more obvious.

A third method for founding chapels was introduced as Archdeaconry structures were put in place in Aru and a significant number of evangelists were able receive training. This method followed the urban model of greater centralised control. The diocesan centre at Boga quickly realised that Archdeacon Munege Kabarole could not effectively oversee the rapidly growing northern churches from Bunia, 320 km south of Aru. So Mukasa Nasanairi, the Ugandan missionary, came out of retirement in Kampala to be the first Archdeacon of Aru in 1984.[36] Kabarole Baguma became the second Archdeacon in 1986. The number of untrained *walimu* was so great and the number of chapels increasing so rapidly that a Bible School was removed from Komanda to Aru. In 1988 a CMS family came to Aru to assist with training, administration and development in the new archdeaconry and two other mission

---

[35] Interview, Asiki David, Aru, English, 22 August 2000.
[36] *Hadizi ya Archidiacone ya Aru*, 5.

partners, an agriculturalist and a doctor, were to follow. Their presence symbolised the global connections of the EAC and raised hopes of greater *maendeleo*. During this time the northern church changed from most closely resembling an informal grassroots movement to becoming an institution structurally linked with the older church on the escarpment, expected to follow its traditions and be subject to the rulings of diocesan synod.

The Anglicans in the north had no desire to be a loose network of grassroots chapels, nor to be an independent church. They wanted church workers who had formally studied the Bible and the Prayer Book, to guide members in the Anglican way. They wanted to quash outside criticism that this new church was merely a new local sect led by illiterates with no history or legitimacy. They also wanted to be more closely connected to an institution of power and potential development. The Anglican Church, as they understood it from Uganda, was an influential, global institution, providing *utaratibu* and *maendeleo* for its members. This is what they wanted to replicate. Adoroti explained it thus:

> ...the things of Anglican [sic] from Uganda should be for Congo...I would like everything we do in Congo and which they do in Uganda to be uniform.[37]

Pastors saw in this increased uniformity an opportunity for greater control over the work of *walimu* and thus the possibility of avoiding 'clanism' between different villages. The rapid growth of the EAC meant that this centralised model for church planting continued to operate alongside the grassroots models. In Kumuru Archdeaconry, particularly, the demand for trained church workers continually outstripped the resources to train them.[38]

Scholars of African ecclesiastical history recognise that *walimu* and *wangalizi*, were the most effective evangelists in the development of the African Church yet their achievements and methods are not well documented. Studying Christians who identified so strongly with the establishment of the EAC in a new location that they became *walimu* and, as the administrative structure developed, moved up the hierarchy of church workers, provides clues to Anglican identity in this area and their contribution will be analysed below.

---

[37] Interview, Adoroti Ombhabua, Kumuru, Swahili, 17 August 2000.
[38] ArchK *Statistiques*, 2000.

Walimu *and* wangalizi

> ...first to Parombo, the village of Mrs Ferdinand, then to Arisi, my village, after to Pathole, and eventually to other corners of Mahagi. My husband and I have travelled all over to open churches. We've gone to each place where the people have asked for a church.[39]

If this sounds like a localised version of the biblical injunction to witness in Jerusalem, Judea, Samaria, and to the ends of the earth, the parallelism would not be lost on the narrator. Marthe Ubotha of Mahagi zone, like other *Wokovu* members, believed that her task was to carry out the Great Commission. *Wokovu* started in their own villages, gathering their extended family, and then went to evangelise in other villages.

Most church workers were expected to re-locate at regular intervals once the administrative structure was in place and when their pastor or archdeacon deemed it necessary. From the beginning some *walimu* enjoyed the itineration or, more often, semi-itineration, of chapel planting. Others felt their loyalty was primarily to one chapel at a time. This reflects slightly different conceptions of the task of the *walimu*: semi-itinerants were often *Wokovu* and emphasised evangelism; those who mainly remained in one place emphasised the local introduction of Anglicanism. Most of those who itinerated did so from a particular base, travelling further and further from it to establish more churches. Marthe Ubothe was one of the few women who itinerated with her husband. Most husbands left their wives at home to look after children, crops and livestock: the story of *walimu* is still largely a story about men. Marthe found that the difficulties of day-to-day living made evangelism hard and demanded initiative if it was to succeed. Most *Wokovu* had developed the necessary Christian commitment for itinerant evangelism through their conversion and membership of the group in Uganda. For others, the dislocation of forced migration caused a change in life direction involving conversion and commitment to church work. Below are the stories of three church workers who started work as the EAC entered their area. The events they chose to narrate illustrate their Christian identity.

Asiki David's story is one of striking dislocation. Of Congolese parentage, he was born in Uganda. In 1975 he joined the airforce, working as a radar technician at Entebbe airport. He had been baptised and

---

[39] Interview, Ubotha Marthe, Mahagi, Alur, 27 August 2000.

confirmed but claimed that he 'did not know God' and led an immoral life. He was captured by the liberating Tanzanian army in 1979 and spent time in prison in Tanzania and Uganda. There, nurtured by Revivalists, he had a conversion experience as a result of dreams of his dead mother singing hymns and giving him Bible verses. When he was released in 1983 he went to his father's village of Bongilo in Congo where he volunteered as a *mwalimu* in the emerging EAC. He was semi-itinerant, travelling from the chapel to which he had been appointed, preaching in markets, opening chapels under mango trees, returning to visit them and covering huge distances in Aru zone and beyond. He continued the work of chapel planting once he was ordained in 1996. Asiki, who claimed to have opened about sixteen chapels in three parishes, explained why he made journeys of over 100 km on foot or bicycle to establish chapels among migrated Anglicans:

> ...I need development, and I need people to get Word of God...Because the Bible says, Jesus said, when two or three are gathered in his name, he's there. So by then when I hear they need church, I just go, and open also, just because they want Word of God. I go after this.[40]

His stated aims were development and evangelism, which he describes as bringing the Gospel to places where there were already people with Anglican connections. Asiki and others engendered individual conversions and increased commitment to Christianity. They also introduced another denomination to an area; an action frowned upon by the ECC.

Zamba Asu, erstwhile valet to Idi Amin, also had an abrupt change of life direction as a result of his flight from Uganda. Again he was born in Uganda of Congolese parentage. His father, of whom he spoke at length in his narration, was an evangelist in the COU. Zamba had been baptised but rejected the Christian lifestyle when he went to work in Kampala. In his story there is no mention of sudden conversion but rather the impact of losing everything, fleeing northwards with Amin and returning to his father's village with his father:

> After the war came here I could think about the things I had done...Let's say, I was baptised and my family was Christian and, because I left being a Christian to be something else, I realised that I had really done wrong. It's wrong to deceive my God. I was his child and I left him to do sins.

---

[40] Asiki David.

> Anyway, there, my spirit returned. I no longer like these bad, bad things. I returned to his work, to follow Jesus.[41]

The upheaval of the war caused him to reflect on his life. In his work as *mwalimu* he was following his father's footsteps in his father's village. It was a return to his origins. His work as *mwalimu* was even instigated by his father who, immediately on return to his village, established a Sunday School and, later, joined the EAC when it reached the area.

In Asiki's and Zamba's stories dramatic change is the most obvious dynamic but continuity is an underlying element. These two men developed very different lives for themselves in Congo from that which they had lived in Uganda. They had lost jobs, status, and homes as a result of the war. Their identity as successful, pleasure-seeking, young men had been destroyed as well. In Congo they had to re-form their lives and identity. In doing so they reaffirmed the Christian belief they had been taught by their parents and returned to the behaviour expected of a Christian. They returned to their fathers' villages and also to their parents' religion: the Anglicanism learnt from migration to Uganda. They wanted to transplant *kanisa letu* to their new/original location. The difference between Asiki and Zamba is one of emphasis. Asiki's *Wokovu* conversion made him take *kanisa letu* to other villages and ethnic groups, believing that his denomination was a vehicle for evangelism from which development would emerge. Zamba was pleased to see the EAC spread but his emphasis was on bringing greater opportunities for his locality. He found the peripatetic life of a *mwalimu* difficult.

Samuel Agupio, who later became pastor of Isiro EAC parish, was a surprising candidate for leadership of a chapel. Ozua Samson tells his story:

> Telenga church began in the year 1981 . . . And it was my father [a *Wokovu*] who started it . . . He spoke with us, his children. Then he spoke with his brothers and other people, . . . Immediately they formed the first committee and we began the church, it was *kanisa letu* . . . Now we arranged its order: who would be its *mwalimu*? They did not see any one amongst us. Now they said, "No, the one who has lived in Uganda is Samuel Agupio. Even if he doesn't come [to church] now we chose him. He will become our *mwalimu*." Samuel was not yet saved. He was a drunk, a real drunk . . . They took him the news . . . He gave his answer two weeks later, saying if God

---

[41] Interview, Zamba Asu, Kumuru, Swahili, 18 August 2000.

had chosen him to be the leader he would do it. We prayed for him and immediately he started work...[42]

Agupio appears an unsuitable *mwalimu*; drunk, inexperienced, uninterested. He was, however, a villager who had lived in Uganda and whose parents were *Wokovu*. He was also open to the advice of elders and their belief in God's choice, as he himself confirmed:

> They needed to choose a *mwalimu* for our village... It was now the way for me to be saved... I left some time, two weeks, to wait before giving my reply. People came and gave me advice, they said I [should] go and pray to God. He knows that I am a bad person, but they had thought a lot about who could be *mwalimu* there. If they had chosen me it was God...[43]

Although Agupio's case was perhaps the most extreme, it was not uncommon for *Wokovu* members to appoint young non-*wokovu* men to the job. It is striking that the *Wokovu*, for whom public confession, personal Christian commitment and high moral standards were vital signs of a true believer, chose a person who had none of these qualities to lead a local church. There are several reasons why it happened. The *Wokovu* wanted to form a church that was clearly Anglican and not simply a fellowship group. To do this they knew they had to win over non-*wokovu* Anglicans who saw revivalists as spiritually proud. So they appointed *walimu* with previous Ugandan residency and thus a knowledge of Anglicanism. They also wanted to ensure local credibility, particularly in the eyes of a hostile CECA 20. So they targeted men of local families who had had some schooling.[44] The older *Wokovu* themselves often had only the most basic education. Importantly, they also believed they could influence these young men because they knew their families. The young *walimu* took up the challenge because it replaced the lost possibilities of Uganda, giving them status and purpose. A spiritual experience of conversion may have been part of this. Certainly once they accepted the appointment they knew that they would be expected to follow a particular code of behaviour. In these three stories of *walimu* the motives, conscious and unconscious, for taking on leadership roles are mixed. To suggest, however, that parental example, status, and success were influential is not to deny commitment to the Christian faith and engagement in a demanding religious way of life. Respect as a church worker had to be earned.

---

[42] Ozua Samson.

[43] Interview, Agupio Samuel, Aru, Swahili, 9 August 2000.

[44] Personal communication, Titre Ande, 15 November 2000.

Unlike the EAC hierarchy on the escarpment, these men were societal juniors who had few connections with the local social elite and *heshima* was not immediately conferred by status. The northern *walimu* had not been groomed through school and Bible school for church work nor did they come from prominent families in the wider community. They did, however, often come from Anglican families and were returning to a familiar way of worship. Those men who felt the dislocation most keenly often became *walimu* in the new church. In doing so they were engaged on two different levels which reflected the reality of their dislocation. On the local level they were attempting to bring their brand of global—the Anglican Church—to their father's village and its neighbours. They increased their sense of belonging to the village by establishing *kanisa letu*. On a regional level they were bringing the global to new areas by using networks of *Wokovu* or returned-migrants.

There is an irony in this: during the 1980s, the majority of *walimu* were untrained and knew little of the Anglican Church except the individual chapels in which they had worshipped in Uganda, that may have been some distance from the parish or diocesan centre. There was an effort on behalf of all these individuals to conform to their conception of an organised religious institution. When it arose, the opportunity for training was perceived by *walimu* as personal *maendeleo*, providing greater confidence to lead and filling, to an extent, the educational lacuna created by an abrupt end to life in Uganda. Young men could, potentially, rise quickly to the rank of pastor. They experienced *uhuru* from the social constraints of those who did not have the connections normally expected of church leaders. Thus their appreciation of Anglican *utaratibu* grew through a process considered in terms of *uhuru* and *maendeleo*. Their religious commitment made sense of the returned-migrant situation and offered them purpose and status. Through their own progress they gave hope to others, offering them the *uhuru*, *maendeleo* and *utaratibu* which they felt they had left behind in Uganda. All this they understood as being part of the Gospel message of freedom through Jesus Christ. For these *walimu* personal identity was linked to the developing Anglican identity.

Consolidation

Whilst chapel planting continued through the 1990s individual chapels began consolidating their presence in the villages. The brief descriptions of church life in the *Histoire de la Paroisse de Azangani* give some clue of the extent to which Anglican aspirations for *utaratibu*, *maendeleo* and *uhuru* had become reality at chapel level. They say nothing about Sunday worship but provide a list of projects and groups for social and spiritual improvement. The descriptions of the chapels stress the elements of commonality between them and other Anglican Churches. The desire to copy the COU and belong to the EAC encouraged the replication of groups that were familiar to Anglicans, although not all were exclusively Anglican. Most chapels had a Sunday School, a Mothers' Union and a youth fellowship group. Some participated in seminars and Theological Education by Extension organised at parish or archdeaconry level. The numbers baptised, confirmed and those being prepared for confirmation are mentioned. These groups demonstrated their Anglican credentials and asserted their membership of a global Christian institution. The development projects listed hint at the liberty to address perceived local needs. Some emphasised buildings, others agriculture, others animal husbandry, and one chapel possessed a sewing machine. At Gombe where, unusually, some Muslims had joined the church, a service was also held on Friday. Individual chapels could respond to the local situation within the limits of what the congregation considered acceptable for an Anglican Church. Congregations saw value in belonging to a bigger group. They desired uniformity rather than innovation. This uniformity was expressed in the *utaratibu* of Anglican liturgy and hierarchy. These descriptions present a paradox; the Anglican Church at its most local was consciously trying to be international, that is, to replicate the COU that was assumed to represent universal Anglicanism. Small EAC chapels developed, not because little groups wanted to do their own thing, but because they wanted to be a part of an inclusive global group, which was seen to accord with their aspirations and which lent status to their socially marginal position. An official, national and international church was introduced to respond to local issues, described as the need for *uhuru* and *maendeleo*.

Peter Yobuta, reflecting upon the rapid growth of the EAC among the Kakwa, explained how he saw the influence of *uhuru* and *maendeleo*:

> Well, firstly the Anglican Church is pretty good. Its *uhuru* is there... The second thing, people like Anglican more because they see *maendeleo*... [In] CECA, they don't like young people to lead... The real work of leading the church they leave to the elderly. Yes, people see this as really bad. When they opened Anglican [sic] they saw young pastors and *maendeleo* going well. Now, we have agriculturists and what not. Now people can see that this church can truly provide *maendeleo*—physical and spiritual... There

are even CECA members who start to ask us to provide their children with work, eh! Because the Anglican Church is—that's to say, the Bible or studying theology is *uhuru*. To study at university is *uhuru*. To do some sort of *maendeleo*—every one is *uhuru* to do it. Yes, people like this a lot.[45]

Yobuta suggested that *uhuru* and *maendeleo* were linked in peoples' minds to the EAC. The meaning of the words were closely entwined; northerners wanted both freedom to develop, and to develop in freedom. One way this was achieved was by junior members of society having more opportunities to be involved in church leadership. Seniority by age or status was not required to lead an EAC chapel; there were not enough senior Anglicans to make this viable. Those searching for freedom from adherence to a limited code of behaviour and freedom for study and employment joined the EAC. Yossa Way, for example, was a talented young man who felt he had no opportunities in CECA 20 for ordained ministry but who was quickly accepted by the EAC becoming first a head-teacher, then pastor and theological college tutor. In each parish a host of small projects were set up for improvement of living standards and community co-operation. Different groups within the parish also had their projects. The Mothers' Union, for example, made clothes, mats, baskets, kept animals and grew food.[46] An office of *Bien-Etre Social* was created in Aru by 1990 to encourage the projects and teach new skills. Yuma Ajule, as development worker for his parish explained that instruction was given at parish level and then disseminated locally through the chapels.[47] The projects encouraged the development of common resources—fields, fishponds, tree plantations, sugar mills—which involved the whole community at a basic level. With the EAC as the institutional driving force behind these initiatives *maendeleo* was not considered a separate wing of the church, as some urban migrants thought, but rather a natural development of Christian life.

EAC members were committed to their church and worked hard for its success. A common Congolese perception was that a significant part of the mission of the church was to offer development because religious beliefs were expected to be manifest in the improvement of life. A religion whose influence was not perceived to aid day-to-day living was not

---

[45] Interview, Peter Yobuta, Kumuru, Swahili, 19 August 2000.
[46] Interview, Janette Sinziri, Kumuru, Swahili, 18 August 2000.
[47] Yuma Ajule.

worth following. Different denominations were assessed in terms of what they offered beyond religious worship. As government was increasingly unable to deliver, churches, as the few remaining functioning national institutions, assumed greater responsibilities for health, education and agricultural improvement. In the neglected corner of North-east Congo a denomination which arrived announcing its commitment to *maendeleo* was attractive to those beyond its immediate group and gained members from other denominations. Returned-migrants' understanding of Uganda and the COU provided them with aspirations that gave an impetus for *uhuru* and *maendeleo*. The *utaratibu* of Anglicanism was for them not a conservative force but one that provided a socio-religious structure in which *uhuru* and *maendeleo* could be (partially) realised. It allowed them to be legitimately Congolese without leaving Uganda entirely behind: to have a foot in both nations.

Difficulties

As the EAC grew in the north it faced a number of difficulties. The call to *maendeleo* was as much a hope as a promise. It may have encouraged people to join but it often set unsustainable standards. When evangelists promised *maendeleo* they may have assumed that the EAC would rapidly resemble the COU, or they may have been convinced by their rhetoric and desire for church growth. The parlous economic and political state of the country and the relative lack of wealth and education of EAC members meant that even grassroots, small-scale *maendeleo* was increasingly difficult to deliver. Members constantly compared the progress of their church unfavourably with that of the COU and they perceived themselves to be less successful. Some rationalised the different standards of *maendeleo* between the EAC and the COU as the difference between two countries.[48] Others were disappointed and denigrated achievements that were made in comparison with Uganda. Chapels that had been promised significant development projects found their membership dwindling when these were not realised. Whilst some compared the EAC favourably with CECA, others compared it with the COU and found it wanting.

---

[48] Ozua Samson.

As the EAC grew it encountered the issue of increasing linguistic diversity, ethnic and cultural plurality. The EAC leadership desired a common language in which to express the inclusiveness of Christianity and through which to carry out administrative control. The frustrated exclamation of 'Tower of Babel!' was not uncommon when linguistic diversity provoked particular communication problems that were said to prevent *maendeleo*. The diocesan centre at Boga imposed Swahili as its *lingua franca* for training and administration and encouraged its use in worship.[49] *Utaratibu* was disseminated in Swahili and so the Bible Schools at Aru, Kumuru and Mahagi used Swahili. Many trans-border migrants knew Swahili from their time in Uganda. However, in the northern area, Bangala was the trade language. As the EAC grew in the north, people who did not know Swahili came forward for leadership positions. Personal *maendeleo*, as ministerial training, was only available to those who knew, or were willing to learn, Swahili. The levelling effect that the Swahili medium had afforded in the urban churches from the 1970s could not be replicated in the north. A policy which had been introduced to be inclusive and to topple Runyoro from its position of 'sacred language' was repeated in an area in which it created the same problem that it had been designed to solve. Fortunately the *Book of Common Prayer* had been translated into Alur, Kakwa and Lugbara in Uganda and, except in the larger centres, church services were often carried out in the local language. This encouraged the *uhuru* to use local songs and musical instruments in services. Thus worship was not contained within the framework of escarpment *utaratibu* and *upole*. Alio Samweli, pastor and mainstream revivalist, for example, acknowledged in interview that worship in the EAC in Aru and Mahagi *territoires* had been greatly influenced by Boga. However, when he was pastor of Ekanga, he mixed the "Boga style" of worship with "doing it in our way to get alive in the service" because, he thought, the people, "shouldn't be suppressed" by *upole* services.[50] Amid the Morning Prayer liturgy Alio led his congregations in lively dancing and singing that understood to be related to traditional Lugbara forms of worship that he, as religious leader, was expected to initiate. This approach challenged

---

[49] Titre Ande, "Authority in the Anglican Church of Congo: The Influence of Political Models of Authority and the Potential of 'Life-Community Ecclesiology' for Good Governance" (PhD Birmingham University, 2003), 147.

[50] Interview, Alio Samweli, Arua, English, 3 September 2000.

the belief that worship was nothing more than the *upole* ritual of the Prayer Book.

Not all church-workers, however, knew the local vernacular. In an attempt to combat potential ethnic division or in response to the pragmatic considerations of availability, *mwangalizi* and pastors were frequently sent to work with an ethnic group other than their own and so used the Swahili Prayer Book for services. The EAC struggled to find a position in which *maendeleo* was neither stunted by linguistic pluralism nor hampered by a lack of commitment to their vernacular or regional trade language. Issues of the local and particular and the universal and inclusive were raised in worship as well.

Northern Impact on EAC

Widespread migration and the resultant church growth had forced apart the coalition of the EAC with escarpment culture and provided alternative identities. Trans-border migrants regarded Anglican order in terms of change and improvement rather than in terms of the preservation of a tradition. The relationship of ordinary members to the *utaratibu* of hierarchy and liturgy was interpreted according to *maendeleo*. That is, the actions of the whole community to improve their standard of living, providing the primary development they perceived as unavailable elsewhere in the area, arose directly from their membership and worship as Anglicans. Anglican *utaratibu* was understood as a framework for opportunity rather than conformity.

This dynamic approach was further encouraged by historical and social factors. In an area of acephalous, segmentary societies highly stratified social order was antithetical to northern village values and respect accorded to centrally appointed church workers was much less evident in the north than the south of the EAC. Yet prior labour migration and colonial intervention had influenced the introduction of greater stratification enabling Anglican *utaratibu* to be better accepted than it might otherwise have been. Furthermore, returned labour migrants were distanced from particular Alur, Lugbara or Kakwa social structures and also possessed confidence enough to challenge them. Thus junior migrant members were likely to take leadership positions in the EAC and encourage the definition of *utaratibu* as *maendeleo* and *uhuru*. The plotting of *utaratibu* with these identity signifiers made for a different imagining of the central basis of EAC identity. It challenged the assumption that social status and seniority influenced ecclesiastical rank.

The northern church also altered women's roles in the EAC. Archdeacon Kabarole noticed a difference between women in the Aru area and those in the Boga area:

> Some women can even preach...Some can't even read but they really work hard in the church. I see a big difference in other places, Boga for example. Women [there] are really very frightened. Only a very few of them can stand amongst people and preach. But here they preach.[51]

Women in the north were more likely than women in the south to take a public role in ritual *utaratibu*. The change was slight; the handful of women who took the evangelists' course in Aru were usually considered to be training for MU posts. Nevertheless, a few women acted as unofficial *walimu* in charge of chapels. In the north, because of its interpretation by *uhuru*, ritual *utaratibu* could be uncoupled from hierarchical *utaratibu*. Thus women who did not hold authority within the EAC structure might take a public role in community worship. Women's leadership of worship was enhanced by a less formal approach to the Prayer Book. The influence of Revivalists meant that many were involved in or aware of Anglicans worshipping regularly without following a written liturgy. The northerners began to introduce spontaneous and egalitarian forms of worship in the vernaculars that had greater resonance with their popular culture.

The changes instigated by the northern EAC as a result of their different interpretation of *utaratibu* were tempered by the tendency for Boga to send clergy from the escarpment to work in the north. This policy maintained links between the two areas when travel and communication was difficult and provided mutual learning at a personal level. It was also an attempt by Boga to mould the northern church into its own image, assuming that the historical centre of the EAC provided best Anglican practice. Archdeacon Kabarole Baguma acknowledged proudly the influence of his Boga origins in his own ministry in Aru:

> ...I grew up there in Boga, I studied there in Boga, so the doctrine of [Boga] I brought here. Everything that is done here I taught to these people, so they were taught those [things] of Boga.[52]

---

[51] Interview, Kabarole Baguma, Aru, Swahili, 09 August 2000.
[52] Ibid.

Kabarole expected conformity to the escarpment hegemony that he understood as faithful to universal Anglicanism. The northerners were ambivalent about this assumption. In areas where escarpment practice was familiar to them from their experience of the COU they were willing to accept it. If it offered *maendeleo* in terms of ministerial training they saw its benefits. But there were areas, like that of worship, in which northerners worked for greater autonomy. Tensions might have been much more severe had centralisation by the escarpment church been more successful. The diocesan centre at Boga did not have the resources to impose its identity on areas where the EAC had recently been introduced.

Furthermore, some northerners began to develop a discourse about the escarpment church that labelled it an undeveloped backwater of insufficiently rigorous morals. This gave further legitimacy to a resistance of the escarpment definition of EAC identity. Northerners visited Boga to attend Bible School, diocesan synod and nursing college. They were dismayed by what they found: a small, isolated village, which seemed to take commitment to 'true religion' very lightly. There were few obvious signs of the *maendeleo* they had seen in the COU. Some criticised the lack of infrastructure, the unimpressive school buildings and hospital, and the overgrown areas of the church compound. Unfairly, perhaps, northerners had imagined that the historic centre of the EAC would be bigger and more impressive than it actually appeared to be. More serious and more frequent, however, were the criticisms of the moral and spiritual life of the people of Boga. Northerners were shocked by what they considered to be the church's moral laxity and its intimate relations with traditional cultural values. Isaac Agele accused people in Boga of being spiritually weak, he said only the wealthiest members of the congregation were expected to give to the church, and services were attended by drunks.[53] Others claimed that Hema Christian practice was 'syncretistic'[54] because the chief maintained a cultural role whilst being a significant figure in the church and because the marriage service was surrounded by traditional practice. The dislocation northerners experienced through labour migration, then sudden return, had distanced them from the detail of their own indigenous social structures. Thus

---

[53] Agele Isaac.

[54] Interview, Ubaya Uchaki, Mahagi, Swahili, 30 August 2000 and Kapondombe Wiyajik, Mahagi, Swahili, 27 August 2000.

their expression of Anglican Christianity was dismissive of those elements of indigenous culture most closely associated with customary
governance and traditional religious practices. Northerners criticised
Boga's attempts at ecclesiastical hegemony from a sense of moral and
spiritual superiority.

By the end of the 1980s, the northern ethnic groups were represented in decision-making at synod whilst escarpment Anglicans were
fast becoming the minority members of the EAC and could no longer
direct its path. The specific cultural assumptions of the escarpment
could no longer automatically underlie discussion. If membership of
the EAC had allowed northern migrants to *feel* at home in the place
they *called* home, their re-ordering of the EAC 'furniture' challenged
the sense of homeliness that had emerged on the escarpment. Later
chapters show the emergence of a new communal identity as the EAC
began to develop a public discourse of unity, *umoja*. The *umoja* discourse
attempted to acknowledge diversity with the EAC and accept regional
differences as the results of Anglican migration continued to challenge
the identity of the EAC.

Conclusion

The migration of Congolese living in Uganda caused a re-assessment,
however subconscious, of their identity. The refugees may have been
returning 'home' to their 'father's village' but it was an unfamiliar place
in which they needed to re-establish themselves and re-form their identity. They had not chosen to return. They could not display the rewards
of their labours and assume the status of the experienced travellers,
as others had done before them. They had fled and no longer had
recourse to the 'good life' they had known in Uganda. They wanted to
belong but their experience of life beyond the village prevented them
from easily returning to local traditions and encouraged them to challenge to the *status quo*. They negotiated the disruption of migration by
bringing together the experience of belonging to two nations and to
two different lifestyles in their religious identity. Forming an Anglican
chapel meant creating home. It brought something familiar to the location to which they felt they ought to belong, thus changing that place
to their advantage. It bridged the identity gap of belonging to one's
father's village in Congo and belonging to Uganda where they were no
longer welcome. In establishing the EAC in their area these migrants

demonstrated themselves to be both dislocated individuals who needed to belong to their locality, and independent initiators who were seeking order, freedom and development in all aspects of life. They sought social freedom from constraints not considered conducive to development and emphasised the dynamism of new opportunities rather than respect for family tradition. The continuity of practice they desired was continuity with the COU that they interpreted as encouraging change and development.

CHAPTER FIVE

CONTESTING UNITY AND ORDER:
INTER-CHURCH CONFLICT

Introduction

The migration of Anglicans has been shown to challenge the identity of the EAC because migration acted as a catalyst for widening identity choices, providing more options from which to re-construct identity in a new location. Anglican migration was also considered a threat to the identity of other denominations because it encouraged an awareness of various church structures and practice and of different loci of religious power, and it promoted the construction of alternative ecclesiastical spaces that presented alternative interpretations of religious identity. The most significant external conflict in the North-east was between the EAC the *Communauté Evangelique du Centre de l'Afrique 20* (CECA), the largest Protestant denomination in the area. The conflict influenced the sense of home Anglican migrants developed within the EAC and it demonstrates the way in which group identity is partially created by relationship with those outside the group. This chapter shows how two mission-initiated Christianities related to each other and it provides an understanding of Anglican identity as seen by those outside the EAC. The dynamics of denominationalism reflected the debates about unity and difference taking place in the national, political and ecclesiastical sphere from 1960 and this background is presented first.

National and ecclesiastical unity

The 1960s decade was a turbulent one for the newly independent Congo. After five years of civil unrest and factionalism President Mobutu came to power in 1965 promoting national unity and centralised government. His *Mouvement populaire de la révolution* (MPR) became the sole legitimate political party of which all citizens were members. He re-coded traditional ideas of leadership to encourage this form of unity and maintain his power. To retain religious control Mobutu demanded that all Protestant Churches in Congo belong to one organisation, the

Eglise du Christ au Congo, (ECC), established in March 1970 from the Congo Protestant Council (CPC).[1] The CPC had experienced many internal conflicts during the 1960s, including schisms, the formation of new denominations, and the establishment of churches in areas previously barred to them by missionary comity. In an attempt to avoid Protestant division and competition the ECC defined unity as working towards shared goals in different geographical locations. This had been a key ideology for the CPC as it upheld the denominational boundaries established by missionaries. The Protestant call for unity was heavily infused with one party government rhetoric; Protestant disagreements were likened to the political rebellions of the 1960s and considered disloyal and unnationalistic.[2] By 1970 the ECC was presented as the national, united Protestant Church for Congo comprising of many *communautés*, or denominations. As one church it upheld for its member communities, "...strict observance of the existing territorial boundaries."[3] However, since State-recognised denominations were permitted to practice throughout Congo, the ECC could only recommend its approach and could not prevent the spread of denominations into different areas. The ECC rhetoric of unity coupled with a contradictory national law heightened tensions between many ECC members.

By 1970, CECA 20 was playing a prominent role in the ECC, abandoning the stance of the previous decade when its AIM missionaries resisted the ecumenism of the CPC. As the largest Protestant denomination in the North-east, its leaders were influential in regional and national meetings and they adhered to the ECC position on unity through the maintenance of separate spheres of Protestant influence. Protestants of any denomination migrating to an area of CECA influence were expected by CECA to join it. Following the ECC policy on intra-Protestant unity maintained CECA's position of influence in the region.

Since 1912, CECA had guarded its internal unity by emphasising clear standards of moral and sacramental conduct, the observance of which was essential to membership. Theologically speaking, salvation from sin was through faith alone, but right living in accordance with CECA's standards was imperative to demonstrate salvation and remain

---

[1] Philippe Kabongo-Mbaya, *L'Eglise du Christ au Zaïre: Formation et adaption d'un protestantisme en situation de dictature* (Paris, Kathala, 1992), 7.
[2] Ibid., 125.
[3] ECZ, *Dieu et le Monde: Procès Verbal du 4e Synode National* (Kinshasa, ECZ, 1977), 19.

in right relationship with God and others. These moral standards provided a particular kind of order that was fundamental to CECA's identity. Christian identity in CECA was intended to be unambiguous. Belonging was clearly defined and members included or excluded through weighing their behaviour against CECA's standards to determine their Christian commitment. As a result wider social cohesion was also preserved. Titre Ande, who grew up in CECA in the 1960s and 1970s, remembers the care and constraint provided through church membership:

> ...when you have a problem, you have a bereavement at your house, you are ill, things like that, they could help you. So many became members of the [CECA] church thanks to that. And sometimes one was constrained by the family because if you refused to become a member of the church, at that moment you were rejected.[4]

The opposing realities of support or rejection encouraged unity at a grassroots level. So did the influence of the leadership. As had happened with the EAC in Boga, the CECA church leadership and the social elites became closely connected in many areas of the North-east. Ordination in CECA was the result of lengthy training and experience, and frequently took place only in later life. As senior members of society, great respect was conferred on the old pastors and the authority of their leadership was rarely questioned. They were able to bestow or withhold the approbation of social virtue through the use of church rules and thus maintain internal unity. The internal unity of the EAC contrasted with that of CECA. The EAC attempted to preserve unity through respect for the *utaratibu* of the Prayer Book and hierarchy of church workers. Salvation and right living were theologically important but belonging to the EAC depended on right practice and structure. The EAC frequently compromised on exactly how *utaratibu* was interpreted.

The EAC in the 1970s was less concerned with intra-protestant unity than its own expansion. The desire of members to locate EAC chapels outside the areas agreed by missionary comity placed it on a collision course with CECA which followed the ECC ideology and considered that it had most to lose by this incursion. Adrian Hastings recognised that the reality of mobility across Africa mitigated against ideologies of unity like that propounded by the ECC:

---

[4] Interview, Titre Ande, Edinburgh, French, 25 September 1999.

...a "mixed" Christianity...was emerging across the continent...Africans themselves showed a marked dislike for 'comity' arrangements agreed between Protestant societies whereby any particular area would be designated for a single denomination. African society had become too peregrinatory for that to be acceptable.[5]

In Congo the Catholics and Protestants had always been territorially 'mixed' to some extent but different Protestant denominations had not. The movement of peoples broke down clearly defined boundaries—both geographical and religious—that missionaries had attempted to erect. Africans, by and large, did not wish to observe them. However, Hastings' observation does not allow for the significant number of Africans for whom these boundaries had proved useful in providing identity by marking out their Christian beliefs, obtaining influence, or sustaining tradition, and who were, therefore, unwilling to relinquish them easily. This was the case for CECA in North-east Congo. CECA wanted to maintain its Protestant monopoly in the areas it influenced; it was wary of alternative church structures, and its members believed fervently that the gospel message was best packaged in the system they had inherited. The EAC was not necessarily any different in this regard but its situation was different. The heartland of Congolese Anglicanism, the sixty mile radius round Boga walked by Apolo Kivebulaya, was so isolated that the influence of other denominations was very slight until the late 1990s. Thus the issue of denominational competition only arose in a one sided way; that is, the small, flexible and growing EAC reaching beyond its traditional borders into the territory of other denominations rather than experiencing such an incursion itself.

Local conflict

The issues of unity and the mix of denominations were continental problems that were played out locally between CECA 20 and EAC. As previous chapters show, most migrating Anglicans defined themselves as Protestants and worshipped in the local Protestant Church, usually CECA, when they first moved. They establish EAC chapels to replicate Anglican worship and to feel at home in their new location.

---

[5] Adrian Hastings, *The Church in Africa, 1450–1950* (Oxford, Clarendon Press, 1994), 578.

As Kabarole Munege says they often felt that they did not properly belong elsewhere:

> Before the [Anglican] Church was here…some were with CECA. But even so they saw themselves as if at someone else's house, not at their own home. This pushed them to begin to think about their church.[6]

Many Anglicans worshipped for years in urban CECA churches. When they left CECA, leaders felt betrayed, accusing EAC evangelists of stealing their members.[7] CECA resented the establishment of the EAC because they considered it an attempt to fragment the united Protestant group in the area and an illegitimate presence on their patch:

> …the boundaries inherited from the missionaries must be respected.… [but] the Anglicans followed their Christians who were here, who worshipped with us at CECA…in Bunia. They were told, "No this is not your field of evangelism, it's for CECA."…Despite that they insisted, they didn't obey…[8]

CECA also considered that the EAC disseminated false teaching and false practice. They disliked another form of 'mixed' Christianity that the EAC brought; it claimed to be Christian but condoned certain traditional practices, it claimed to be Protestant but observed infant baptism and confirmation and followed a liturgy similar to the Roman Catholics. An erstwhile member of CECA makes clear what he had been taught: "…a church which resembles the Catholics is not a church".[9]

When the EAC was introduced in the zones of Aru and Mahagi from 1979 there was already disquiet among the CECA leadership about EAC growth elsewhere in Ituri. However, it was in this northern area that the most serious and long-lasting rifts developed between the two denominations. In the north the most common reason given for installing or joining the EAC was the unwillingness to follow CECA's stipulation to be rebaptised. A large number of refugees who had arrived in the area claimed to belong to local villages but possessed different cultural, social and religious experiences. They began to challenge CECA's control over Protestant Christianity. Change was inevitable but the leadership of CECA 20 wanted to maintain the *status quo*. Some migrants established Anglican chapels in refugee camps.

---

[6] Interview, Munege Kabarole, Bunia, Swahili, 13 September 2000.
[7] Interview, Beni Bataaga, Bunia, English, 15 September 2000.
[8] Interview, Etsea Ang'apoza, Bunia, French, 18 September 2000.
[9] Interview, Baba Atseko, Aru, French, 14 September 2000.

This was accepted by CECA 20 because it was seen as a temporary arrangement catering for foreigners.[10] But many refugees returned to their fathers' villages and, once they felt they had been rejected by the CECA congregation, formed an EAC chapel. In establishing an alternative ecclesiastical space and asserting a different Christian identity they were accused of destroying the Christian unity of the village. The migrants themselves, felt unwelcome in CECA, and considered that they were building a home for themselves in which their identity as returned-migrants could flourish. The issues surrounding unity were discussed inconclusively at a popular level.

God, Prophets, Baptism and Chapels

Janette Sinziri's parents were members of CECA 20. Janette had been brought up in CECA but had spent time in Uganda where she had joined the Church of Uganda (COU) because it had not demanded of her the literacy standards that CECA expected in order to accept someone for baptism and membership.[11] She married Sinziri Onadra who, on their return to Congo, became the first EAC catechist in their village. In this quotation she explains how her parents resisted the local leaders of CECA when they attempted to force her return from the EAC to CECA:

> My parents were happy because they said that religion is one. Even if there are different religions, God is one. They refused to say this [EAC] is a different religion. They were just happy. They said all is one God, like this. . . . my father was there [when] the CECA people came and really upset me. They wanted to send me back to CECA.[12]

Her narrative revolves around the belief that *Mungu ni moja*, God is one. The exasperation is almost palpable; if God is one, different religious expressions are basically the same, so one should be able to choose which denomination to join. Exasperation was also felt by CECA members; yes God is one, so why is different religious expression necessary? We can worship God in the same way. For Janette disloyalty to the church of her village was less important than freedom to follow the experience of baptism and membership in the COU. This story illustrates

---

[10] Yobuta Peter, Kumuru, Swahili, 19 August 2000.
[11] Janette Sinziri, Kumuru, Swahili, 18 August 2000.
[12] Ibid.

that *umoja* was discussed at grassroots level. There was an awareness of common Christian beliefs and aims but issues raised as a consequence of migration militated against institutional unity. Baptism was the most serious of these, as Airene Ayike explains:[13]

> First of all I was baptised in the Anglican Church. Our catechist taught us that no one can be baptised twice. So when the CECAs (sic) wanted to rebaptise us so that we could participate in Holy Communion we refused and left CECA.[13]

For Anglican Christians this was the pivotal issue. If they were pressed to be rebaptised by CECA they usually left. Etsea Angapoza, President of CECA, explains its policy on baptism as it was when faced with an influx of returned migrants in the northern area.

> ...when our Congolese Christians were there in Uganda, they had what we call baptism of repentance...when they came with that to us at CECA we posed the question, "Have you received baptism, and afterward has the Bishop confirmed your baptism?" If he said no, we said, "No, you can't be received. You can study the catechumenate...until we baptise you." In the past if someone comes with the confirmation it was fine, now there are a few questions that are asked. It's necessary to see if his behaviour...really demonstrates that he leads an exterior life that shows that he is truly transformed internally. So he is observed a little. Because at CECA there is a discipline, there is no smoking. If someone says, "I'm confirmed" but he smokes, he is already doubted...But with us when you are baptised you can't be rebaptised...With us the baptism by immersion is obligatory, you immerse yourself in water. If you haven't had that sort of baptism, your baptism can be questioned.[14]

The CECA 20 ideal of adult baptism following conversion and improved moral life style was challenged by EAC practice. In Irumu and Nord-Kivu this was because of the Anglican acceptance of infant baptism as initiation into the church community. In the Aru and Mahagi zones the issue was not one of infant baptism but of guarding access to communion. By talking about "baptism of repentance" Etsea seems aware that in West Nile particularly, where the COU had been established by AIM missionaries, many Anglicans had not been baptised as babies but as older children or adults after catechism and recognition of sin. Since Anglicans were permitted to take communion after being confirmed and CECA members participated in it after believers-baptism and had no

---

[13] Interivew Airene Ayike, Kumuru, Kakwa, 17 August 2000.
[14] Etsea Ang'apoza.

confirmation rite, CECA thought non-confirmed Anglicans ought to be re-baptised when joining CECA. This would maintain the respect and solemnity of communion. Etsea goes on to say that even confirmation might not confer automatic access to CECA communion; proper conduct was paramount. CECA believed that the holiness of communion was attained by guarding it from anyone who was judged to fall from the moral code. There was also suspicion of anyone who had not been baptised by immersion. The outward details of the sacramental rite were regarded by some in CECA as a vital sign of the spiritual grace it was intended to confer. So the Anglicans, who practised aspersion, were also considered guilty of questionable baptismal practise. With the introduction of the EAC in the area, Protestant unity as conformity to a single practice was unravelling.

CECA's policy also changed the self-perception of Anglicans. To be asked to be re-baptised was, in their eyes, to be considered 'pagan' rather than Christian. They thought CECA doubted their Christian identity. Anglicans, whilst living in Uganda had learnt to identify themselves, in opposition to Catholics, as Protestant Christians. The reaction of Anglican migrants on finding that CECA was unwilling to accept them as members was to highlight their identity as Anglicans rather than simply as Protestants. Thus it reaffirmed the importance of Anglican *utaratibu* in their socio-religious practice.

When Kabarole Baguma became the first EAC pastor in Aru in 1982 he faced accusations and attempts to discredit him:

> When I arrived here, they said I was a false prophet. "The church of the false prophets...has arrived [laughs]. It will give bad teachings to the Christians."[15]

It is difficult to know whether these accusations were deliberate smearing or whether they were born out of ignorance, fear and presupposition: *Nabii yauli*, 'false prophet' was a standard accusation used against rival church workers. Potentially more grave, the EAC was also accused of being a 'sect'. In Congo this was the name given to a religious group not recognised by the government; its beliefs, heterodox or otherwise, were secondary to its illegitimacy. An accusation of this kind meant that the state administration could be called upon to eliminate the group. Local CECA churches accused the EAC several times before

---

[15] Kabarole Baguma, Aru, Swahili, 09 September 2000.

local government of being illegitimate but each time the EAC proved it was a legitimate member of the ECC.[16] The accusations of CECA members increased antagonism between the two denominations but they could not deter a legitimate member of the ECC from operating in the area. EAC chapel building continued apace.

Gboŋa Amuel, who returned to Congo from Uganda in 1979, tells his chapel building story:

> We wanted to have a church and we built our church. Actually we had already built this church and afterwards we sent a report to them, the people of CECA to say, "We have completed building our church," and they said, "We have not permitted a church there." When we came to hear this report…we said, "Well, this is something God wants, he wants church, but you, you come to argue with us. We have our church." So we said we had already built the church and we would join the Anglicans. So we are here. [Evangelist Adoroti] came here to see us, to enter our church here. The year was '84, the date the 19th of August, when this church here joined the Anglican [Church]. And many joined the Anglican [Church].[17]

On his return to Congo Gboŋa had been accepted back into CECA because he had been confirmed in the COU. He organised his village, Bongilo, into building a chapel but the central church refused to acknowledge it. The village decided *en masse* to join the EAC and ten years later Bongilo chapel became the centre of Kumuru archdeaconry headquarters. For CECA the initiative was a worrying one. CECA's administration was organised to ensure internal unity and thus the construction of churches was carefully vetted. Bongilo village had not deferred to the section office before beginning the building, and permission to use it was not granted. Prior to the return of the migrants from Uganda that might have ended the matter. Returned migrants, however, were unimpressed by this controlling attitude. It contradicted their desire for *maendeleo* and *uhuru* (development and freedom). So they joined another church, one with which they were familiar and which allowed freedom for such initiative to bear fruit. In establishing its boundaries on these issues CECA unwittingly encouraged what it was trying to avoid—Protestant division and the establishment of a more lenient church ready to adapt itself to circumstances. When CECA perceived Anglicans to be a threat to the order and unity they had

---

[16] Thumbe Ferdinand, Mahagi, Alur, 29 August 2000.
[17] Interview, Gboŋa Amuel, Swahili, Kumuru, 18 August 2000.

achieved the Anglicans became such a threat, establishing an alternative Protestant Church with an alternative identity.

There is another interpretation of the Bongilo chapel story that raises another problem for unity. In refusing to allow worship to take place at Bongilo, CECA claimed it was trying to avoid the 'clanism' mentioned in the previous chapter, which also worried Anglican leaders. The nearest CECA church to Bongilo was four kilometres away, situated on the land of another clan. Gboŋa claimed his decision was based on distance; this was too far for children and the elderly to walk every week. CECA thought, however, that the desire for a church at Bongilo was being dictated by potentially divisive clan interests, a problem already perceived within EAC and CECA ranks. Yeka Idroru, a CECA pastor, explained it thus:

> ...the church is becoming more clannish than a universal church... By 'clannish church' I mean that almost every clan wants its pastor or its catechist. That's why you see lots of churches.[18]

More churches were built at the expense of greater cohesion. The Anglicans, by asserting an alternative identity and claiming their own ecclesiastical space, could be accused by CECA of not simply dividing Protestants but of encouraging the separation of individual clans into their own religious units, competing with the clans around them. *Umoja* appeared to be dissolving on several levels. Groups—whether confident migrants or competitive clans—asserted their identity by affiliating themselves to a denomination of their choice and staking out their own space.

Social influence

As has been demonstrated, CECA's position of authority in the community allowed it pervasive social control through moral guidance and ecclesiastical administration. Smoking, drinking, polygamy, and dancing were some of the things considered unfit for the converted. CECA applied rigorous standards to a whole gamut of social issues. A look at two complex socio-economic and cultural issues, chosen because they were of great concern to members of both churches, will demonstrate CECA's attempt at social and moral cohesion and how the EAC

---

[18] Interview, Yaka Idroru, French, Kumuru, 19 August 2000.

undermined it. The complexities are not investigated fully, rather the contrasting ways in which two denominations dealt with the issues in a changing society are the focus.

"If smoking is bad so is the growing of the raw material," reasoned CECA. Members were, therefore, banned from growing tobacco. Yeka Idroru explains the consequences:

> CECA 20 doesn't accept this cultivation. So when the Christians do this cultivation, they leave the church and all the spiritual activities and other activities. This diminishes the number [of members].[19]

The tobacco industry threatened social cohesion and family health. The cash crop was grown in private fields and provided a chance to earn a lot of money. More often, however, families came under the thumb of the British and American Tobacco managers who placed stringent demands on cultivation and discouraged the growing of food crops with the result that poor families slipped further into poverty.[20] If CECA members followed their church's ban they were probably being saved from greater misfortune. EAC leaders also worried about the effect this had on their members. Several of them, including Sinziri Onadra and Yobuta Peter,[21] had grown it before they became church workers. They knew the consequences but were unwilling to make the issue a matter on which to determine good standing within the EAC. The EAC had no clear policy, members had *uhuru* to make their own decisions and individual church workers provided guidance only in particular circumstances.

Marriage was another issue of concern. CECA weddings brought together western Christian and traditional African teaching and practice. They could only be conducted between a couple who had not lived together beforehand.[22] They took place once there had been parental agreement, a bride-price had been set and paid, and a civil ceremony had taken place. In the 20th century bride-price rose comparatively to average wealth and young men found it increasingly difficult to pay.

---

[19] Yeka Idroru.
[20] Conversations with Jessé Leku, EAC Development worker, and Ezati Ezayi, Head Nurse of EAC Medical Service, Aru, and observations of tobacco growing in Kumuru *collectivité*, August 2000.
[21] Conversations with Sinziri and Yobuta 17–20 August 2000.
[22] Lalima Tagamile Dhulembe, "L'Exercise de la Discipline dans une Eglise Africaine: Examen Théologique de l'Application de l'Article VII de R.O.I. de la CECA/AIM, Zaire" (Maîtrise diss., Faculté libre de Théologie evangelique, 1984), 21–22, 91–92.

Couples would attempt to force their parents' hands by living together before it had been paid in full, or paid at all. CECA as the guardian of social and moral norms as well as ecclesiastical rites resisted this disintegration of a social system, upheld the bride-price, and insisted that full membership of CECA could not be sustained if a couple behaved in this way. The man was said to have 'abducted' the woman—even though the woman was usually complicit. The marriage was considered 'illegal' because the parents had not given their consent.[23] Such actions normally resulted in excommunication for the couple.

The approach to marriage in the EAC was little different in theory. The EAC made no attempt to reform the system of marriage that had evolved. What was different was the leniency in applying the system. In interview Thérèse Pasa of CECA expressed her incredulity at Anglican practice:

> ...in the Anglican Church there are some marriages that they do when you have eight or three or four children, eeee! They say that they bless these marriages! I don't understand in what way or how![24]

Remo Mawa, a CECA youth worker, was also shocked by EAC practice. He highlighted the fact that people could be considered worthy of church leadership in the EAC even though they had been living together for years without a church blessing of their marriages. They were only required to have such a blessing before studying at Bible School.[25] The EAC's response to individuals caught between poverty and the economic attraction of growing cash crops or the cultural pressure to marry and have children was ambiguous. Its lenient approach was not always helpful. In certain circumstances the EAC effectively condoned a series of 'trial marriages' before blessing the union considered by the man as the 'real' marriage, thus further weakening the position of some women in marital issues, whereas CECA's stricter approach might better protect the societal status of some women. However, the EAC outside Boga, having few connections with social elites, was sympathetic to the problems of junior members of society and appreciative of the difficult social and cultural realities. As a result it gained new members. Those who had been ostracised by CECA's clear social boundaries could still

---

[23] Kokole Idrng'i Loding'o, "Le Chrétien fâce au Mariage par Rapt (Cas de la Tribu Kakwa)" (Diplôme de Graduat diss., ISTB, Bunia, 1986), 18–31.

[24] Interview, Thérèse Pasa, Bunia, Swahili, 18 September 2000.

[25] Interview, Remo Mawa, Kumuru, French, 19 August 2000.

be members of a recognised Protestant Church and not have to adhere to the rigorous code of practices expected by CECA.

CECA upheld a particularly strong emphasis on the institutionalisation of strict moral standards and a concurrent discipline system for those who fell short of the stated aim of making all African Christians committed and not nominal Christians. Pastor Yaka proudly proclaimed that, "CECA 20 is very strict in discipline, in life."[26] Anglican opinion was much the same but the tone was different, as a disapproving Anglican articulated:

> ...the CECA Church, they rather watch people very, very, very much. If you do [even] a little thing they excommunicate [lit. shut] you.[27]

Excommunication was used in order to maintain the 'purity' of the church.[28] Drinking, smoking and adultery, non-attendance at Communion, *inter alia*, incurred excommunication. In 1981, for example, 16,444 CECA members were under some form of church discipline. In 1982 that figure was 22,103. For many years excommunication was accompanied by physical punishment.[29] Etsea Ang'apoza, President of CECA explained the system in the 1970s and 1980s and how it changed:

> One must repair one's fault physically so physical work was prepared; perhaps carrying bricks, 200, 300 bricks—following the seriousness of the sin—or perhaps filling a cubic metre of wood...Eventually our council decided to forbid corporal punishment. If someone sins against God, if he repents, he is pardoned, he is taken back...Certain leaders knew the period for repentance. You were told you were sanctioned for so many years or so many months...We have also found that that was not good. If someone falls into sin, he must be excommunicated and give time to examine himself...In the past if someone repented, he was not admitted to Holy Communion, one waited to see if the repentance was genuine.[30]

Since CECA was the only church in many villages these rigorous standards were set for the whole society. Members often found themselves on the wrong side of church discipline but they bowed to it because of

---

[26] Yaka Idroru.

[27] Peter Yobuta.

[28] Article 7A, *Reglement d'Ordre Interieur de la CECA/AIM Zaire*, in Lalima "L'Exercise de la Discipline," 21–24.

[29] Obitre Biya, "La Discipline ecclesiastique selon le Nouveau Testament et son Exercise dans le District de Aru" (Diplôme de Graduat diss., ISTB, Bunia, 1982), 111.

[30] Etsea Ang'apoza.

the risk of being ostracised from the community. With the arrival of
the EAC this social and ecclesiastical cohesion broke down at village
level. CECA felt frustrated that its standards were compromised and its
unity threatened by the more lenient practice of another denomination.
Here is a conversation between an older woman and a younger woman,
both CECA members, on the subject of church discipline:

> Alo: The system [of excommunication] continues until today and I en-
> courage it because it's one method of putting the guilty person on the right
> road. By depriving them like this one lets them think about their error.
>
> Bhako: Often, however, the person leaves the church.
>
> Alo: If he acknowledges it he could plead before the elders and ask for-
> giveness. These [elders], after a meticulous examination, release him to
> re-participate at the holy eucharistic table.
>
> Bhako: In the past they demanded that bricks be made or that straw be
> found to build a house. I don't know if it continues because there are lots
> of sects. One can decide to join a sect instead of doing the discipline.[31]

Alo Cecile supported strict discipline and wished for the days when
CECA had more control over its members. Bhako Fibi accepted the
reality that religious choice made discipline difficult to implement.
CECA began to change its disciplinary system during the 1980s. Etsea
suggested that this improved church practice. Bhako thought it was
changed because CECA was losing members.

A system designed as a way of forming a new cohesive community
of committed Christian believers with an unambiguous identity had
become, by the 1970s, a rigid code of behaviour enforced by fear of
ostracism that, according to one CECA researcher, caused some CECA
members to join the Anglicans and the Pentecostalists.[32] Others formed
a breakaway group, *CECA 20 Réformée*, in the early 1990s. CECA wanted
to maintain clear boundaries between right and wrong, member and
non-member. In the 1970s and 1980s CECA faced a rapidly changing
society because of internal and trans-border migration. It proved too
wary of losing its principles to adapt to changes with enough speed to
retain Anglican migrants and even some of its own members. Ideology
and circumstance committed CECA to maintaining its boundaries,
allowing only gradual change.

---

[31] Alo Cecile, Bhako Fibi, Swahili, Bunia, 18 September 2000.
[32] Obitre, "La Discipline ecclesiastique," 45.

For migrants and some CECA members, change was attractive and ostracism worth risking for the opportunity of improved liberty and self-determination, as Titre Ande discovered:

> Now, when they had the possibility to have another community, people thought that it was good to free themselves in order to be more autonomous. But that created lots of problems since, actually, when one decided to change there was no longer a good relationship with the family. But all the same, people were encouraged by the new community into which they integrated in order to constitute a sort of family.[33]

The EAC provided the necessary sense of belonging, a familial home, along with a sense of freedom and development, *uhuru* and *maendeleo*. It actually possessed moral ideals not dissimilar to CECA but it did not expect all members to adhere to them—an attitude that was considered by CECA as proof of lax moral standards and underhand competition. CECA felt that the EAC was more lenient in order to gain members. The EAC was also aware that its approach resulted in more members and it is probable that it exploited this in some cases. The Anglican tendency to be flexible on behaviour codes and discipline was made more so by circumstance. Boundaries in EAC had become more permeable as members crossed geographical boundaries.

Umoja or uhuru

CECA's concern over the disintegration of Protestant unity, and the effect this had on socio-religious cohesion, was justified by appealing to the stance of the ECC and the legacy of western missionary societies. CECA's desire for a pure church of committed Christians followed a strong Christian tradition. These views bolstered CECA's belief that it was the rightful actor in the area and the EAC was an impostor. However, in independent Congo unity as promoted by the ECC was not working. Attempts to maintain the comity agreements of missionaries provoked antagonism among indigenous churches. As people moved location they wanted to take the church of their ethnic group with them, as escarpment Anglicans demonstrated, or they wanted freedom to develop alternative ways of worship and society, as the migrant labourers from Uganda illustrated, and this was permitted by

---

[33] Titre Ande.

the state. These conflicts can be understood as the search for a place to feel at home.

CECA's identity was embedded in a strict moral order arising from individual Christian conversion. In an area in which it had the Protestant monopoly this was upheld through the support of social elites. Anglican unitary identity was centred around liturgical and hierarchical order that allowed members greater flexibility on issues of moral and social control. Its identity was not fundamentally threatened by a reasonable variety of moral standards. Furthermore, the developing rhetoric surrounding its internal unity allowed it to accept the emphasis on freedom and development propounded by northerners that so irked CECA's authorities. Because of the historical events surrounding Anglican migration the gulf between CECA and the EAC in the 1980s appeared to be very wide, their identities very different. Later chapters will demonstrate that common identity features were to emerge by the late 1990s that made possible a more consensual relationship that recognised unitary aims.

Conclusion

There are three paradoxes in the story. Firstly, it seems that throughout North-east Congo the threat to CECA's membership from new EAC chapels was not large. The EAC attracted more local Catholics to join them than local Protestants yet the Catholics appeared unconcerned. Secondly, in the north, once migrated Anglicans left CECA and obtained the *uhuru* and *maendeleo* they sought, they adhered to a more rigorous moral standard than that observed by the Anglicans in the escarpment area. They retained the conservative evangelical ethos they had learnt in the AIM-influenced COU in West Nile or from the *Wokovu* revivalists. In the third paradoxical twist CECA found the *Wokovu* even more difficult to deal with than mainstream Anglicanism even though the *Wokovu* too had a strict morality which followed similar rules to CECA, and set clear boundaries on who was 'saved' and who was not. It is to the *Wokovu*, who initiated the arrival of the EAC in the north, that we turn now. Their challenge to the orthopraxis of western initiated churches was rejected by CECA and seriously threatened the internal unity of the EAC.

CHAPTER SIX

HOMELESS AND FREE FOR THE GOSPEL: REVIVALISTS IN THE EAC

Introduction

The EAC had begun to portray itself as an inclusive church that united different groups of people who could feel at home within it. The interpretative discourse of home helped to create a sense of common identity and to maintain unity (*umoja*). Yet the need to feel at home was not universal among EAC members. The most significant internal challenge in the EAC resulting from its migratory growth came from Anglican *Wokovu* (Revival) groups, who did not possess the same home-making desires as the non-Wokovu majority. This chapter studies the radical revivalist groups of the EAC and the way in which their belonging to the church was negotiated. *Wokovu* provided a dissenting voice within the church especially in the north where they were more numerous and influential than in Irumu and Nord-Kivu areas. Most wanted to operate within the same ecclesiastical space as the Anglicans, claiming unity with them, but they offered an alternative religious identity that proclaimed spiritual freedom to be paramount to liturgical and hierarchical order and that emphasised homelessness more than home. The rifts that emerged became almost too great to sustain institutional unity. Their alternative Anglican identity demonstrates the pluriform membership of the church and the importance of *umoja* for the EAC.

Strivers and resters

Small groups of *Wokovu* (lit: salvation) were present in Aru and Mahagi zones from 1960. They were obvious by their activities; evangelism at markets using home-made loud speakers and lively singing and dancing, weekly meetings at the houses of members where exuberant worship was used to tantalise the curiosity of neighbours, and confident preaching outside churches as worshippers left the Sunday services. They preached salvation through the cleansing quality of Jesus' blood, accessible by the public confession of sins and the subsequent living of a strict moral life in fellowship with other 'saved' ones. Most of the *Wokovu* in Congo came from radical tendencies within the East African Revival.

The mainstream East African Revival, or *Balokole* movement, which emerged from 1933 in Rwanda and South and Central Uganda, aimed to revive the COU from the inside, challenging nominal Christians to become 'saved' ones and to focus on spiritual rather than politico-socio religious issues. Most of the *Balokole* remained faithful to the COU, intent on reviving it from within. Tensions in Northern revivalism were much greater. At times revival groups were so critical of the COU that their continuing membership was burdensome and some broke completely from the COU.

The Revival was brought to North-west Uganda about 1948 by Dr. Lubulwa Elija working at Arua and Moyo hospitals. Like the *Balokole* in the south, the northern revivalists called for public confession of sin, a commitment to fellowship and evangelism, and provided a radical critique of local, traditional customs. In contrast to the southern *Balokole* they developed a suspicion of educational *maendeleo* aspirations, expressed in a condemnation of worldly achievement and wealth and a claim of greater reliance on the spontaneous guidance and provision of the Holy Spirit. One of the early converts, Ajuku Dronyi Sothenes, was particularly zealous. He called on *Balokole* to abandon their teaching and nursing jobs and to eschew material reward in order to carry out vigorous evangelism. He preached a thorough dislocation from both modernity and tradition and attracted the socially disenfranchised.[1] As has been said of revivalists elsewhere, 'Christians who lacked other forms of status had an interest in asserting a distinctive identity.'[2] The actions of Ajuku and his followers were seen by mainline Anglicans and *Balokole* as disruptive but discipline and even imprisonment were greeted by them as signs of success; persecution was expected for those who showed loyalty to Christ's command to preach salvation.[3] They also used local cultural influences more than their southern counterparts, including traditional melodies and vertical jumping styles of dancing. Although revivalists were firm in denouncing traditional rites allied with

---

[1] Adraa Mokili, "The Growth and Impact of Chosen Evangelical Revival (C.E.R) in Ayivu County, Arua District, West Nile-Madi Diocese" (Diploma diss., Makerere University, 1986), 11–14.

[2] Meredith McKittrick, *To Dwell Secure: Generation, Christianity and Colonialism in Ovamboland* (Portsmouth, Heinemann, 2002), 261.

[3] Margaret Lloyd, *Wedge of Light: Revival in North West Uganda* (Rugby: private, n.d.), 20.

socio-religious power they were less removed by education, work patterns or colonial privilege from popular expressions of local culture.

There was an attempt to bring the Northern movement under the norms of the southern and central Ugandan *Balokole* movement at the Kako Convention in 1954. It failed and resulted in two distinct movements: Ajuku's followers became known as Trumpeters (from their loud-speakers) or Strivers, and called themselves Chosen Evangelical Revival (CER). One observer, who described the *Balokole* Revival as 'a movement of the Spirit of God bringing people into an experience of Christ's power to save from sin, and into a new understanding of what Christian fellowship and brotherhood is,' described the CER as a 'lunatic fringe'.[4] Insults were not one-sided; mainstream *Balokole* were called by the CER, *Wapumzifu*, 'the resting ones'. Each movement had its own organisational structure that, in attempting to encompass the local and the international, paralleled that of the COU. Both groups initially remained in the COU, although at times parts of the CER left it. The next forty years saw violent division and painful reconciliation between the two movements and the COU. The entire West Nile church was affected by one movement of Revival or the other.[5] For example, Janani Luwum and Silvanus Wani, both Archbishops of Uganda, Rwanda, Burundi and Boga-Zaïre during the 1970s, were mainstream Balokole from the north. In Congo, almost all the *Balokole* or *Wokovu* of Mahagi zone were members of the CER movement, often called, *Wokovu ya Nguvu*, 'Strong Salvation'.[6] In Aru zone there was a mixture of mainsteam Revivalists and CER as well as many ordinary Anglicans. Although mainstream Revivialism and CER may be better understood as two points on a continuum of revivalist belief and practice between which individual *Wokovu* moved at different times, separating them allows clarity of analysis. For example, mainstream Revivalists were largely willing to accept the common identity features of the EAC. CER, however, maintained a sectarian stance within (and occasionally outside) the EAC and contested the validity of dominant EAC identity.

---

[4] J. H. Dobson, *Daybreak in West Nile* (London, Africa Inland Mission, 1967), 36.

[5] Interview, Alio Samweli, Arua, English 08 August 2000.

[6] For information on different groups see D. Bagatagira, "Split in the Revival Movement in Uganda," *Occasional Papers in African Traditional Religion and Philosophy 4* (Makerere University, Kampala, 1972), 1–5.

CER in Congo

A number of revivalists who had returned from working in Uganda were already preaching in the Aru zone when revival was preached in Mahagi zone in June 1964. Ajuku and eleven others, including three female evangelists, preached in Mahagi-Port to a crowd that included people internally displaced by the Simba rebellion. Those who converted as a result of this visit soon fled to Uganda to escape the rebellion where they met other Congolese influenced by Revival preaching. In the late 1960s they began to return to Congo and the CECA Church. The noisy confidence of their evangelistic enthusiasm and their insistence on the necessity of public confession made them unpopular, although the actual message preached—summed up as, 'Jesus said, "Confess your sins, find salvation, you will go to heaven",'[7]—was in keeping with CECA's evangelicalism. CECA church leaders considered them a dangerous nuisance; loud, bumptious, uncouth, disobedient and disruptive. They disliked *Wokovu* refusal to submit to the church authority, displayed in overt attacks on pastors' Christian credentials and the holding of meetings without their permission. CECA members were offended by detailed public confession.[8] They were uncomfortable with the use of traditional Lugbara, Alur and Kakwa instruments, melodies and dance patterns, and were irritated by the nuisance the *Wokovu* made of themselves in public places in the name of evangelism. CECA regarded the *Wokovu* as contorting Christian identity by noisy behaviour and convictions of spiritual superiority that posed a threat to internal unity. One of those who publicly confessed his sins in 1964 was CECA pastor, Aloni Ngomu. His attempt to reform his parish along *Wokovu* lines was met with disapproval by CECA authorities and he was forced to leave his church.[9] Ubotha Marthe and her husband, a CECA catechist, also converted in 1964. They were surprised that their *Wokovu* lifestyle was not welcomed by CECA:

---

[7] Interview, Sila Bileti, Aru, Swahili, 10 August 2000.
[8] Interview, Alo Cecile, Anamwasi Paluku, Bhako Fibi, Pasa Therese, Bunia, Swahili, 18 September 2000.
[9] Ang'omoko Tek'akwo Upio, "Mouvement des 'Barokole' dans le diocèse de Boga-Congo; cas de l'archidiacone d'Aru" (Diplôme de Graduat diss., ISThA, 1997), 4.

...Even though we did the recommended work, the offerings, and all other sacrificial acts, we were all [put] outside. This was the result of our salvation (*wokovu*).[10]

For *Wokovu* the memories of these years of alienation are recounted in narratives which express both dismay and pride: dismay at being rejected by CECA leaders simply for being, so they believed, better Christians than the rest; pride at having their faith tested through persecution.

During the 1970s several groups were arrested and imprisoned for their activities. In all these cases it was CECA leaders who were believed to have alerted the secular authorities to the disruptive behaviour of the *Wokovu*, accusing them before the civil authorities of "coming to destroy our country."[11] Such an accusation could be percieved as a ruse to encourage the desired imprisonment, or it could be understood as the extent to which CECA leaders were disconcerted by the seemingly unsociable behaviour. Ugen Lambert remembers being arrested:

> ...the *collectivité* chief called us to him and said, "Leave this thing completely. Don't ever do it again." We said that we couldn't leave these things because before we drank, we swore and quarrelled with people, we led a bad life. Now when we received Jesus in our lives we found joy and so stopped all the other things...On the 17th he sent us for three months to Mahagi zone [prison]. When we arrived they took off all our clothes, they said...we had introduced an unknown religion...[12]

Imprisonment did not stop *Wokovu* activity but it subdued it and moved it to the private sphere. From 1971 *Wokovu* in Mahagi were no longer welcome in the CECA Church and met only in each others' homes. In their own eyes they were Christians without a church—a contradiction for most Revivalists. In the eyes of the state they were a religious group without government recognition, a legally untenable position. In 1979 when they heard that an Anglican Church existed in Congo they became members. Had CECA found a way of accepting the *Wokovu* they would have probably remained within it. *Wokovu* believed in the importance of *umoja* with the church that they were called to revive from within. With this principle they could be members of any denomination which permitted their adherence. Their identity as confessing Christians was more important to them than denominational loyalty. The break

---

[10] Interview, Ubotha Marthe, Mahagi, Swahili, 27 August 2000.
[11] Interview, Uzele Salatiel, Mahagi, Alur, 28 August 2000.
[12] Interview, Ugen Lambert, Mahagi, Swahili, 29 August 2000.

down of relations with CECA, their own belief in revival from within a church, and the threat of State persecution for un-aligned Christian groups encouraged them to seek a covering body for their activities. The Anglican Church was the obvious choice because revivalists operated within it in Uganda. One *Wokovu*, aligning Anglican membership with issues of freedom, declared, "...this [Anglican] Church came to free us from certain yokes from other churches in the area."[13] Immediate circumstance as well as prior familiarity encouraged identification with Anglicanism. *Wokovu* now expected to work for revival within the EAC. For Otuwa Simeon, membership of the EAC was a fulfilment of God's plan for the area. He understood his return to Congo in 1959 as analogous to Ezra's return to Jerusalem to rebuild the temple. He quoted Ezra 9:9, "He has given us new life to rebuild the house of our God and repair its ruins, and he has given us a wall of protection...." For Otuwa, the institution of the EAC was the "wall of protection" which enabled *Wokovu* to rebuild spiritually the true church.[14]

Uhuru

Wokovu found genuine relief in the confession of their sins, assurance of salvation and sustaining relations in fellowship groups. They regarded the term 'Christian' as a social as much as a religious term. It denoted those who had accepted the social *utaratibu* of the church and its accompanying aspirations for *maendeleo*. Christians had participated in baptism and confirmation, which were important for *Wokovu*, but they had not openly confessed their sins and therefore could not, according to the *Wokovu*, have assurance of salvation.[15] Ubaya Ucaki, for example, confessed his sins publicly because he feared death. Seeing two corpses being carried for burial on the same day made him reassess his life. He announced to his astonished friends. "Today, I want to receive Jesus." And he went to a church where:

> They said, "[Tell] these things which hurt you..." Now truly, as the Spirit spoke through me, I recounted all these things openly. I said, "Truly I am a sinner. Jesus, forgive me! I stole things like beer..." [They said] "Before returning to the Lord's table go to the Christians and explain

---

[13] Interview, Ukethi Amos, Mahagi, Alur, 29 August 2000.
[14] Interview, Otuwa Simeon, Aru, Lugbara, 11 August 2000.
[15] Lloyd, *Wedge of Light*, 52.

everything." So I said, "We used to steal without anyone knowing. Now no sin is hidden from God. I did this. Jesus, forgive me and cleanse me with your blood."[16]

Ubaya expressed his sense of relief as a result of this public repentance. This sense of relief was often described as having freedom, *uhuru*; freedom from the fear of death, freedom from regular blood sacrifice, freedom from anti-social living (drunkenness, lying, stealing, adultery) freedom to do the will of God, freedom to preach and teach without having a certain educational standard.[17] Personal conversion led to changed behaviour exhibited in a strong dichotomy between the lifestyle of the 'worldly' and that of the 'saved'. The *uhuru* advocated by the northerners was understood primarily as freedom from social constraints. For Wokovu, however, *uhuru* was primarily spiritual and was paramount to Anglican *utaratibu*. This spiritual freedom entailed the rejection of some social norms and the manufacturing of other strictures. These included the refusal to wear ties, jewellery or elaborate hair-styles, a ban on holding end-of-mourning ceremonies for their dead, and on accepting indigenous medicines, as well as more widely accepted prohibitions like temperance and monogamy.[18] These social conditions developed a new culture of the initiated that set them apart from the community, Christians and non-Christians alike, and earned them the criticism from mainstream revivalists of being legalistic.[19]

As Derek Peterson points out in his article "Wordy Women: Gender trouble and the Oral Politics of the East African Revival in Northern Gikuyuland," conversion upsets categories of identity that affect the wider culture.[20] Revivalist conversion pits spiritual, spontaneous belonging against literate, bureaucratic and hierarchical belonging. The freedom to preach and to teach gained through *Wokovu* confession was a freedom extended to those who were often considered deficient in the necessary education. The identity of the preachers and teachers was challenged within the church. Whereas the majority of untrained *walimu* sought education, the CER presented a model of leadership

---

[16] Interview, Ubaya Ucaki, Mahagi, Swahili, 30 August 2000.
[17] Interview, Ozua Samson, Aru, Swahili, 10 August 2000, Adoroti Ombhabua, Kumuru, Swahili, 17 August 2000.
[18] Ang'omoko, "Mouvement des 'Barokole'" 12.
[19] Interview, Sengi Lupanzula, Bwakadi, Swahili, 06 October 2000.
[20] Derek Peterson, "Wordy Women: Gender trouble and the Oral Politics of the East African Revival in Northern Gikuyuland," *Journal of African History* 42 (2001): 471.

in which the uneducated and socially marginalised could be confident Christian leaders. They included many women who preached and taught alongside men, as the following chapter will demonstrate. The *Wokovu* made their lack of education a point of spiritual superiority, spurning opportunities for learning and claiming the inspiration of the Holy Spirit was the key to spiritual leadership:

> If someone already believes in Jesus there's no need to study again because the Spirit of God helps them...You are going to destroy [what you already have]...the Word of God is not studied.[21]

In claiming *uhuru* through public confession of sins the most radical *Wokovu* eschewed the *maendeleo* which was the foundation of identity and reason for *uhuru* for many other Anglicans. In the northern area there were Anglicans who most espoused *maendeleo* as a way of interpreting *utaratibu* and there were Anglicans who were the fiercest critics of it. The noisy and disruptive evangelistic behaviour of the CER became an embarrassment to *maendeleo*-minded EAC members and a threat to mainstream EAC identities.

Migration to a heavenly home

Migration particularly shaped the CER movement. The interpretation given by the *Wokovu* to their migratory experiences further encouraged disdain for *maendeleo*. They incorporated the idea of regular movement into their daily life and gave it theological purpose. During the 1960s and 1970s those who became CER had found it necessary to cross physical borders; sometimes they were economic migrants, sometimes they were refugees. Revivalism enabled them to perceive migration as part of God's greater purpose. The deliberate crossing of national, ethnic or just parish boundaries was now done at the prompting of the Holy Spirit. The freedom gained through salvation included the freedom to travel in order to preach the gospel. Sometimes CER felt prompted to leave good employment and return home to evangelise their own families. Sometimes they left home to evangelise neighbouring ethnic groups. At other times they used their migratory networks to further their evangelism—perhaps staying with someone who had once worked on the same plantation. Uketi understands this as an obvious result of

---

[21] Ubaya Ucaki.

his conversion. He should not stay calm in church, like Christians or mainstream Revivalists, rather:

> My faith has given me strength to explore lots of unknown places. When I was saved I went by foot to Aru, everywhere...yesterday I was in Nebbi, Uganda. Following this faith I don't worry about my tiredness.[22]

The discourse of tireless itineration is a frequent one; overcoming check-points, border officials and language barriers to preach the Gospel. In Congo *Wokovu* itineration resulted in the development of many small chapels from the 1970s onwards. This 'striving' to promote salvation was contrasted by *Wokovu* with the lack of activity of other Christians, who they accused of 'resting' inside churches. Inevitably, other EAC members refuted such accusations since they were busy building chapels, worshipping in them and encouraging social development.

The EAC provided the majority of its members with a locus in which to ground their social, spiritual and personal identity. They were making a home-from-home or adapting their 'strange home' to fit the aspirations they had learnt in familiar foreign parts. *Wokovu* simply did not find such ideas of home important. By developing or aspiring to peripatetic existences they challenged the self-understanding of other Anglicans who spread the EAC through migration. All Anglicans expected the EAC to be involved in the proclamation of the Gospel; all Anglicans anticipated eternal life. However, they did not all expect to reorient their lives in order to evangelise others, or to abandon a sense of home that connected religious observance with family and land. For CER the importance of specific geographic location, family ties and traditional rites were no longer considered important. Their need for an earthly home was diminished and the journey to their heavenly home was emphasised. Along this journey radical *Wokovu* wanted to share the intense feeling of freedom they felt through conversion. Public proclama-tion of the Gospel was for them a duty and a joy. Homeliness could be found in the *Wokovu* allegiances, in the international conventions, and the networks for evangelism (explained later in this chapter) for which one needed to travel. However, ultimately, for radical revivalists, home would be reached in the future. It was a point of pride that as 'saved ones' they need not worry about belonging to society and conform-ing to its standards. They resisted assimilation into their immediate

---

[22] Uketi Amos.

surroundings because their personal, social and spiritual meaning had an eschatological locus.

Different theological emphases on home and migration can be seen in the selection and interpretation of Biblical texts. It is not uncommon for EAC members to plot Biblical narratives with their personal stories. In the previous chapter, Ozua Samson described his flight from Uganda in terms of the Israelites' exodus from Egypt. The emphasis of his narrative, however, was on the Congo as the promised land, the land to which he belonged with his family, the home given to them by God. The radical *Wokovu*, on the other hand, considered themselves to be acting out the Great Commission of Matthew 28. Ubotha Marthe, in chapter four, described herself and fellow *Wokovu* as being peregrinatory, going to all peoples, teaching and making disciples. Otuwa Simeon's choice of text in this chapter might, from the lips of someone else, be used to indicate a settled form of Christianity in which building God's house was to be equated with establishing an earthly home. For Otuwa, however, it indicates his revivalist restlessness for restoring proper worship of God among a fragmented people in a fractured land. The EAC as a 'protective wall' is only a useful tool to this end. Nevertheless, as a tool the EAC must be an effective one and the *Wokovu* considered that part of their role was to ensure the church was revived from within.

The 'soap' of the EAC

The initial reaction of the EAC towards the *Wokovu* was different to that of CECA but it soon found itself dealing with similar issues of identity and unity. When the Mahagi *Wokovu* wrote to Bishop Ridsdale, he and other Anglican clergy were delighted that people should ask to belong to their church. It fitted Ridsdale's belief in the universal attraction of Anglicanism and a potential rise in members gave increased status to Congolese Anglicans. They wanted to expand and become more significant in the regional ecclesiastical scene. Secondly, they were aware that the request came from people who had been members of the COU. They could claim that they were not acting contrary to ECC policies by attempting to influence members of other denominations but were merely providing for migrant Anglicans accustomed to a particular way of worship. Thirdly, several church leaders already had personal experience of conversion through the Revival movement in Boga. Beni Bataaga and Munege Kabarole, who visited Aru and Mahagi from 1979 to meet the *Wokovu* and later to establish the church there, had both belonged to Revival groups. Mukasa Nasanairi, who became the first Archdeacon of Aru in 1984, had introduced Revival spirituality to the escarpment EAC from 1947. They soon realised they were engaging with revivalists more radical than themselves who held more tightly to their revivalist convictions than to their loyalty to the Anglican Church. For their part, the *Wokovu* were disappointed that the EAC was little affected by revival and they took on the task of being 'soap' to 'purify' the church.[23]

When Bileti Sila, the Aru *Wokovu* leader, and others returned from the Convention in Mahagi in January 1980 and proposed that the *Wokovu* join the EAC their vote was split. Some, including Bileti's wife, resisted the introduction of the Anglican Church to the area because they thought they would lose their influence and radicalism. When they did agree to the idea they thought it inappropriate that Bileti be both *Wokovu* leader and church leader.[24] This difference of opinion caused tension in the Aru zone until discussions with the second Bishop of Boga, Njojo Byankia, in 1986 after which all *Wokovu* agreed to come under church authority.[25] The church spread quickly in this area, as chapter four illustrated, in large part through the work of both mainstream revivalists and CER. The fact that the desire, expressed by most Anglicans in the north, for trained centrally appointed clergy was not realised immediately probably kept more radical *Wokovu* within the EAC structure. They had greater leeway in establishing and leading their own chapels for a number of years until the Anglican structure that they knew from Uganda began to take hold. In Aru zone *Wokovu* evangelism, lively worship and a stricter moral code than that adhered to among southern Anglicans fed into the mainstream EAC and rendered the church more dynamic. The problems in Mahagi zone were more intractable. The CER were particularly zealous and uncompromising. Some of the leaders were both charismatic and dictatorial and they criticised the EAC ruthlessly. Pastors sent from the escarpment area found the situation bewildering and intolerable. Yet it was the mid-1990s before a local *Wokovu* pastor was available because of the resistance of the CER to theological study. The EAC spread much more slowly in

---

[23] Interview, Ndiritho Paulo, Mahagi, Swahili, 29 August 2000.
[24] Interview, Alio Samweli Arua, English, 8 August 2000.
[25] Conversation, Adoroti Ombhabua, Arua, Swahili, 31 August 2000.

Mahagi zone as a result of internal wrangling. It only became a viable Archdeaconry with four parishes in 2000.

Complex relationships and radical Christian behaviour were to test the patience and diplomacy of local church leaders and the unity of the EAC. The problems played out differently in Aru and Mahagi but the underlying issue was the same in both areas: the relationship with the institutional church. All Anglicans, *Wokovu* or not, had a relationship with the EAC. This relationship can be seen to fall on a continuum between the acceptance of institutional structure, practice and doctrine of the EAC at one end and a rejection of it at the other. Groups and individuals did not remain at a fixed point on this continuum but moved along it as they responded to circumstances. Analysed below are the points on this continuum of ecclesiastical relationship that shed light on Anglican identities and Anglican unity.

Ecclesial identity

For all Revivalists the institutional church comprised of two groups, nominal Christians, and 'saved ones'. The two groups worshipped together on Sunday mornings but their behaviour and activities separated them. The aim of the Revivalists was to make all Christians saved ones. The CER adhered to this principle as well but displayed more zealous moral behaviour and more fervent evangelistic activities. CER desire for unity within the church was overshadowed by their radical anti-*maendeleo* behaviour and their stringent criticism of the spiritual quality of church leaders. One pastor explained that *Wokovu* attacked the church by saying, "In the church there is sin, the church is full of sinners."[26] In including church leaders in their criticism, the *Wokovu* effectively contested the *utaratibu*, upon which the EAC had maintained its identity and unity.

The emphasis of the Congolese *Wokovu* was on their own close-knit spiritual group. It provided fellowship and stimulated evangelism. Belonging was primarily to the *Wokovu* rather than the EAC. These groups had their own order that was very different to the stratified, formal *utaratibu* of the EAC. It can be no coincidence that the CER existed in cultures like the Kakwa, Lugbara and Alur that are tradition-

---

[26] Interview, Tabu Abembi, Bwakadi, French, 06 October 2000.

ally segmentary. Leaders were those who showed most ability or zeal in preaching; they were often charismatic individuals to whom a great deal of loyalty was shown by group members. The influence of the leadership was tempered by democratic voting systems for decisions on whom the leader of open-air evangelism should be, or which theme was to be chosen for the Sunday afternoon meeting.[27] All *Wokovu* were expected to participate to some degree in evangelism and in fellowship meetings. *Wokovu* events were self-supporting. Their leaders received no financial remuneration.

The migratory paths taken previously for employment or security were repeatedly followed for spiritual fellowship with a wider network of *Wokovu*. They maintained international networks via Uganda that included local and regional leaders, meetings and conventions, through which a sense of heavenly homeliness was engendered. *Wokovu* maintained transnational connections at a time when the EAC and COU were emphasising national ecclesiastical structures.[28] Geographical boundaries were no barrier to fellowship. Possessing a sense of divine purpose *Wokovu* could confidently travel to brothers and sisters in Christ.

Wokovu declared greater affinity for this fictive kin structure of *Wokovu* 'brethren' throughout East Africa than for the EAC members in their own village and their allegiance to it meant they were less inclined to accommodate themselves to the works of parish or diocese.[29] The *Wokovu* preferred a network system, rather than a chapel system. The network had influence but little direct authority over local groups as the history of division and reconciliation within the movement has shown.

The alternative structures of the *Wokovu* conflicted with the mainstream EAC system and caused suspicion on both sides. The *Wokovu* were suspicious of the institutional church and its desire for educated, salaried (albeit poorly) leaders who did not sufficiently challenge themselves or their congregations to repentance and right-living. Their *heshima* for EAC leadership was noticeably lacking. Through these attitudes they were contesting the values of mainstream Anglicans and the identity of the EAC with *utaratibu* and *heshima* as its way of government, worship and social interaction. The previous chapters illustrated the ways

---

[27] CER meeting, Bunia, 17 September 2000.
[28] Ibid.
[29] Interview, Wiyajik Kapondombe, Mahagi, Swahili, 27 August 2000.

in which EAC identity maintained continuity with cultural structures of the escarpment that upheld the values of the socio-religious elite. *Wokovu* demonstrated different lines of continuity with a different culture. They eschewed elite structures and condemned rites that upheld those structures, embracing instead a popular, pneumatological religiosity that would inevitably clash with *utaratibu* as defined by EAC leaders. Ubaya Ucaki explains the tension between EAC *utaratibu*, to which most *Wokovu* submitted on Sunday mornings, and *Wokovu* worship:

> Well, in the morning service they follow the *utaratibu* of the church completely. They sing praises as well here at church but [at *Wokovu* meetings], as it's evangelism, they really dance. At the church they only do *utaratibu* because it's the place particularly to respect God, of real *heshima*. There at the place of evangelism people really show Him, they really dance.[30]

Now a deacon, Ubaya recognised the identity of the EAC service—its *utaratibu* and *heshima*—and respected it as displaying reverence for the Almighty. He considered *Wokovu* meetings more fun and therefore more likely to attract outsiders. Worship was exuberant and spontaneous and followed local dance and musical influences. *Wokovu* used their own compositions alongside the hymnbook, singing its songs with more gusto than was customary in church. They preferred their own style of worship to the formal, Prayer Book style. More importantly, at a lively evangelistic event, suggested Ubaya, God was revealed through dance and music in a way, it is inferred, that God was not seen in the *utaratibu* of a church service! This is a striking claim that prioritises attendance at the *Wokovu* meeting.

Most *Wokovu* considered there was a division of labour between them and the church, as Bileti explains:

> I want the church because the work of the church...is to baptise, give sacraments. It does this work that I don't do. Mine is to preach as evangelist....[31]

The EAC authorities, however, expected their programme of church services and even evangelism to take priority over *Wokovu* activities. The *Wokovu* felt differently. The issue that most threatened EAC identity is the reversal in the minds of the *Wokovu* of the importance of roles within

---

[30] Ubaya Uchaki.
[31] Sila Bileti.

the church. Sengi Lupanzula, the Lese pastor of Mahagi between 1992 and 2000, believed that the *Wokovu* wanted to have authority over the church, "They wanted the church to be below them and them to be above the church."[32] The *Wokovu* believed that this authority was rightfully and biblically theirs. Mahagi archdeaconry evangelist and *Wokovu* leader, Ndiritho Paulo, explained:

> We go about the country, looking for other people outside. If we find people there we take them to the church worker...As the Bible says, "We will chose seven people to stay here but we will go out to preach."[33]

His application of the role of the diaconate in Acts 6:2–4 to contemporary ecclesiastical structures put the *Wokovu* in a position parallel with the first apostles. It placed official EAC workers as those appointed by the apostles to carry out tasks of secondary importance, an inversion of the *utaratibu* model of the EAC. Ndiritho, however, insists; "There are differences but we are all in *umoja*."[34] Although this sort of argument may have persuaded members of the CER to remain within the EAC it was unlikely to endear itself to ordinary *walimu* and pastors. Instead of seeing *wokovu* activity as secondary to church worship and hierarchical structure, *Wokovu* believed it to be so spiritually and socially significant that it had priority over the institution of the EAC. By this approach the CER effectively attempted to uproot the *utaratibu* of Prayer Book and hierarchy from its place of paramount importance in EAC identity to a secondary place below the *uhuru* of fellowship meetings and open-air evangelism important for CER identity. They inverted not only dominant EAC order but also mainstream Revivalist order. These differences caused great strain as *Wokovu* of different movements and non-*Wokovu* tried to co-exist within the one institution. The *umoja* between the EAC and some *Wokovu* groups was stretched very thinly indeed.

In asserting *Wokovu* unity with the EAC and spiritual superiority over it Ndiritho is not content to contest biblical hermeneutics. He also provides his own interpretation of the story of Apolo Kivebulaya:

> [The EAC] was introduced by Apolo Kivebulaya...He preached the Good News to every one...at the end of his life, he returned to heaven and he left work for his own people [to do]. But this work did not come

---

[32] Sengi Lupanzula.
[33] Ndiritho Paulo.
[34] Ibid.

to our area....Now we [*Wokovu*] are very happy with the work that the
servant of God [Apolo] has left...we want to build up *Wokovu* and the
church. But, you see, when Apolo left Boga his work ceased.[35]

The people of Boga, he said, did not continue the evangelism of Apolo.
Wokovu were his true followers. Chapter two suggested that the narration
of Apolo's story by escarpment Anglicans was used primarily to support the retention of the tradition he had brought them, which led to
the indigenisation of Anglican structures. Chapter three suggested that
those emulating Apolo may have given a more expansionist slant to his
story, but their mission was still seen as implanting Anglican tradition
among Anglican migrants throughout Congo. Ndiritho's interpretation
questioned the narrative that claimed escarpment *utaratibu* as the prime
legacy of Apolo. Ndiritho claims that *wokovu*-style evangelism was the
commission his followers should have undertaken after his death. In
his view, escarpment Christians should have taken the Gospel further
into Congo and should not have become locked into the tradition of
an ecclesiastical institution. Those who are willing to leave their homes
are the true followers of Apolo who demonstrated his own renunciation
of home by being buried with his head pointing away from it. Ndiritho
audaciously appropriates a fundamental narrative of EAC identity to
assert the superiority of *wokovu* evangelistic homelessness and to criticise
the tradition of escarpment Anglicans.

Conclusion

Radical *Wokovu* shunned specific traditional religious forms and encouraged popular participation in worship. The belief in the power of the
Holy Spirit to act directly to solve daily problems resonated with popular
religious expression that had often been stifled by an elite preoccupation
with status and education within the church. Spiritual progress affecting the whole of life was expressed in ways that challenged the close
association between the church and traditional social elites. This did
not mean that traditional social structures evaporated. Revivalist groups
commonly started as fluid, popular, junior movements and transformed
in the lifetime of their leaders into autocratic, gerontocratic institutions.
Nevertheless, worship within these groups tended to take a spontaneous,

---

[35] Ibid.

charismatic form; a characteristic also observed in revival-influenced mainline churches in Tanzania.[36] Like mainline churches in Tanzania, the EAC was "...torn between adherence to tradition on one hand, and to the manifestations of the Holy Spirit, on the other."[37] The Spirit influence would spread further through the EAC with the changes wrought by women and young people, examined in the following chapters. In Tanzania, however, unlike the EAC, many revivalists left mainline churches to form their own. Members who found spiritual and social satisfaction in the old order, that provided for them a 'uniform' of belonging, exerted centralised, bureaucratic authority over the reformers who then felt alienated and left. The rapid migratory growth of the EAC meant that the leadership could not attempt to exert the same control over the *Wokovu* and a serious split was averted.

Radical *Wokovu* suggested that the Anglican pattern of *utaratibu*—whether interpreted by *upole* and *heshima* or by social *uhuru* and *maendeleo*—presented a modernity which spiritually neither tackled the sinful ways of the present nor rooted out the evil of the past. Thus they inverted the identity of the EAC and upset the sense of 'home' created by the majority in their chapels. The CER tested almost to breaking point the elasticity of EAC rhetoric on *umoja*. Yet the mutual recognition of the importance of internal *umoja* as an identity signifier held them together. CER gradually accepted the importance of attendance at EAC services and ordination for some of their members. The EAC leadership gave them leeway and benefited from their enthusiasm for evangelism. The EAC provided a home for many. For a few, it provided a vehicle in which they could be homeless migrants travelling for the sake of the Gospel.

---

[36] Josiah Mlahagwa, "Contending for the Faith: Spiritual Revival and the Fellowship Church in Tanzania," in *East African Expressions of Christianity*, ed. Thomas Spear and Isaria Kimambo (Oxford, James Currey, 1999), 304.

[37] Ibid., 305.

CHAPTER SEVEN

WEAK VESSELS OR CHURCH FOUNDATIONS?
WOMEN IN THE EAC

Introduction

...we women are very weak vessels. Even if we force ourselves...our work just dies...we are people of real shame...we mistrust each other.[1]

...women are the foundation of the church... ...they have strength. Your church will stand through the ways of women...They have strength and unity.[2]

From these contrasting assessments made by two friends who worked together as women's leaders, it is apparent that the self-perceptions of women in the EAC are complex and at times contradictory. Anglican women in North-east Congo both disparaged their church work as ineffective, blaming their own defective characters, and also proudly proclaimed themselves as the basis of the church without whom it would not function. A glance round almost any chapel of the EAC on any Sunday morning between 1960 and 2000 would tell the observer that women in the congregation clearly outnumbered men yet few women took public roles during services. Such a situation of men as actors and women as receptors in acts of worship belies, however, a complex gendered interaction in the EAC within and beyond Sunday morning worship in which women became more assertive within its structures. Women's identity—expressed negatively and positively—was formed as they negotiated the ecclesiastical, social and economic expectations of their roles.

This chapter assesses the identity of migrant Anglican women examining how and why such polerised evaluations are possible. It assumes that gender is "...culturally diverse, historically dynamic and inflected by differences of age, class, race, ethnicity and nation,"[3] and it traces

---

[1] Interview, Tumusiime Rhoda, Kumuru, English, 18 August 2000.
[2] Interview, Janette Sinziri, Kumuru, Swahili, 18 August 2000.
[3] Dorothy Hodgson and Sheryl McCurdy, "Introduction," in *'Wicked' women and the Reconfiguration of Gender in Africa*, Hodgson and McCurdy (Portsmouth, Heinemann, 2002), 5.

the expression of demands made by men and women, and their relative and changing exercise of power. The assessment will develop the theme of religious change and continuity during migration. Along with the following chapter, it shows how, during the 1990s, groups of second generation migrants became influential in the EAC and further altered the identity of the church. The chapter analyses the shift in the role of women's groups and the developing relations with women in other churches. It demonstrates ways in which migrant women influenced the leadership and orientation of the predominantly male-led, male-oriented EAC and provided a force for identity-change within the EAC in the 1990s. In doing so it enters the debate about the extent to which Christianity enabled or constrained the lives of African women.[4]

Migration by women

Rural-urban migration from the Semeliki escarpment was experienced differently by women than men. Basimasi Kyakuhaire, mentioned in chapters two and three, demonstrated that colonial employment opportunities usually favoured men. Married women were often expected to maintain family stability in the upheaval of migration. Husbands, sometimes accompanied by school age children, might go to the town for employment and education, leaving their wives to cultivate the family field in the village. If the husbands established themselves sufficiently wives might move to town later.[5] Alternatively, marriage could be a cause of migration for women. An urban businessman might return to his village to marry, taking his bride back to the town with him. Anglican women moving to the towns used the Mothers' Union (MU) to provide for themselves the stability they were expected to offer their families. In the first instance women replicated the form of the escarpment MU in which the MU provided them with religious and developmental opportunities within traditional male dominated social structures that were perpetuated and enhanced by the EAC. However, migrant women came to challenge the narration of gerontocratic authority by older women that was plotted with discourses of *heshima*

---

[4] See Elizabeth Isichei, "Does Christianity Empower Women? The Case of the Anaguta of Central Nigeria," in *Women and Missions: Past and Present*, ed. Fiona Bowie et al. (Oxford, Berg, 1993).

[5] Valdo Pons, *Stanleyville: An African Urban Community under Belgian Administration* (Oxford, Oxford University Press, 1969), 44.

and *utaratibu*. Increasingly, they considered that providing a home-from-home by replicating escarpment values was unhelpful in their migrant situation. Their need to adapt to urbanisation altered the identity of the MU and the EAC.

Trans-border migration also had different consequences for women than for men. Those who took refuge in Aru and Mahagi zones when Amin fell from power in Uganda generally fled in family groups. A married woman was usually expected to accompany her husband to his father's village, which often increased the sense of loss and dislocation, especially if she had not lived in Congo before.[6] For others sudden migration contributed to marital break up,[7] or was the result of it.[8] Such women found in the MU companionship and spiritual support in dislocation. Many MU members in the north were also *Wokovu*. Their Christian experience, studied towards the end of this chapter, shifted the roles normally ascribed by church and culture to women.

Migration instigated socio-religious change for women by providing lifestyle alternatives unknown in the village and different to ethnic customs.[9] For Anglican women its effects became most apparent in the late 1980s and early 1990s in the context of greater economic and political decline. Plantation farming had diminished and state institutions were in terminal decline. Schools and hospitals operated at a basic level and salaries and morale were low. Most people, even in urban areas, relied on subsistence agriculture for survival. Husbands' ability to earn salaries was reduced and many migrant women became petty traders to supplement the family income. Women, who had always performed much of the agricultural work, took greater responsibility for the monetary income of the family: a situation not always appreciated by their husbands.[10] Women were not only expected to provide family stability they also needed to be socially adaptable and economically flexible. The customs with which they had grown-up did not always appear relevant to their migrant situation and, whilst gender norms did not

---

[6] Tumusiime Rhoda.

[7] Interview, Adili Janette, Kumuru, Swahili, 18 August 2000.

[8] Interview, Aiye Joanne, Arua, Lugbara, 12 August 2000.

[9] Pons, *Stanleyville*, 45–47.

[10] Ch. Didier Gondola, "Popular Music, Urban Society and Changing Gender Relations in Kinshasa (1950–1990)," in *Gendered Encounters: Challenging Cultural Boundaries and Social Hierarchies in Africa*, ed. Maria Grosz-Ngaté and Omari Kokole (New York, Routeledge, 1997), 81.

disappear, women could act in a wider sphere without abrogation if their actions were perceived to benefit the family. Some women saw these opportunities as empowering and enjoyed their greater economic and social independence. It is these women, consciously adapting to the worsening socio-economic situation, who were most likely to encourage change in the EAC that would respond to change elsewhere in their lives. They desired greater self-determination that was not based upon social hierarchies or education. Because the EAC remained their home, the place in which their identity was grounded, their push for social change was expressed most cogently in their religious life. They wished to re-order their home to make it more habitable in the contemporary situation. Others, often the older first generation migrants, regarded new opportunities as bewildering, even frightening; they considered themselves 'weak vessels' in the face of greater responsibilities. They wished to possess in their religious home the comforts of the familiar. Although EAC affiliation was perceived to provide support during this time of change the nature of the support they required proved to be quite different.

Migration was responsible for an increased mix of denominations throughout the country as their members established churches in new locations and disregarded the old boundaries of missionary comity. The EAC had been at the vanguard of this trend in the 1970s in the North-east. By the 1990s many other *Eglise de Christ au Congo* (ECC) members were present in towns. Even in rural areas there might be two or three different churches present. Unpleasant relations, like those between CECA 20 and the EAC examined in chapter five, continued to occur but the contact between churches, including that of CECA and the EAC, became increasingly harmonious. Large towns with a greater mix of denominations set a trend for greater co-operation that was significantly influenced by the women's movement in which Anglican women played a part.

Church planting

The growth of the EAC as a result of urban migration afforded some women the opportunity to exercise initiative in the ecclesiastical sphere. Mahirani Melena, the daughter of Basimasi, instigated the EAC in Butembo. She had the support of her husband, the patronage of a wealthy trader and the blessing of Mukasa Nasanairi, the Ugandan missionary. The men provided the ecclesiastical and civil legitimacy considered necessary in starting a church. However, it was Mahirani who met people, ran seminars and organised market place evangelism. She worked mainly with the women. About 1972 she began visiting the town market place, "To search out those without faith so they could come to meet together."[11] She gathered non-Christians, Anglicans from Uganda and the escarpment, and members of other churches not represented in Butembo. Her approach was basic evangelism but her aim was to establish an Anglican congregation. Most other women who claim similar initiatives in the establishment of EAC chapels come from the Revivalist tradition. Most of them appear to have had an informal but recognised status within the nascent Anglican community, usually through their husbands, but occasionally in their own right as significant traders.[12] However, their contribution was not always officially remembered if they worked alongside husbands or *walimu* to whom credit was often accorded.

In establishing or providing for new EAC chapels these women did not overtly challenge official gender specific roles within the church but could work within them because of their own personalities and positions. The EAC leadership regarded them as committed Christian women whose work was an example to others. The fact that some women did initiate EAC chapels and many more gave support to these initiatives demonstrates the significant part the EAC played in their social-religious identity. It also shows that the male-led EAC could permit female initiative in new migrant situations.

Mothers' Union

The MU was frequently the first group to be started in a new chapel. Evasta Kusuna, for example, started the MU group in Bunia in 1970 whilst her husband helped to establish the EAC chapel there. Women married in church adopted the aims of the international MU body as interpreted by the escarpment Anglicans. It was seen as desirable by all members of the church to have a strong and active MU harnessing the physical and spiritual potential of women for the good of the congregation and providing a supportive, developmental group for the betterment

---

[11] Interview, Mahirani Melena, Komanda, Swahili, 21 September 2000.
[12] Interview, Bonabana Christine, Beni, Swahili, 17 June 1998.

Illustration 6   Photograph of Mothers' Union Members processing during the centenary celebrations, 1996. Androsi Kasima, interviewed for the book, is front right. Used with permission of Sarah Roberts.

of women. The MU on the escarpment presented an idealised western early 20th century view of women as dutiful wives and mothers which was mixed with compatible customs from local cultures. In doing so, it maintained women's social dependence on their fathers and husbands whilst providing skills, teaching and fellowship which enlarged their opportunities within that dependence. When they migrated, Anglican women used the MU, with its hybrid understanding of motherhood and domesticity, as a network to enable adaptation after dislocation. Initially the MU provided a similar role to that of the wider EAC during migration; it offered a home to those who, as a result of migration, found themselves in an unfamiliar place. It replicated the socio-religious values of the previous home and functioned in creating a group of mutually supportive friendships for migrant women. Through it they could develop a network of fictive kin on whom they could call when family members were absent or with whom they could share memories of life experienced in their previous home. The MU mitigated against the isolation a woman could feel in a new town or in her husband's village. The members shared a set of presumptions about their Christian faith. They also shared skills to supplement the family income. When economic decline meant that embroidery and knitting became luxury items from which regular income was less frequently gained some women took up the buying and repairing of second-hand clothes for resale[13] or reintroduced traditional weaving skills.[14] Skills learnt at the MU group could enhance the trading capacity of migrant women.

Leadership in the MU, in the first instance, was based on customary expectations and traditions that had developed within the EAC. It replicated the village tradition of *wamama wazee* (lit: elder mothers) in which post-menopasual women advised younger ones and were sometimes granted positions on community councils. In the MU similar relations to the traditional generational ones were maintained as women attempted to uphold continuity between the old location and the new one. In addition to *wamama wazee*, the wives of church workers were prominent in the leadership of the MU. Their marriage gave them seniority even if their age and previous social status made them otherwise junior. Grace Peter was expected to lead the MU prayers in Kumuru and ensure they were understood and orderly. Her marriage

---

[13] Adili Janette.
[14] Interview, Alio Samweli, Arua, Swahili, 08 August 2000.

to the pastor gave her a responsibility to pass on the MU teaching. Her status within the church depended on the proficiency with which she did this. Pastor's wives who did not perform well were considered very 'weak vessels' indeed, so training was often provided in order to fulfil these expectations. Janette Sinziri recounted what she learnt when her husband was training for ministry:

> ...to be the wife of a minister they like you to care for your body, to have good habits, to do good deeds towards others, to be happy, to remain happy with everyone, to be dutiful, to obey your husband as a husband and so on.[15]

Such virtues were expected of all MU members, but pastors' wives were to set a particular example. In this case, the obedience of a pastor's wife to her husband did not simply have personal or familial consequences it affected the running of women's groups. Order and status in the MU was linked to the hierarchical *utaratibu* of the EAC because many of the leaders of the MU, through marriage and through training, were intimately connected to the male leadership of the EAC. Depending on individual marital relationships negotiated within the clergy home, these arrangements could engender more control by the pastor over the group or greater freedom for the group in direction and agenda. Janette found the course helpful, giving her '...strength in my spirit.' Women, like Janette, who lacked formal education and family status, found the training enabled them to carry out the extra tasks of their particular marital role and to fulfil the expectations of church members. The MU in the early years of the migrant church functioned in such a way as to perpetuate male and gerontocratic power linked to hierarchical *utaratibu*. Male-control was, however, only ever partial. Its exclusively female membership gave the MU greater scope for female orientation in socio-religious practice.

Many MU groups were structured around weekly meetings that had three parts; the learning and sharing of domestic skills and crafts to improve the home and earn money, choir practice for performance of contemporary Congolese songs (discussed in the next chapter) and prayer and Bible study. Bible study provided spiritual guidance and prayer addressed problems by accessing of divine power. Asuŋe Ella explained the importance of the MU prayer group in Aru:

---

[15] Janette Sinziri.

...women can have power before God. Once a week we have women's prayers...[a woman] can explain her problems before God and we can see that this wife really has problems. Then we pray to God together. Sometimes we can see the power of God who can help her.[16]

Asuŋe infers that this was one of the few ways power was conferred on women. In corporate prayer women shared problems in the presence of God and had direct access to the divinity who responded to these prayers: an access which by-passed liturgical and hierarchical *utaratibu*. Although, in form and in content, MU prayer groups were far removed from indigenous possession cults, in terms of the understanding of the proximity of the spiritual realm as a result of corporate action they were not so distant.[17] They were expressions of popular religiosity that were oriented towards the concerns of women and seen as vehicles through which positive change could be effected.

As has been observed in women's organisations elsewhere in Africa, the MU had given 'a new primacy to motherhood' as well as 'new challenges to Christian mothers'.[18] As well as expectations of particular behaviour, hospitality on behalf of the chapel or parish was seen as women's preserve. MU members also visited and prayed for the sick, thus providing an important service of pastoral care. They raised money for the EAC. They cleaned and adorned the church building. Women usually gave more than men at church collections; a point noted by women with pride and only partially explained by their larger numbers. Women articulated their activity within the EAC in terms of service, prayer and giving: a role within the parameters of the MU model of motherhood, domesticity and community building. Church teaching and cultural expectations colluded in maintaining a domestic role of service for MU members in the EAC. Muhindo Tsongo summed up this attitude by saying with pride that a woman, "...plays an important role in the church because she is used to serving."[19] This was a supportive, background role to the public male roles of leadership and decision making. It maintained male control within the EAC whilst

---

[16] Asuŋe Ella, Aru, Swahili, 12 August 2000.

[17] Matthew Schoffeleers, "Pentecostalism and Neo-Traditionalism," in *Christianity and the African Imagination* ed. David Maxwell and Ingrid Lawrie (Leiden, Brill, 2002), 235–236 and 263–266.

[18] Deborah Gaitskell, "Power in Prayer and Service: Women's Christian Organisations," in *Christianity in South Africa: A Political, Cultural and Social History*, ed. Richard Elphick and Rodney Davenport (Claremont, David Philip, 1997), 266.

[19] Interview, Muhindo Tsongo, Edinburgh, French, 17 December 2000.

allowing women skills and fellowship that they perceived as immediately beneficial to their life and faith. It was by these criteria that EAC women had been accustomed to judging themselves "weak vessels" or "strong foundations."

The MU was a conservative organisation, which, as migration took place, emphasised the continuity of EAC *utaratibu* with its clearly defined expectations for women as wives, mothers and servants of the church. As such it could be perceived as controlling women by limiting their role to one of domestic service for church and home. This approach was not perceived to be problematic by most women. They regarded motherhood as a highly valued role and saw these tasks as an extension of it. They wanted support and advice on how to be wives and mothers. Their daily work was onerous enough and many did not want additional tasks or increased responsibility. They appreciated the provision of friendship and spiritual care to migrant Anglican women. In this way the MU empowered women to adapt to their new circumstances, provided them with skills and networks of support which gave them "strength" and "unity." The dichotomy of empowerment and control was alien to most. As Elizabeth Isichei highlights in an article entitled, "Does Christianity Empower Women?" the "most passionate concern" of African women, "is not with power but with life."[20] That is, many MU members were less concerned with wielding public power than having access to divine, life-giving power for assistance in daily life. If the MU provided them with quotidian support, many were content with that. Change, however, occurred because an increasing number of MU women were *not* content with the *status quo*. They wanted to play a role in church and society beyond the boundaries laid out by the escarpment MU. The scope for female-orientation in socio-religious practice within the MU grew as young migrant women began to feel that MU practice inherited from the escarpment no longer met their requirements.

Change

In providing women with friendship, fellowship and skills in their new location the MU was already open to change. The issues of a migrated

---

[20] Isichei, "Does Christianity Empower Women?" 227.

life in North-east Congo, including economic loss, urbanisation, denominational and ethnic mix, inevitably altered the dynamics of the MU.
From the late 1980s onwards, the migrant MU members slowly dis-
entangled themselves from the influence of escarpment Anglicanism,
a process still underway in 2000. Younger migrant women became
aware that their MU model was not universal. Some left the group or
attended irregularly. Others expressed dissent over the limited range of
roles women were allowed to fulfil within the church. They undermined
the presuppositions on which the MU was based. They disliked their
"inferior" position vis-à-vis men and resented the passive role allotted
to them in public.[21] It was these dissatisfied women who provided the
vanguard of change for the EAC in the 1990s.

An event I witnessed in 1995 presents in microcosm some of the issues
for Anglican women in the 1990s as a result of migration. In this particular case the issues surrounded the urbanisation and modernisation
of a church with rural roots. On 25 March, "Mary's Day," the women
of Bunia parish had their usual service and meal to commemorate the
immaculate conception of Jesus Christ and celebrate the virtues of
motherhood. The Archdeacon, pastor and evangelist, assisted by four
other male church workers, supervised the event. During the day the
election of a new committee of the MU took place. There was much
dissent during the election and several of the elected women declined
the posts, saying they felt unworthy to assume such responsibility. To
emphasise their point they walked out of the church. These women were
among the most confident and well-educated in the room. A number of
them were also married to prominent local clergymen (none of whom
was present). For the male church workers in charge of the election
they seemed the ideal choice. Their dramatic exit from the building
demonstrated the strength of their reluctance to be involved and their
discontent at the way in which they were being coerced to accept MU
posts. The church workers attempted to maintain order and cajole those
elected into accepting the posts. The women were eventually persuaded
and led the group competently. However, the events surrounding their
election were much discussed over the next weeks.

The women who had been elected were wary of leading the Bunia
MU group because it had been dysfunctional for some time. However,

---

[21] Interview, Damali Sabiti, Mukono, English, 20 October 2000.

this reason was eclipsed in later discussion by their dislike of the role men had played in the elections. The male church workers had staged-managed the elections to achieve a result they thought would be best for the group. The elected women felt manipulated into positions of responsibility about which they had reservations. This incident brought to the fore the issue of men controlling the affairs of women in the church, of men organising the day set aside for a celebration of mother-hood. Some of these women were married to clergy and held positions in the church from which they felt able to criticise the *status quo* and refuse to show *heshima* (respect) towards male leadership. However, they were also aware that by refusing a role expected of pastors' wives they would be perceived as shamefully shirking their responsibility. So their refusal was couched in the language of inferiority. They stereotyped themselves as weak, timid women, unable to lead and make decisions; a discourse frequently used of women by men. EAC women wished to be considered respectable and moral and, in so far as these values were defined by male social and ecclesiastical leadership, their identity had remained under male control. Male leaders were often wary of shar-ing their public roles of leadership and decision making. They might pay lip-service to increased public participation by women in church leadership but they continued to attempt to control the manner of this participation and limit its scope by recourse to traditional and national narratives of the importance of women's domestic roles and their subordination to men. This discourse was now being turned back on men when they least wanted it. The actions of these women, however, contested male control over the MU roles and prompted debate on the proper influence of male leadership over MU affairs.

The dysfunctionality of the MU group was also a result of contested control. Prior to the elections members had criticised the leadership of the group and demanded new leaders. The leaders felt betrayed by this response and there was much tension and mistrust. Meetings were postponed or poorly attended. The breakdown of relations justified, in the eyes of church leaders (and some women) male intervention in the elections. It was proof that women were indeed "weak vessels" needing guidance and support in all things. Those who demurred at their manipulated election to MU posts were conscious that leadership of such a disunited group would be difficult. The quarrel within the MU was at base a generational issue and had much to do with the altered expectations of some women vis-à-vis the characteristics of a good MU leader.

The challenge to the leadership was made by younger women who wanted a faster pace of change and new ideas and skills. The older women thought the younger ones disrespectful and immoral as Damali Sabiti, the MU Provincial Training Officer, explained:

> The elderly women were blaming the young ones. They said, "These ones don't want to listen to us. They are bad people." And the young ones said, "These ones are teaching us old-fashioned things. All the time we go there they are teaching us the same topic."[22]

The older women followed the values of the escarpment where age and experience improved status. The status of older women within the village community had often perpetuated the lowly position of younger women whose fertility and exogamy had disqualified them from taking decision-making roles, an attitude which had been assimilated into the EAC.[23] The younger women in the urban MU groups knew little of the village. Many had lived in towns all their lives. They were distanced from traditional power structures, less willing to cede position to older women simply because of their age, and found gerontocratic advice irrelevant because it was rarely based on the realities of a migrant situation. In Bunia in 1995, church workers recognised these generational tensions and were hoping that the leadership positions would be taken by women with a different kind of status within the church—younger clergy wives. This did happen. But not before the educated, young, clergy wives they had chosen had demonstrated their reluctance to be manipulated by church leaders and had distanced themselves from the decisions of the male hierarchy.

Some of those involved believed "tribalism" rather than generational differences to be at the root of the discontent. Evasta Kusuna, one of the most prominent older leaders, believed that she had given herself tirelessly to the MU in Bunia since its inception, encouraging new skills, and forging links with women's groups in other denominations,[24] and was being criticised unfairly for her old-fashioned ways by younger women. She rather saw the whole quarrel as a means by which the Hema majority was attempting to assert their influence in all areas of church life. She herself was from the Nyali ethnic group who had

---

[22] Ibid.

[23] Marie Tabu, Joyce Tsongo and Emma Wild, "Unity Must Adapt to Diversity: Congolese Women in Dialogue with Christianity and Culture," *Anvil* 15 (1998), 38.

[24] Interview, Evasta Kusuna, Bunia, Swahili, 16 September 2000.

often felt themselves to be marginalised and disdained by neighbour-ing Hema. The bias of colonial rule and the pattern of development of the EAC only reinforced this feeling. In articulating a problem in ethnic terms the stakes of dissent were raised in the ethnically unequal situation of North-east Congo. Evasta could understand herself to be a victim, not a cause, of tension. In this particular situation Evasta was in the minority. Her niece and other younger non-Hema, like Damali Sabiti, did not feel that it was primarily an ethnic issue. They wanted younger women to lead regardless of ethnic origin and both played a significant role in the MU themselves. The influence of ethnicity in this debate was understood differently depending on the relative age and influence of the women. Younger, urban women were less likely to see the influence of the rural client relationships in the disagreement.

Mary's Day 1995 brought into focus the issues of status—gender, generational, marital, ethnic—all being renegotiated in a church rap-idly changing as a result of its migratory growth. The results were a shifting of control, minuscule in many ways, but not insignificant. By 1997 the women in Bunia were left to organise their own Mary's Day without the assistance of the clergy. Younger women began to take over MU positions while older women were increasingly sidelined in leadership. Change also took place in the format of MU meetings. Tindyera Kaberole gave a positive description of the women's Bible study in 2000:

> Everyone reads a verse...then the explanation begins, "I saw this and that..." two, three or four people agree on a word and we leave with that as our spiritual aid.

Then she describes favourably the way in which the skills workshop operates:

> The one who knows something comes to teach the other. It's not that it's you who will teach everything. No. This one here might have the gift of knowing one thing, another, something else. We teach each other.[25]

These quotations suggest that the *modus operandi* of the MU group had become more collaborative; a sharing of problems, insights and skills, rather than the group learning the skills known by their leader. The group dynamics had come to reflect the primary function of the MU among migrants: mutual support and sharing, rather than transferring

---

[25] Interview, Tindyera Kaberole, Bunia, Swahili, 19 September 2000.

advice from one generation to another. The quotations also imply that the generational factors mentioned above could be contradicted by personality. Tindyera, an older woman, founder member of the Bunia MU, the archdeacon's wife and raised on the escarpment, appreciated the new consensual approach and appeared relieved to relinquish leadership responsibility. Tindyera also noted that attitudes towards church marriage also changed. Previously, only women married in church could join the MU but in 2000 MU membership in Bunia was no longer assumed to be concomitant with the regularisation of martial status. The group insisted "...that it's only the one who believes in Jesus who is really in order with the church, we will go with her."[26] Unmarried women were accepted into the group as other members recognised their Christian sincerity. In interview this was given as an example of the way in which the Bunia MU no longer followed most of the MU rules, "...because here in town the custom is not appropriate."[27]

Adaptation to local situations and recognition of alternative customs, including the realities of modern conjugal arrangements, challenged the *utaratibu* of the MU. Younger women began to question the certainties of the old *utaratibu* and *heshima* of male control and gerontocratic female authority that had continued in the EAC. Because of migration the MU, like the EAC, was now larger and more dynamic outside its original power base on the escarpment and it could no longer be interpreted through escarpment social and cultural norms. Those who remained within in the MU increasingly emphasised *maendeleo* rather than *utaratibu* as the primary function of the group.

Maendeleo *and international connections*

The emphasis throughout this study has been on the local grassroots expansion of a church with international roots, a global network and a world-wide affiliation. The importance of adhering to locally adapted Anglican patterns of liturgy and hierarchy has been noted but relations between the EAC and the global Anglican Communion have not been fully explored. In this and the following chapter mention will be made of the local impact of transnational connections as they were made more tangible through improved communications and travel.

---

[26] Ibid.
[27] Ibid.

Most EAC members were proudly aware that they belonged to a world-wide movement and thus had connections more influential than their size or infrastructure in Congo would suggest. The pride in their local Anglican identity was influenced by the sense of international belonging. Clergy often articulated an awareness of Anglican heritage and strove to maintain the liturgical and hierarchical order as necessary characteristics of Anglicanism. Women, through the international movement of the MU, emphasised the local variety within the Anglican Communion and articulated this variety as an opportunity for change within Congo.

The MU offers training for its leaders and provides funds to assist travel or establish projects. MU members in Congo were proud to be part of it, felt encouraged by the international aid they received, and always hoped they would receive more. This connection afforded a few women opportunities to visit other countries, often Uganda or Kenya, for training. They were expected to return home and share what they had learnt. They became aware of altered women's roles in church and society elsewhere in Africa and as they shared their training they also called for change in Congo. Younger women who advocated change in the EAC often had an awareness of change taking place in other Anglican Provinces.

The change women required was spoken of in terms of *maendeleo*, a word frequently used to refer to education, health care and income generating skills. However, some women began to apply it to anything they believed would ameliorate the lot of women socially and ecclesiastically. Damali Sabiti spoke of improving self-esteem and challenging cultural assumptions:

> We need development really...some women refuse to do things because they look down upon themselves, they think they are nothing, they just refuse...a woman is not supposed to stand in public...[28]

In the 1990s some church leaders began to ask women to participate publicly in services but some were unwilling to perform roles they had been taught were male ones. They declared themselves weak and unfit. Damali believed attitudes had to change before such a development could happen. She wistfully recounted the women's leadership she had experienced elsewhere in the Anglican Communion, declaring that, in

---

[28] Damali Sabiti.

Congo "...we have not yet been given real liberty."[29] Opportunities for *maendeleo* required *uhuru* (freedom) to take them, suggested Damali. For her *maendeleo* did not simply cover the social work of the EAC or the service rendered by MU members but denoted personal development and cultural change towards gender equally. It was this she saw as the primary role of the MU. The wider network of African Anglican connections appealed to women who felt that the pressure on them to conform to local cultural norms that stifled the *maendeleo* they sought.

The experience of seeing women's progress in other African countries caused some EAC women to blame local indigenous customs and attitudes for retarding their progress. Although escarpment women had probably led forms of popular religious expression prior to the arrival of Anglicanism the EAC had colluded with particular elements of escarpment social structure to contextualise itself, thus reinforcing male power structures and unequal gender customs. Younger, educated women considered that the church should disentangle itself from such customs.[30] The common perception among second generation migrants that the customs of their home village were regressive was strengthened when men who expressed reservations about women's leadership in the church argued that it was "un-African" because it contradicted gender norms. The public ecclesiastical power of women was contested in terms of tradition. Muhindo Tsongo attempted to persuade Anglican traditionalists by appealing to Apolo Kivebulaya:

> ...follow the example of Apolo Kivebulaya who...worked with women and men in all church activities. He educated women and taught them without discrimination.[31]

Muhindo invoked Apolo's memory to press her cause. She reminded the EAC of his regard for women before the alliance of social and ecclesiastical structures began. Once again the story of Apolo was narrated to support the position of a particular group within the EAC with the expectation that other members would be persuaded by his example. Attempts at identity shift were made by the plotting of the founder's ministry with significant present concerns. Whether the appeal to Apolo was convincing in this instance or not, it was apparent that

---

[29] Ibid.
[30] Interview, Androsi Kasima, Boga, French, 08 October 2000.
[31] Muhindo Tsongo, "The Role of Women in the Anglican Church in Congo: A case of the Diocese of North Kivu" (M.A. diss., Trinity College, Bristol, 2000), 51.

gender expectations were shifting when the Diocese of Boga accepted women's ordination and, in 2003, Muhindo was the first woman to be ordained.

By 2000 there was a younger generation of women active in the MU who rejected the organisation as a way of managing and marginalising women's involvement in the EAC. Rather they perceived the MU as a vehicle for enhancing the self-esteem and social and economic independence of women through Christian fellowship and development skills. They were determined that the group should be led and oriented by women. *Maendeleo*—as more widely defined above—was the major paradigm through which they saw faith and life. It necessitated *uhuru* to practice it. Their understanding of *maendeleo* and *uhuru* was informed by their transnational Anglican identity. Women who travelled abroad, however, were a minority. Most MU women in Congo were more directly influenced by meeting with other Protestant women.

Wamama wa Habari Njema

"We have one God but it's religion that divides us,"[32] said Wadhiko Dina from her experience of the denominational rivalries in Aru zone. Yet the truth of this statement was at least partially subverted by Christian women in North-east Congo as they began to meet, worship and work with women from different denominations to their own.

When Mahirani Melena evangelised in the market place to gain converts for the EAC chapel in Butembo in 1972 she went with other women from *Wamama wa Habari Njema*.[33] The "Mothers of the Good News," is the name used by women's groups in other member *communautés* of the *Eglise du Christ au Congo* (ECC), which are similar to the MU. It seems that Mahirani was helped in her efforts to establish the EAC in the town by a group of women from different churches, including the Baptist Churches already present in Butembo as a result of missionary comity agreements. Indeed, Mahirani could be seen as continuing the collaborative effort of her mother. For when Basimasi moved to Nord-Kivu in 1939 she did not entirely abandoned her church work. She had helped a CBFMS evangelist to catechise a group of new Christians. Women appear to have been ready to help

---

[32] Interview, Wadhiko Dina, Aru, Swahili, 10 August 2000.
[33] Mahirani Melena.

each other in establishing denominations but men working formally for the EAC found no such encouragement from the leaders of other churches. Lukumbula Kihandasikiri, who officially started EAC chapels throughout the Butembo area, experienced strong opposition from the leadership of the Baptist Churches.[34]

Many women seemed unconcerned about the proliferation of denominations usually considered a divisive issue by male leaders. Women understood that different denominations provided a way in which members could feel at home in a new place. Few ECC member churches had official leadership roles for women and it seems that a lack of influence in ecclesiastical leadership may have made women more open to working together. Indeed, collaboration across denominational boundaries appeared more satisfying than working alone. The dislocation resulting from migration facilitated this openness to a greater degree than if the women had remained in their original home because they had greater opportunity to forge relationships with women who came from different denominations. It is also apparent that this approach was more common in urban centres where the mix of peoples and denominations was far greater than in rural areas. This phenomenon demonstrates the importance of different networks for Christian women. These networks would eventually engender a greater heterogeneity of practice within their denominational groups.

The example of Mahirani's daughter, Estella, may provide another reason why women were less concerned about denominational proliferation than men. Brought up in Butembo by parents who had worked hard to introduce the EAC in the town, when Estella married she joined the church of her husband, CECA 20 *réformée*. She explained that her sisters had followed the denomination of their husbands whilst her four brothers had remained Anglicans. When asked whether husbands could follow their wives' denomination, Estella, her mother, and the audience who had gathered to hear the interview, all laughed at the unusual suggestion.[35] Denominational affiliation in North-east Congo usually followed the male line and widespread migration since the 1960s increased the possibility of marriage across denominations. Estella said that the issue should not cause domestic discord because all churches

---

[34] Interview, Lukambula Kihandasikiri, Kampala, Swahili, 25 July 2000.
[35] Estella in Mahirani Melena.

worshipped Christ. *Mungu ni mumoja*, God is one, was the underlying basis on which Christians operated.

These gender specific expectations, however, produced a situation, where many women, unlike their husbands, were familiar with at least two denominations; the one in which they grew up and the one into which they married. This facilitated relationships with those from other churches and respect for their religious traditions; they recognised that they were all "Mothers of the Good News." Denominationalism may have led to mistrust among churches but an alternative story was emerging among women that would eventually begin to spread to male church leaders. The gendered position of women in ECC churches better placed them to traverse denominational boundaries. The group in which this potential was most clearly manifest was the *Fédération des Femmes Protestantes* of the ECC.

The *Fédération* brought together *Wamama wa Habari Njema* groups from all its affiliated denominations. At local level it was probably the most active arm of the ECC. Bhako Fibi from CECA 20 explained its significance:

> So we, with the Anglican women, we got to know each other well through the Federation...one Sunday a month we meet together to listen to the Word of God, to bring our needs, to pray on behalf of our nation, and to pray for *maendeleo* work...[36]

The Federation held monthly services as well as organising literacy classes and work in a communal field. The services were well-attended and lively, with enthusiastic chorus singing and dancing, choir participation, spirited preaching, fervent prayer and a shared meal. The singing at Federation meetings was led by an *animatrice* who enthusiastically encouraged exuberant praise. Many of the songs were in Lingala, the language of Kinshasa and its musical tradition, and were accompanied by clapping and dancing. The dominant mode of worship was one of Spirit-led joyful spontaneity that was described as *uhuru* and *furaha* (joy). The theological emphasis was on the power of the Holy Spirit to heal. Prayers for healing with laying-on of hands were a significant part of Federation meetings giving a central place to direct divine action for sick or infertile women. These new emphases were introduced by members of the Federation who attended Pentecostal Churches. By the 1990s

---

[36] Interview, Bhako Fibi, Bunia, Swahili, 18 September 2000.

there were about eleven ECC member churches in North-east Congo at
least three of which were Pentecostal. Even when the monthly service
was held by Anglican women in the Anglican Church there was little
sign of formality or the demure, timid demeanour displayed by them
on other occasions.[37] Women expressed themselves in *uhuru* without the
encumbrance of men whose presence inhibited their vivacity and openness. Such vibrant public worship was new to many Anglican women
but reinforced the belief, expressed in MU prayer meetings, of the
power and proximity of the spiritual realm.

The activities of the Federation challenged the socio-religious framework in which Anglican women had participated in the EAC. The
importance of *maendeleo* for women was maintained—that is, the
Federation organised literacy classes, communal fields, and so on. An
alternative to *maendeleo* was also offered in which the *uhuru* of spiritual
power was presented as a way of directly and immediately tackling
the problems of everyday life. Through the Holy Spirit, divine power
could be accessed without being mediated through knowledge, status,
institutions and hierarchies; *utaratibu* was circumnavigated. The power
which EAC women sought through prayer to aid them in daily life
seemed most immediately available in the freedom of emotive prayer
and praise in Federation meetings.

The Federation worked particularly well in urban settings with growing
number of denominations. It was introduced into rural areas as they
became more denominationally mixed. Women were usually willing to
learn from each other. The women of CECA 20 in Bunia, for example,
were favourably disposed to their Anglican counter-parts because they
knew them personally and had worshipped and worked together. As a
result each group invited the other to special events organised by their
own churches, further fostering relationships of understanding and
trust.[38] Women cited unity (*umoja*) and fellowship at times of difficulty
as a major strength of the Federation.[39] The word *umoja* is used here
not as a cohesive force internal to the EAC but as the connection
between women from different denominations in the solving of common
problems and in mutual support. The amelioration of ecumenical rela-

---

[37] Emma Wild, "Working with Women in Congo," in *Anglicanism; A Global Communion*,
ed. Andrew Wingate, et al. (London, Mowbray, 1998), 281–282.
[38] Tindyera Kabarole.
[39] Interview, Caroline Mwanga, Butembo, Swahili, 16 June 1998.

tions between ECC members went beyond the Federation because its activities enabled cross-fertilisation of denominational ways of worship and service as women returned to their own denominations influenced by Federation meetings. Anglican women experienced a new way of praying which included laying on of hands and loud supplication, sometimes in tongues. The songs learnt at the Federation were often repeated at MU meetings and, via the MU choir, were introduced to Anglican worship on a Sunday morning. During the 1990s changes were introduced into EAC practice as a result of ability of the women to engage with those of other denominations. This engendered a greater cohesion between Anglican worship and that of other ECC members and encouraged co-operation between leaders of the denominations.

The change, engendered by women, in the EAC's understanding of its identity in relation to other denominations was generally met, by those other denominations, with increased cordiality. For example, CECA 20 largely changed its perception of the EAC during the 1990s from considering it a threatening competitor to regarding it as a companion who shared the same ultimate objectives. Jockeying for power still occurred but, in the narration of interviewees, events stressing *umoja* were more likely to be emphasised than those stressing tension and strife. By 2000 EAC members were interpreting grassroots relationships with CECA and others as increasingly unified and of mutual benefit.

Women did not directly challenge the liturgical and hierarchical *utaratibu* of the EAC but they did influence the way in which it was performed. Their actions questioned the interpretation of *utaratibu* by *upole* and *heshima* as the EAC in the north had already begun to do. Quiet, formal services led by respected men were no longer considered the only way, or even the most desirable way, in which Anglicans could worship. Women interpreted *utaratibu* by *maendeleo* in the public ecclesiastical sphere and by spiritual *uhuru* in corporate worship, thus influencing identity change. Similar changes were being introduced from other quarters and will be analysed in greater detail in the next chapter. This chapter now turns to the influence upon women of the Revival movement. Like the Federation meetings Revival emphasised the Holy Spirit as enabler. For the *Wokovu*, however, the Spirit was primarily an agent of salvation rather than healing and *maendeleo* was considered unnecessary if one was sustained by the Spirit. Nevertheless, both groups claimed that it was the Spirit that empowered women to act in ways that challenged the *status quo*.

Wokovu *women*

The East African Revival is recognised as a movement in which the roles of men and women were less obviously gendered than in other areas of society. Thus women were able to criticise traditional hierarchies and church bureaucracy and assert moral and spiritual authority.[40] The movement allowed local leadership by women and influenced the Church of Uganda to an early acceptance of women priests.[41] This move was by mainstream revivalism that espoused education and modernity as the proper social responses to a Christianity of personal piety and corporate confession and fellowship. *Wokovu* in Congo came both from the mainstream tradition and from the Chosen Evangelical Revival (CER) tradition which was critical of education, *maendeleo* and church hierarchy, emphasised *uhuru* in the spontaneous mediation of the Holy Spirit, and utilised traditional forms of music and dance in worship. Whilst socially conservative in many ways, the Congolese *Wokovu* were more encouraging of the public, vocal ministry of women than the mainstream EAC. Although they rarely became senior leaders, *Wokovu* women took prominent, decision-making roles in Christian life, church planting, preaching and voting in *Wokovu* elections.[42] These practices addressed traditional gender assumptions but rarely resolved them in the lives of *Wokovu* women.

The opposing forces of traditional and *Wokovu* expectations and the ambiguity of women and men bending gender roles are articulated in the quotation below:

> There, where we opened churches, I went with [Marthe Ubotha]. We went with them. Our husbands helped draw water because there wasn't anyone else there. They went to open churches and we accompanied them. The churches from here to Avari were [opened] by us.[43]

Njang'u Esther first declared that she and Ubotha opened churches with their husbands. Then she said the opening of churches was the job of their husbands and they merely accompanied them. Elsewhere in the interview, it was clear that the women preached, evangelised and

---

[40] Derek Peterson, "Wordy Women: Gender trouble and the Oral Politics of the East African Revival in Northern Gikuyuland," *Journal of African History* 42 (2001), 471.

[41] In 1994, when the first women were ordained in the Church of England, Uganda had thirteen women priests in five dioceses.

[42] Interview, Anzukaru Marita, Aru, Lugbara, 21 August 2000.

[43] Interview, Njang'u Esther, Mahagi, Alur, 28 August 2000.

taught alongside their husbands but there was an ambiguity about the role of a *Wokovu* woman; was a wife the helpmeet of her husband or an evangelist in her own right? The gender ambiguity was also apparent for men. The lifestyle of itinerant evangelists demanded that the men helped with their wives' domestic tasks, fetching water for cooking and washing. These couples developed a partnership in which domestic tasks were shared beyond normal gender boundaries when the primary task of evangelism demanded it because they believed that preaching salvation was an exigency that over-rode the necessity to observe gender boundaries.

This equivocal situation was underlined by Ubotha when she attempted to establish her credentials as a dutiful wife who, as a women's leader, taught others to obey Alur custom with regard to their husbands:

> ...be docile in all things. When the husband returns to the house, give him water for bathing and tea and food. When you speak with him do so in a polite tone to show respect. And, as our [Alur] tradition expects, kneel before your husband...you can give him honour by washing his feet.[44]

Domestic tasks and relationships were still gendered for the *Wokovu* and Ubotha believed that gendered customs were in keeping with Christian teaching. However, Ubotha also insisted that a woman's first loyalty was to God. If a husband sinned his wife should correct him:

> Of necessity you must remind him of the wrongdoing without feeling inferior or superior and promptly put him back on the right path.[45]

A *wokovu* wife had the same moral and spiritual obligations to her husband as he had to her, she was his equal in spiritual matters, a position that conflicted with the customary 'honour' and obedience which an Alur woman was also expected to give. The self-identification as good wives and mothers by N'jangu and Ubotha comes from both the conservative elements of *Wokovu*, mainstream EAC and MU discourses as they melded with indigenous ideas of women's roles. Outside the *Wokovu* community itineration and public preaching were considered to be male tasks. Non-*wokovu* men and women often looked askance at the unwomanly activities of certain *Wokovu* women, criticising them for neglecting their domestic duties, leaving the home untidy or the children unruly, whilst they were evangelising. *Wokovu* women were aware

---

[44] Interview, Ubotha Marthe, Mahagi, Alur, 27 August 2000.
[45] Ibid.

that they were walking a cultural tightrope. They evangelised publicly,
they claimed a spiritual right to challenge male authority—albeit pri-
vately—and they questioned the need for material homemaking when
the journey to the heavenly home was of paramount importance. They
were in danger of being regarded as "wicked" women who threatened "respectability" and the "norms of 'appropriate' gender roles."[46]
Wickedness did not cohere with the perception of themselves as saved
and, for this reason, although they pushed gender boundaries, they
were careful not to overstep them. Where *Wokovu* women knew they
were stretching the boundaries to the point of societal disapproval
they insisted that salvation made them better wives and mothers. It is
this tension which probably prevented *Wokovu* women from taking main
leadership positions of *Wokovu* groups. It is also this that encouraged
them to insist that, where gender roles were being contested, it was as
a result of following more closely the commands of Christ or being
obedient to the call of the Holy Spirit.

Paradoxically, for those mainstream EAC members who argued so
passionately for development for women, it was their anti-*Maendeleo*
stance, accompanied by their reliance on the Holy Spirit, which
allowed *Wokovu* women to take a public religious role without having EAC authority or training. *Wokovu* argued that the authority to
carry out a public role in the church came from the Holy Spirit. If
a particular spiritual gift had been given then it should be used. Nor
should traditional expectations render women unfit for preaching or
decision-making if the Holy Spirit has been seen to use them. Njang'u
said emphatically,

> Women who preach [are] led by the Spirit. They stand up amongst people
> and speak. And the problem with other people is the problem of reading.
> It makes them frightened of standing in front of others.[47]

Since most Anglican women had learnt that education was necessary for
public roles in church and society, and since they were generally less
educated than men, many understood themselves to be less able to take
the leadership and decision making roles they considered the preserve
of educated men. The *Wokovu* emphasis on the role of the Holy Spirit
offered a critique to this attitude, declaring that Christian leadership

---

[46] Hodgson and McCurdy, "Introduction," 6.
[47] Njang'u Esther.

was a spiritual quality for which education was not necessary and may even be a hindrance; an argument which gave *Wokovu* women confidence to preach and evangelise. Indeed, where MU groups were led by a woman who was not married to a church worker she was often a revivalist, confident enough of her spiritual gifts to lead. *Wokovu* stress on direct obedience to the Spirit, an authority higher than men, provided them with a way of contesting, although not entirely overcoming, the dominant gender roles.

The *Wokovu* movement provided women with an identity in which the gendered aspects were configured to allow them a public religious role that necessarily conflicted with customary and traditional MU identities. The assertions of *Wokovu* women appeared less radical to those women influenced by the *Federation* and adapting to necessary socio-economic change. Both groups were galvanised by migration: *Wokovu* women gained a heightened perception of the need for evangelism and an ability to itinerate to meet that need; mainstream MU members gained experience of other ways of worship and increased social independence that encouraged greater public participation in church affairs. As they exerted their corporate will on Anglican practice it became increasingly female-oriented.

Conclusion

The changing identities of EAC women over forty years conflicted and coalesced to different degrees with the Anglican 'norm' that had emerged from the escarpment. Women were often enabled to cope with the instability of migration by membership of the MU and the Federation, drawing from them "strength" and "unity" from which many were able to declare themselves "foundations of the church." This confidence was, however, achieved through "shameful" generational conflicts that engendered mistrust. Second generation migrant women, distant from village values and aware of other national or international alternatives, wanted to make the EAC and the MU vehicles for the further development of women in self-esteem, education, and church leadership. Some women denigrated themselves as "weak" and "untrustworthy" because they failed to live up to the old expectations or felt threatened by change. Other women measured "strength" or "weakness" to the extent to which they could maximise the new opportunities presented to them.

Migratory dislocation presented women with different social choices and thus permitted them to re-assess their position within the male-led and male-oriented EAC. They negotiated the constraints of gendered roles formed on the escarpment to present a more confident public identity for Anglican women to develop an EAC that was more oriented to female concerns. Through widening the significance of *maendeleo* to challenge gender norms and encompass a spiritual element, and through a greater appreciation of *uhuru* and *furaha* in worship and pastoral care, migrant women were altering their religious identity and introducing change to the EAC. They used what they knew of global Anglicanism to encourage diversity within the church. They were in the vanguard of a steady adaptation to an Anglicanism that embraced a popular Congolese expression of Christianity.

CHAPTER EIGHT

"YOUNG PEOPLE, KEEP YOUR FAITH:"
YOUTH, SPIRIT AND CONTEMPORARY
CHRISTIAN EXPRESSION

Introduction

The world is extremely drunk...
Everywhere we hear,
News of war,
People are dying day and night,
Children are left as orphans...
It's sad, it's very sad.
...Everyone is looking after their own interests
Looking to enrich themselves,
Through wealth from stealing.
It's sad, it's very sad.[1]

These lines, written by an EAC youth choir, to be sung during Sunday worship express the sense of hopelessness bred in many young people by the political instability and economic decline in Congo. Yet the song is framed by the words of the Lord's prayer, 'Your Kingdom come, Your will be done,' words sung with hope for a divinely improved situation. This chapter examines the way in which the youth movement developed over twenty years and how it responded to the socio-political situation in North-east Congo. It analyses how migrant young people (*vijana*) introduced a new understanding of *maendeleo* within the EAC and brought Anglican worship closer to a popular contemporary expression of Congolese Christianity. It highlights generational issues as it presents the youth movement as another vehicle for change in the EAC.

In instigating change *vijana* created a church in which they felt at home. Young people do not always find the church of their elders to be a homely place. In their study of American immigrant religion, Helen Rose Ebaugh and Janet Saltzman Chafetz suggest that the majority of young, second generation migrants do not attend their parents' place

---

[1] Imani ya Kweli choir, 1997 collection.

of worship.[2] Linguistically less isolated than their parents and culturally and spiritually less conservative they join churches that are informal, egalitarian and multi-ethnic. Paul Gifford suggests that African young people abandon mainline churches to older congregations. They are drawn to new Pentecostal churches because they address the "preoccupations of youth" and "re-order society for the benefit of youth."[3] Young EAC members displayed aspirations for youthful Christianity yet, in opposition to these findings, they did not leave their church in any significant numbers. Indeed by the 1990s the EAC was attracting youth from other churches. Nevertheless, young people challenged the *utaratibu* of Anglican identity and emphasised *uhuru* in worship and *umoja* in the social conflicts that rent North-East Congo at the end of the 1990s.

North-east Congo in the 1990s

The Youth movement interacted with wider politico-economic issues affecting Congo in the 1990s. In 1992 democratic process was instigated by the *Conférence nationale souveraine.*[4] The population was hopeful of great improvements in the country but the influence of the *Conférence* was too distant and too brief—suspended as it was by Mobutu—to effect directly the population in the North-east. It marked the beginning of the end of Mobutu's totalitarian hold on power but the weakening of the President accelerated the, already steep, decline of civil services and national governance.[5] Meanwhile there was a rise in ethnic alliances within the political and economic spheres that challenged earlier nationalist political discourse.[6] Daily survival became a more pressing issue than democracy in the minds of most. Many young people could not afford to complete twelve years of schooling. If they did, there was little employment beyond the army and gold mining. Even in towns most people relied on their fields for food. Almost 50% of Congolese were

---

[2] Ibid., 129–130.

[3] Paul Gifford, *African Christianity: Its Public Role* (London, Hurst, 1998), 88 & 347.

[4] Georges Nzongola-Ntalaja, *The Congo from Leopold to Kabila: A People's History* (London, Zed Books, 2002), 190–196.

[5] Winsome Leslie, *Zaire: Continuity and Political Change in an Oppressive State* (Colorado, Westview, 1993), 131.

[6] Tshikala K. Biaya, "Parallel Society in the Democratic Republic of Congo," in *Shifting African Identities*, ed. Simon Bekker et al. (Human Sciences Research Council, Pretoria, 2001), 52.

under nineteen years of age and there were few organisations targeted particularly for them. A generation of disaffected youth was emerging that was vocal in its disappointment of government and ripe for recruitment as boy-soldiers in the internal wars which ended the decade. In 1997 Mobutu was overthrown by Laurent Kabila. The following year, Kabila's erstwhile supporters, the governments of Uganda and Rwanda, rose against him and began several years of warmongering, pillage and population displacement. Throughout the 1990s, churches attempted to provide alternative discourses to those that stirred up violence but many of their members had competing loyalties or felt helpless in the face of such turmoil. Mainline churches also struggled to maintain health programmes and development projects. State neglect, poverty and disorder widened the fissure between the hopes of *maendeleo* and the needs felt by many Congolese.

In this context mainline churches, like the EAC, who had encouraged the concept of *maendeleo* as skills and material provision to improve physical and economic well-being, were disadvantaged since this definition of *maendeleo* was no longer perceived to be a sufficient answer to the problems of the nation. Skills and material provision were not universally available and they did not respond entirely to spiritual, cultural and political issues. The continued influence of therapeutic concerns provides one example of a search for a more holistic approach to life. During the 1970s and 1980s traditional healers were encouraged to practice as a result of Mobutu's authenticity policy whilst mainline churches preached against their skills and provided hospitals and clinics.[7] In the 1990s churches tried to provide health programmes with limited resources. Clinical health care was beyond the means of many, or it was deemed not to work for certain 'African diseases'. There arose an increased interest in traditional African therapeutic practices that Christians had been taught to consider evil. Previously outlawed Pentecostal and African Initiated churches responded to such concerns through healing by prayer. These churches re-emerged as Mobutu's grip on power waned and the threat of state action against non-ECC member churches was diluted. New denominations condemned traditional healing methods but invoked God's power through the Holy Spirit to intervene in people's lives. They offered an alternative, but obviously

---

[7] Buyana Mulungula, "Conflit entre la Foi Chrétienne et le Ufumu dans le Milieu Urbain: Bukavu et Bunia" (Licence diss., ISTB, 1996), 18–20.

Christian response, to clinical methods of healing and a more holistic understanding of people's daily needs. Reliant on spiritual intervention they provided an alternative to *maendeleo*, challenging the development paradigm as understood by many ECC churches. The new churches interfaced with local culture and responded to issues of contemporary society at a different point from many mainline churches.[8]

The choice of Christian denominations in North-east Congo widened considerably from the late 1980s. In Bunia, for example, there were at least nineteen new churches by 2000.[9] A number were local; two of the churches in Bunia had split from CECA 20, one split from the Catholics, one from *Communauté Baptiste du Kivu* (CBK). Another six had origins elsewhere in Congo. Although these churches differed—some consciously attempted to incorporate African customs (*Eglise Evangelique des Rites Africains*, EERA), others emphasised exorcism (*Eglise Jésus Christ, Esprit de Verité* also known as *Bima*, 'leave,' in Lingala)—many had characteristics in common. They were Pentecostal in style in that they highlighted the spontaneous, dynamic action of the Holy Spirit through healing, exorcism and lively, emotive worship music. They expected dramatic conversions demonstrated by change in moral behaviour. Their church choirs composed popular, rhythmic songs which blended indigenous musical styles with those of the contemporary Kinshasa music scene and fused religious worship with a popular, national pastime; the performance and appreciation of Congolese music. Catchy songs and enthusiastic, participative, evangelistic preaching, often through loudspeakers in the open-air, attracted many spectators. Often originating as an urban phenomenon, larger denominations like FEPACO ('Nzambe Malamu' or the 'Hallelujahs') had spread throughout Aru zone and to Boga by the late 1990s. Western initiated churches maintained their membership, in part, to the extent to which they were able to engage with similar, contemporary expressions of Christianity.[10]

Youth from EAC and other ECC churches were attracted by these new influences coming into Ituri and Nord-Kivu and sought to emulate

---

[8] See similar situation in David Maxwell, *Christians and Chiefs in Zimbabwe: A social history of the Hwesa people, c. 1870s–1990s* (Edinburgh, Edinburgh University Press, 1999), 114–116.

[9] "Eglise Independantes et Sectes Implantées à Bunia," report by Yossa Way and students of ISThA, April 2003. This excludes the Kimbanguists who are recognised by the government.

[10] Katrien Pype, "Dancing for God or the Devil: Pentecostal Discourse on Popular Dance in Kinshasa," *Journal of Religion in Africa*, 36 (2006): 298.

aspects of them. The leadership of the Catholic and *Eglise du Christ au Congo* (ECC) Churches, however, saw the growth of the new wave of Pentecostal Churches as a threat to their own growth. They questioned their social and ecclesiastical legitimacy, calling them *sectes*. They claimed a sense of superiority over these 'upstarts' but they were jealous of their success, wary of spiritual manifestations akin to traditional trances and spirit possession, and fearful of a loss of influence. They warned *vijana* away from them. Anglican leaders perceived *sectes* as an attack on the order, stability, power and unity provided in the solemn hierarchical and liturgical *utaratibu* of the EAC. In *African Gifts of the Spirit*, David Maxwell suggests that Anglicans, Roman Catholics and Methodists have adopted Pentecostal approaches as a deliberate strategy, "to maintain numbers, particularly among the young."[11] In the EAC there was no strategy of adoption. The young negotiated charismatic innovation whilst the first generation migrants looked on in alarm. The generational tensions mentioned in chapter three were manifest in the different reactions to the style of Christianity apparent in the new churches.

'Vijana keep your faith'[12]

The generation gap was visible in the 1970s in the provision for the older migrants of a familiar pattern of church life within the EAC and the attraction of their children to other ECC denominations that worked with young people. Parents expected their children to attend the family church but children wanted to attend a Christian group of their peers. The response of these *vijana* to being brought up in an EAC which catered for their parents' needs as migrants but not their own as those at home in the urban setting, prepared the way for change in the 1990s. Irene Bahemuka, for example, who had been disparaging about the Bunia EAC because it seemed 'cold', 'Catholic' and 'Hema', attended the CECA 20 youth group in Bunia.[13] *Vijana* articulated their struggle within the EAC as a desire to study the Bible with their peers free from the unnecessary rites, unappealing solemnity and ethnic hierarchies that they associated with the escarpment Christianity of

---

[11] David Maxwell, *African Gifts of the Spirit: Pentecostalism and the Rise of a Zimbabwean Transnational Religious Movement* (Oxford, James Currey, 2006), 223.

[12] Song by *Gospel* choir, 1996.

[13] Interview, Irene Bahemuka, Boga, French 30 September 2000.

their parents. They joined CECA 20's youth activities although they
did not join the church. These positive experiences of CECA 20 by
vijana were to be the precursors of improved relations between EAC
and CECA 20 in the 1990s, particularly in the towns. Young people
who moved out of the Ituri and Nord-Kivu areas were also exposed
to charismatic practice. Kalume Sivengire from Kainama studied in
Kisangani in the 1980s:

> There were frequent manifestations of the Holy Spirit although there
> wasn't any in our Anglican Church. That caused me concern. Why did
> it happen in other churches? It also tempted me to leave the church
> but...I have persisted with the Anglican Church...[14]

For Kalume, the lively, participative, spirit-filled worship was an attractive alternative to the formal *utaratibu, upole* and *heshima* of an Anglican
service in which the Holy Spirit was rarely mentioned.

Kalume, Irene and many of their peers remained loyal to the church
of their parents, choosing it as their own church in adult life. As *vijana*
they had searched for an intensification of their Christian experience
among their peers beyond the EAC. As adults they both appreciated
some of the traditions of their parents and they embraced changes to
those traditions for which they had previously hoped ten or twenty years
earlier. As second generation migrants, they were willing to question
family loyalty to a particular denomination because they emphasised
the importance of their Christian identity above their ethnic identity.

In 1975 Bishops Ndahura and Ridsdale had expressed concern
about urban young people, saying "the youth gravitate to the towns,
where there is no employment, and they have nothing to do on leaving school."[15] However, it was to be fourteen years before the EAC
leadership formed an organisation specifically for its own migrant
vijana. Known as *Agape*, this youth movement was started in Bunia by
newly appointed Youth co-ordinator and CMS mission partner, Judy
Acheson, with the support of the young pastor, Bezaleri Kahigwa.
Funding from Britain allowed *Agape* to buy a bar and turn it into a
youth centre and to train leaders in a variety of development skills.
Irene Bahemuka joined it immediately and found in it the group for
which she had been longing.[16] By 1994 there were 72 *Agape* groups

---

[14] Interview, Kalume Sivengire, Butembo, French, 11 June 1998.
[15] DBk, 'New Diocese in Zaïre,' Bkbk750825h.
[16] Irene Bahemuka.

in Boga diocese with about 3,500 young people in them.[17] A similar youth movement developed in Nord-Kivu diocese and became part of a provincial *Agape* network. Significantly, *Agape* operated from Bunia, establishing itself as an urban movement, a result of migration, whilst other EAC departments continued to work from the village of Boga. As it worked in rural areas it also disseminated urban Christianity to villages. *Agape* had been established by the church leadership but its groups did not simply exist alongside the orderly adult worship of the EAC, they challenged and changed it. Thus they continued what the northerners' and the women's movement had already begun; they shifted the migrant EAC further from a gerontocratic institution characterised by *utaratibu, upole* and *heshima* to become an increasingly youthful, animated church with an accent on *maendeleo* and *uhuru*. Jon Millar in work on Korean migrants in the USA considers that issues resulting from migration cause religious diversity. He explains that second-generation immigrants, "...move away culturally, linguistically and spiritually from the insularity and conservatism of their elders...still deeply religious [they] are experimenting with innovative religious forms."[18] *Agape* was the vehicle through which many second-generation migrants were able to express their identity as Anglican Christians.

Agape

In outlining the genesis of *Agape* in Aru Archdeaconry in 1990, Anguzu Alfred explains the activities organised by *Agape* and the ideological framework through which *vijana* were encouraged to come to church and become Christians:

> The first way we could attract young people was through songs...sometimes it was through playing football...And we saw that in this work for society there were two ways of *maendeleo*: the first *maendeleo* we saw is spiritual *maendeleo*...to study the Bible together...like a debate, discussion about the Word of God. Each person could give their thoughts about a word or advice that they saw. It began like this. It was really good. And the other development was corporal...like they had a field, they had different

---

[17] Kisembo Sumbuso, "Etude de Mouvement de la Jeunesse Chrétienne 'Agape' dans le diocèse anglican de Boga-Zaïre" (Graduat diss., ISThA, 1994), 7.

[18] Jon Miller, "Missionaries and Migrants: The Importance of Religion in the Movement of Populations" (paper presented at Currents in World Christianity Conference, Pretoria: 3–7 July 2001), 7.

tasks like carpentry and other things...It was extremely good for young people to have the two sides of *maendeleo*—spiritual and physical—because if they lose the physical the spiritual will not survive well...[19]

The entire work of *Agape* was seen in terms of *maendeleo*. Nationally, the development model of provisions of skills and material appeared to have failed but *Agape* presented a different interpretation of *maendeleo* in the EAC. *Maendeleo* had always been used to denote spiritual as well as corporal development in the EAC but, as has been shown in previous chapters, the emphasis in the use of the word had been on the material and, often, on schools and clinics. The teaching of *Agape* re-emphasised the spiritual and social sides of the churches' work as two inseparable sides of the same coin. Although Anguzu used the language of dichotomy he was trying to express their integral nature. He considered that holistic *maendeleo* was ultimately not for the benefit of the church but for society, placing socio-religious aims in the centre of corporate life. In placing this altered understanding of *maendeleo* at the centre of its activity *Agape* were subverting, although never entirely overthrowing, the previous attachment to *utaratibu* as the way in which spiritual activity of the EAC was described. The concept of *maendeleo*, here as a socio-spiritual development, was being brought into the central act of belonging—the EAC worship service—in a more radical way than even the northern Anglicans had done.

In the first instance, Sunday worship remained connected, in the eyes of *vijana*, with the tradition of one's parents but youth Bible study and prayer was seen as *maendeleo*. Anguzu's description of Bible study is contrasted with EAC sermons, and presented as active and participatory, rather than passive listening. It was also different from the rote learning expected in schools. It aimed to give *vijana* freedom to think through moral and spiritual issues for themselves and question biblical passages. It was accompanied by an emphasis on personal conversion. When church workers like Bezaleri took part in the discussions they were effectively relaxing the hierarchical *utaratibu* and *heshima* of the EAC and establishing social relations on a more equal footing. The leadership structure was not altered but some leaders at least were seen as flexible, benign and appreciative of change. There is little evidence that *Agape* borrowed this participatory style directly from the new churches but it resonated with the popular pentecostal sermon style of dialogue and

---

[19] Interview, Anguzu Alfred, Aru, Swahili, 10 August 2000.

response. Some EAC preachers began to adopt aspects of this style in their Sunday sermons and it was popular with much of the congregation. As one interviewee put it:

> ...the preacher tries to interest everyone. If there's a biblical reference, for example, someone tries to read it. Anyone who has a Bible is engaged. There's a little explanation, a little dialogue. The congregation feels really involved.[20]

Involvement, dialogue and recourse to the Bible were all seen as attractive to recipients of the sermons. It aided the spiritual aspect of *maendeleo*.

Anguzu considered the physical side of *maendeleo* to be vital if the spiritual side was to be retained. Skills for employment, infrastructure, health and education services were not abandoned. *Agape* began to provide training in carpentry, agriculture and tailoring, it built youth centres and promoted attendance at school as worthwhile. It also included as *maendeleo* sports events and choir membership, believed to improve the well-being of *vijana*. *Agape* attracted not only committed young people who wished to deepen their Christian faith but those who were simply looking for something to do. *Agape* was responding to the chronic national under-development of the 1990s by small-scale development; that is, the local provision of skills pertinent to the area and economic climate. Development, as the raising of one's living standards through formal education and the learning of skills had not entirely lost its appeal but it required a larger scope than previously. Both Bible study and football fell within its scope. *Agape* enlarged the meaning of *maendeleo* by linking it integrally to every aspect of life—faith, work, leisure, relationships—within the community.

"Jesus wants us to sing for him"[21]

Anguzu mentioned music as a way of attracting young people to the church. It was both a leisure activity and an expression of faith. Most choirs were not established by the leadership of the church but, once formed, were permitted to sing in services. It was through choirs that young people instigated the most pronounced changes in EAC worship

---

[20] Interview, Likambo Tamaru, Boga, French, 09 October 2000.
[21] Popular Lingala chorus.

Illustration 7   Photograph of Imani ya Kweli choir performing during the centenary celebrations, 1996. Used with permission of Sarah Roberts.

services throughout North-east Congo. As in other Protestant churches in Africa, musical change was influenced by pentecostal worship, indigenous music and urban youth culture.[22] Change occurred through a mobile, often migrant, population and they were seen by young and old alike as being significantly different from the *utaratibu* of liturgical ritual, introducing instead an element of spontaneous *uhuru* and *furaha* (joy) which challenged *upole* and *heshima*.

In most chapels there was at least one choir, parish churches had several. By 2000 in Bunia parish church, for example, there were five choirs performing every Sunday, their members constituted about a third of the congregation. In contrast to the early days of the church in Bunia, a large number of mainly young people took an active part in worship every Sunday.[23] Choirs, themselves, were not new. Many mainline churches had used choirs to teach new congregational songs. In the 1990s, however, the form and content of the choirs altered significantly; no longer was the tonic solfa widely taught, no longer were choirs led by church workers, no longer did they sing western hymns or songs.

The primary aim of choirs was to perform—and often compose— religious songs. Some choirs produced a new song every week engendering tremendous musical creativity. Choir directors saw their task as preaching through song.[24] Their compositions were repositories of oral theology, frequently focusing on the intersection of contemporary social reality and biblical faith and highlighting a hope in heaven partially experienced in the joyful performance of the songs.[25] Choirs also led chorus singing using well-known songs from Congo and East Africa. Choruses were simple and repetitive, intended to evoke feelings of heavenly *furaha*. The choirs sang *a cappella* or used traditional drums and stringed instruments unless they managed to obtain the electric guitars and keyboards, used in music from Kinshasa, to which they aspired.

---

[22] See, for example, Matthews A. Ojo, "Indigenous Gospel Music and Social Reconstruction in Modern Nigeria," *Missionalia* 26, (1998); Gerard van't Spijker, "Credal Hymns as *Summa Theologiae*: New Credal Hymns in Rwanda after the 1994 War and Genocide," *Exchange* 30 (2001).

[23] Ruzinga Nobi, "Place et Valeur théologique des Chansons religieuses des Chorales dans l'Eglise (cas de la Paroisse anglicane de Bunia)" (Diplôme de Graduat diss., ISThA, 1997), 15.

[24] Interview, Byaruhanga Isaka, Bunia, Swahili, 13 September 2000.

[25] Peter Wood and Emma Wild-Wood, "'One Day we will Sing in God's Home': Hymns and Songs in the Anglican Church in North-east Congo (DRC)," *Journal of Religion in Africa* 34 (2004): 171–172.

The link with the capital was also perpetuated in the use of Lingala rather than Swahili in many locally composed songs. Thus choirs identified themselves with national, urban music and with contemporary pentecostal worship which had often spread from the west. If, in the 1970s, Swahili had provided young people with an urban semi-national language, by the 1990s the urban *soukous* music and the Lingala in which it was sung provided a strong, cultural symbol of national unity. It was a symbol that spread throughout Congo, introducing elements of urbanism and cultural nationalism to the villages.

Language and musical style were not the only elements that linked Anglican choirs to a wider movement of popular Christianity. By 2000 they were largely given a free rein to compose and perform as they felt led by the Holy Spirit with little interference from church workers. Accompanying this development was the encouragement of oral and spontaneous prayers from individuals during public intercession. Spirit inspired worship could now be found alongside the *utaratibu* of the Prayer Book and the hymnbook. In turn, these books were no longer considered necessary for Christian worship. Tindyera Kaberole explained how music in the church had altered so dramatically:

> Now...you sing whilst miming and dancing. They used to see that as bad. According to the law of our church we don't do that...But we read in the Bible that we must praise God with harps, with songs and dancing so we don't know where they got the idea from...Now, if someone simply says "chorus" every one dances, all the old people dance![26]

Anglican rules, as she had learnt them from Boga, did not permit dancing. It was in keeping neither with the spirituality of the nineteenth century Church of England that the Ganda and then the Hema had adapted, nor with the ethos of *upole* and *heshima* that the Boga hierarchy—customary and ecclesiastical—had encouraged. However, choir members discovered that descriptions of worship in the Bible challenged the old "law" of the EAC. Even the elderly, who might have been expected to criticise new ways and attempt to keep Anglican tradition, danced at the mere mention of a chorus. Most songs were accompanied by mime or dance, and words and music were given equal prominence providing a joyful, vibrant atmosphere intended to evoke the happiness of heaven. *Uhuru* and *furaha* began to vie with *upole* and *heshima* in Sunday services. In the early 1990s, choirs provided bursts of vibrancy and movement between solemn, respectful liturgy and sermons. By the

---

[26] Interview, Tindyera Kaberole, Bunia, Swahili, 19 September 2000.

end of the decade some EAC churches had reversed this; moments of quiet and orderly liturgy were found between participatory preaching and rhythmic music and dance. Worship had departed from the style propagated on the escarpment.

Dance, which had always been the response of ordinary people to religious events, even on the Semeliki escarpment, was manifested in church. Praise was conducted with the whole body and not simply the vocal chords and a large percentage of the congregation were involved in a prominent and public part of the service. The ecclesiastical hierarchy, however, remained apparent with the introduction of this new style of music; children, *vijana* and women danced enthusiastically, some men joined in, church workers maintained their claim on *heshima* by clapping sedately to the songs and demanding *"utaratibu"* when they thought that disorder might ensue. In the northern region, however, especially among *Wokovu*, clergy might dance if they did not feel that they were being monitored by authorities from Boga. Among the Alur, Kakwa and Lugbara, contrary to the Hema, traditional socio-religious leaders had always led the dancing rather than observing it. A re-appropriation of the corporate worship styles of the past—the community at dance—was evident in a contemporary manner. The songs reflected the strong musical tradition of Congo, but it was modern music of Kinshasa, rather than local ethnic music, which was most popular among *vijana*. Vijana had begun to establish different links with Congolese culture than had their parents and grandparents; links with national entertainment rooted in spiritual expression rather than links with local social structure. Once again these links reflected elements appreciated in popular Pentecostalism.

Many choirs met several times a week, for choir rehearsal, Bible study and prayer. The choir directors also met together to plan joint retreats, seminars, prayer meetings and *soirées musicales*. As a result, the growth of choirs challenged the internal networks of authority of the EAC. The voluntary and largely autonomous nature of the choirs transformed the internal dynamics of the local church. No longer were centrally appointed evangelists and pastors in charge of all church activities but voluntary groups appointed their own leaders who developed an important role in the spiritual and communal formation of members. The choirs had no direct link to the church hierarchy but they were recognised as influential in many parishes because they enlivened worship, carried out evangelism and attracted others to the EAC. Technically a ritual, hierarchical institution the rigidity of the Anglican structure had loosened at a local level to allow choirs and *Agape* to function.

As internal *utaratibu* weakened *umoja* was strengthened. This time, however, it was external *umoja* with other churches which was improved by the cross-denominational activities of choirs. Directors liased with those from other denominations to organise corporate events at which choirs would learn songs from each other. Occasionally tinged with competition, these *soirées musicales* usually had an evangelistic thrust and gathered substantial crowds. Musical activities as well as content, form, inspiration and choir organisation all reflected similar characteristics in the Pentecostal churches in North-east Congo. Musical expression linked the EAC to other denominations throughout Congo, many of whom were experiencing a similar influence in their worship patterns. It provided a common language that spoke above doctrinal, historical or ethnic differences. The EAC was able to adapt relatively quickly to these new impulses because its rapid growth through migration had already introduced the hierarchy to inevitable change. Another, increasingly common language which the EAC tried to speak was that of pentecostalism. This further eroded the *utaratibu* of the church hierarchy and proved more contentious than modern choral music. The catalyst for acceptance of a dynamic and immediate role of the Holy Spirit in life and worship came, however, not from a local source but from the Church of England.

Holy Spirit

In 1992 a group of twelve young people from the Diocese of Boga *Agape* group toured the UK for a month, visiting churches. On their return they prayed for an outpouring of the Holy Spirit and were struck by charismatic manifestations similar to those they had witnessed in a parish church in England. They arranged a seminar on the Holy Spirit in the Bunia church and on the following Sunday the congregation observed a sight many found disturbing. One witness described it thus:

> ...arms turned towards Heaven...suddenly the silence was broken by crying, shouting, free falling, trembling and praising. The poor Christians were very upset. Confusion reigned in the church because no one was capable of calming the group down.[27]

---

[27] Buyana Mulungula, "Etude théologique du Boom charismatique de la Paroisse anglicane de Bunia" (Diplôme de Graduat diss., ISThA, 1994), 26.

There were prophesies on the spiritual and political state of Bunia, deliverance from evil spirits and healing. Those directly involved in the experience felt that divine power was more immediately accessed than was common in Sunday services. Those who observed were alarmed by the lack of order and questioned what sort of power would disrupt a respectful act of worship. The most shocking aspect was discussed a week later at a diocesan council in the village of Boga. This is the council's record of events:

> ... [the group] heard that God loves the Anglican Church in Zaïre and this church will develop. Also God loves Bishop Njojo, he will be saved, [he must] 'leave the poison of the fetisher...On the 11/10/92 at Bunia this thing happened again and [some] girls prophesied again about Bishop Njojo.[28]

Teenage girls, claiming direct spiritual guidance, accused the diocesan Bishop, who was also the Archbishop of the Anglican Province of Congo, of evil practice and of not being a true Christian. This behaviour, learnt in the UK and practised in Bunia, disturbed church leaders. The response of the council was as follows:

> The council, having heard these things, greatly regretted seeing how the Holy Spirit was being introduced with speed into the church and how the name of the Bishop was being dirtied in front of our church and in front of other churches. And the council couldn't agree that this was really the result of the Holy Spirit.[29]

The terse few lines of this report show disbelief in this particular prophecy and therefore disquiet about the whole movement. It indicates a lack of clarity on pneumatology and a concern about the shame of public controversy. It also suggests discomfort with young women claiming direct spiritual power and questioning the ecclesiastical authority of an older man. Spiritual *uhuru* challenged *utaratibu* and *heshima*; global influence challenged local authority. The diocesan church leaders showed their disapproval of the events by suspending for three months three local church leaders most closely associated with the movement, Bezaleri, Acheson and Archdeacon Munege Kabarole. In doing so they were criticising them for not upholding the *utaratibu* of the EAC, and for reversing social order by following *vijana* rather than leading

---

[28] DBg, *Conseil executif de Boga.*
[29] Ibid.

them. These charismatic manifestations seemed contrary to the orderly nature of God and to the sense of belonging that had developed in the EAC.

A rural church with a close relationship to cultural practice of a particular ethnic group felt threatened by a migrant, urban, youth movement that understood itself to be embracing an inter/national expression of Christianity. The challenges to ritual and hierarchical *utaratibu* implicit in the activities of *Agape* and the choirs burst to the surface as a result of charismatic activity and pushed the EAC further towards popular pentecostal practice in Congo.

The EAC came through this internal crisis by typical compromise. It rejected the incorporation of charismatic healing and deliverance within its main worship structure but condoned this practice in certain groups and actively pursued a greater understanding of the dynamic role of the Holy Spirit. At Njojo's invitation, SOMA, a voluntary, charismatic Anglican organisation sent international teams to provide seminars for the clergy on the Holy Spirit in 1995 and 1998, emphasising again the Anglican and transnational nature of the theological and pastoral change taking place. The charismatic manifestations caused such tension, fear and elation amongst different members of the congregation that the month of October 1992 can be seen as a significant point in the steady transformation of an orderly hierarchical, rural church into a youth propelled, dynamic, urban one. The strong opinions expressed about charismatic activity demonstrate the contest over EAC identity during the 1990s.

The discourse which surrounded the first appearance of charismatic manifestations shows that conflicting issues often arose along generational lines. For many *vijana* the events fitted with the free and joyful worship already developing in the church. To freedom of expression, informal and vibrant worship, evangelism, Bible study and close friendships was added an emphasis on the workings of the Holy Spirit to overcome affliction and evil, providing an explanation for and solution to sickness. It accorded with the spiritual response to life's difficulties that they observed in Pentecostal Churches. The connection of these events with the visit to a Church of England parish also demonstrated links with a global, interdenominational movement. The charismatic events were proof, to those who supported them, that Anglican Churches did not all follow the EAC model, that variation was acceptable, and that Spirit issues could be addressed by Anglicans. The *vijana* spoke of dramatic spiritual activity as "new," part of the holistic *maendeleo* for which they aimed, thus widening further the definition of *maendeleo* to include a spiritual response to dealing with the difficulties of contemporary life, a process very different to striving for relevant skills.

Those who claimed to have benefited from "this grace" were, however, in a minority. About eighteen months later a sympathetic theological student, Buyana Mulungula, asked people in the Bunia church what they thought of the charismatic activity. Only 10% were positive towards it. Of these most were between 26 to 35 years of age and women were more positive than men.[30] This group was most likely to represent the leadership of *Agape* and women involved in Federation activities. Desirous of change in the EAC, they felt that the old structures of authority diluted power obtainable directly from God's Spirit. The *vijana* who identified themselves most strongly with the Holy Spirit movement were *vijana* not strictly in terms of biological age but in terms of position within the church. 60% of those Buyana interviewed were critical of the introduction of charismatic activity. Anglicans shocked by the events regarded them as undermining the EAC. For many, the legitimacy of the whole experience stood or fell on the truth or falsity of the serious claims against the Archbishop who was respected for his personal character as well as his position. The prophecies against the Archbishop were also regarded as providing a harsh critique of the church hierarchy by presenting spirit-inspired youth as an alternative source of spiritual wisdom. Recourse to inspiration by the Holy Spirit effectively short-circuited access to divine power and made hierarchical *utaratibu* redundant. It was an attack too far on the traditional *utaratibu*, *upole* and *heshima*. Apolo Kivebulaya, they said, had not introduced such activity and his memory was dishonoured by it.[31] Those who vocalised their discontent allied themselves with the expression of Anglicanism connected to escarpment culture. Congolese Anglicans usually expressed pride in their membership of an international network but, in this case, such a link only gave the events increased legitimacy in the eyes of those who were already convinced by the manifestations. To those who were suspicious of these charismatic events, there was a sense of bewilderment that an Anglican congregation in England could display such seemingly unanglican attributes. In this situation such startling results of migration and mobility were seen as a dangerous dilution of a noble tradition.

---

[30] Buyana "Boom charismatique," 45.
[31] Ibid., 47.

Charismatic Influences

The study of popular African Christian movements has engendered a
discourse about the relative influences of the local and the global. Some
scholars assert that Pentecostal religiosity is to be understood within
a discourse of globalisation[32] and modernity because the practitioners
themselves often distance their behaviour from local and traditional
culture. Birgit Meyer in *Translating the Devil*, for example, considers that
Pentecostalism in Ghana is a way of negotiating the individualistic
benefits of modernity within an African context.[33] Others, like Ogbu
Kalu, refute claims that portray a dichotomy with the past and declare
that the phenomenon be understood as a debate about which past continuities are preserved, revived or reinterpreted.[34] One way he observes
continuities is in the widespread cyclical tendency for religious revival
during times of perceived social malaise that pre-dates the introduction
of Christianity. Whilst Kalu's emphasis on past continuities may err
in its neglect of any modern influences, aphorism that, 'Our past is
always in our present'[35] is a reminder that dislocation can only be partial
and that sympathy with charismatic manifestations may have a deep
history. Similar debates took place among EAC members. They were
divided as to whether particular characteristics were more accurately
described as 'traditional' or 'contemporary'. They also disagreed on
the merits of these characteristics, using a discourse of evil to explain
their disapproval.

Theology student, Buyana Mulungula believed that youth involved
in the charismatic movement were, "...increasingly free from the
shackles of the 'contemporaries of Apolo Kivebulaya' to relaunch the
work of Christ in a purely African manner" (note the avoidance of
direct criticism of Apolo).[36] He is suggesting two things; that the EAC
was not sufficiently Africanised by Apolo's contemporaries who did
little but ape western religiosity and that the charismatic movement
represents an African expression of Christianity. Whilst Buyana was not
alone in desiring a "purely African" Christianity, many *vijana* sought a

---

[32] Gifford, *African Christianity*, 321.
[33] Birgit Meyer, *Translating the Devil: Religion and Modernity Among the Ewe in Ghana*
(Edinburgh, Edinburgh University Press, 1999), 211, 215–216.
[34] Ogbu Kalu, "Pentecostal and Charismatic Reshaping of the African Religious
Landscape in the 1990s," *Mission Studies* 20 (2003), 84–86.
[35] Ibid., 86.
[36] Buyana," Boom charismatique," 5.

"pure" Christianity and were wary of one which could be described as "African." They thought that Apolo's contemporaries set the EAC on a course which did not sufficiently distance itself from indigenous customs and societal structure, that it was, in some ways, too African. The problem is raised on several levels. Firstly, migrant EAC youth distanced from the ethnic roots of their parents often possessed a strong belief that Christians should not perform customary religious rituals and considered them evil. This had always been the stated position of the EAC but was often honoured in the breach.[37] Secondly, *vijana* were wary of indigenous social structures, often connected with ancestral rites, which had been accommodated by church structures and which maintained the power of gerontocratic elites from prominent social families. Thirdly, "African" in this discussion was often used to mean "the culture of a particular ethnic group," usually the Hema, rather than a more generic "African." The negative use of "African," therefore, should not be taken as an attempt to deny identity as Africans but rather as shorthand in a particular context for traditional practices which one group no longer wished to perpetuate. This study has shown that many, whose migration had distanced them from the customs of their ethnic group, were wary of a form of Christianity which was close to those customs; they did not entirely understand it and considered it divisive and contrary to expectations of unity in Christ. Those members of the EAC who most wanted change used the language of modernity, contemporaneity and Christian purity when talking of innovation. They spoke of continuity in largely negative terms.

First generation migrants and non-migrants used similar arguments when confronted by the changes introduced to the EAC by their children: the accusations of "paganism" or "African" were mutual, but levelled at different practices. They spoke of continuity with EAC tradition in positive terms but of the introduction of charismatic elements as a frightening revival of elements of traditional religion that they now considered evil. Judy Acheson, who had led the *Agape* trip to the UK, was accused by some of bringing witchcraft from Europe to Bunia.[38] Many first generation migrants considered the congregational participation encouraged in popular song and charismatic worship to be akin to the

---

[37] Emma Wild, "'Is it Witchcraft? Is it Satan? It is a Miracle.' Mai-Mai Soldiers and Christian Concepts of Evil in North-east Congo," *Journal of Religion in Africa* 28 (1998), 460.
[38] Buyana, "Boom charismatique," 27.

emotional rites of popular forms of traditional religious behaviour like possession cults. It lacked order—considered a divine attribute—which was provided by formal liturgy performed by the ecclesiastical elite. Revivalist or charismatic activity suggested to them disorder, insecurity, improper power and a re-emergence of a pre-Christian past; all things that they considered the work of Satan and that they wished to avoid in their adherence to Anglican *utaratibu* as they knew it. Detractors considered the activities similar to those of the mistrusted *sectes*, whose Christian credentials were considered questionable. They might have agreed with Kalu that Pentecostalism regained "...a pneumatological and charismatic religiosity as existed in traditional society,"[39] but they neither liked it nor wanted it in their church.

Similar reactions can be seen elsewhere in mainline churches. Birgit Meyer suggests the assumption within mission established churches in Ghana that manifestations of this nature are evil has left these churches unable to provide an appropriate spiritual response to perceived needs of individuals and has encouraged the rise of Pentecostalism.[40] However, although churches addressing issues of healing and deliverance are popular because they are meeting a need felt by many Africans, many members of mainline churches are not looking for these things and some continue to find them disturbing. In the EAC the introduction of charismatic elements appealed and disquieted for the same reasons; it mitigated against *utaratibu*, *heshima* and *upole* and provided for the needs of those for whom these identity signifiers had become stultifying and irrelevant. It offered *uhuru* in the Spirit that fitted with the *uhuru* and *furaha* of the new musical styles and responded appropriately to the therapeutic issues of those living in a disordered state. Divine power appeared to be more immediately accessible. The desire for church growth and unity within the EAC and the relative lack of effective central control prevented the criticism of first generation migrants and non-migrants from causing a severe crisis in the church. The contested introduction of pentecostal elements indicates a partial shifting of power towards junior members of the EAC. Thus EAC identity could be understood as moving further from escarpment values and towards

---

[39] Kalu, "Pentecostal and Charismatic Reshaping," 106.
[40] Meyer, *Translating the Devil*, 117–119.

a more contemporary, popular national and international expression of Christianity.

If the youth movement increasingly interpreted *maendeleo* as the work of the Holy Spirit who was evoked by prayer and praise were they drawing attention away from social concerns and focusing on spiritual well-being instead? Certainly some of the songs sung in church might be interpreted that way. This one, below, written in the "first Kabila war" of 1996–7 indicates a spiritual and eschatological utopia that understands heaven as the opposite of what its composer was experiencing on earth.

> Heaven, city of the Father
> Heaven, city of enjoyment
> Heaven, city of peace.
> There is no war, refugees, hunger
> There is no innocent blood shed,
> There are no guns,
> There is no looting.

Yet the young people singing these songs, who had often been influenced by *Agape* and the charismatic movement, were those who took most action to care for victims of war, to affect reconciliation, and to offer an alternative discourse to the violence of the final years of the 1990s. As the issues of ethnic and national discourse within the youth movement are studied at time of extreme political tension I will suggest that songs like the one above indicate an urban eschatology that desires the transformation of the nations along heavenly lines rather than an escape into spiritual quietism. As Anguzu Alfred claimed for *Agape*, the spiritual and social were not separate but were expected to inform each other.

...all are one...

In the mid-1990s North-east Congo became increasingly disordered. Between 1996 and 1997 Laurent Kabila, backed by the Rwandan and Ugandan governments, led a war that successfully overthrew President Mobutu. The war between 1998–2005 began as an attempt to overthrow Kabila but became a struggle by neighbouring countries allied with regional warlords to control Congo's natural resources. Violence became localised, stirred up old tensions, and divided people along ethnic lines. Militia on all sides fought with great brutality, killing and raping civilians, and displacing hundreds of thousands of people.[41] Nationalist rhetoric as a political tool had waned and a discourse of ethnocentric divide-and-rule became a feature of politics, economics and regional relations throughout Congo.[42] Johan Pottier contends that the violence is better explained by the exploitation of "poor, unfree and unprotected folk" who were mobilised for the enrichment of those with territorial power and the ability to exploit mineral wealth rather than by simple ethnic loyalty.[43] Nevertheless, "tribalism" was used as an explanation of the violence because exploitation of the poor often followed the manipulation of ethnic allegiance. "Tribalism" was also used because many Congolese essentialised ethnicity, understanding it to be the paramount identification with a small homogeneous group who share the same land, customs, language or bloodline.

Ethnic and national identities are complex topics. They present different, but not necessarily contradictory, options to "the dilemma of selecting an appropriate symbol of cultural identity,"[44] offering a choice of smaller or larger units of belonging. A detailed analysis of the response of young people goes beyond the timeframe of this study because their most co-ordinated work took place after 2001 when Anglican areas were most directly affected. Nevertheless, during the 1990s, *Agape* and the urban church had developed a discourse that enabled them to challenge the ethnocentric view that fuelled the violence. The decline in political structure of the nation-state of Congo and the rise of politically motivated ethnic divisions did not cause a decline in nationalist discourse among many migrant EAC members. It did, however, localise such a discourse. Nationalism was no longer articulated as state-policy in the way it had been in the 1970s, but became the product of the cultural domain where "...the local appropriate[d] the national such that the nation ha[d] various different

---

[41] For a detailed account see Thomas Turner, *The Congo Wars, Conflict, Myth and Reality* (Zed Books, London, 2007).

[42] Kevin Dunn, *Imagining the Congo: the International Relations of Identity* (New York, Palgrave Macmillan, 2003), 158.

[43] Johan Pottier, "Emergency in Ituri, DRC: Political Complexity, Land and Other Challenges in Restoring Food Security" (paper presented at the FAO International Workshop, Tivoli, Italy, 23–25 September 2003), 6–7, 12.

[44] Victor Uchendu, "The Dilemma of Ethnicity and Polity Primacy in Black Africa," in *Ethnic Identity: Creation, Conflict and Accommodation*, ed. Lola Romanucci-Ross and George De Vos (Walnut Creek, AltaMira, 1995), 130.

local meanings."[45] Cultural nationalism proved to be a strong sentiment of identity for many Congolese migrants: "...we were born Congolese, but are also proud to be Congolese...We are proud of our country,"[46] said one interviewee. It was influential in preventing the permanent fragmentation of the nation-state.

Chapter three noted that the sense of ethnic identity, of desiring a home from home, influenced the introduction of the EAC in towns. Yet the church developed as a result of the nationalism of the 1970s. Pride in nation and becoming a national church facilitated greater growth. In the economic and political fragmentation of the late 1990s some national feeling did dissipate within the church as a whole. The discourse of Christian *umoja* did not always provide a convincing framework for action nor did it sufficiently address the appeal of ethnically based identities for certain sectors of the population in particular circumstances. Titre Ande says that:

> ...ethnicism in Congo is a key factor in shaping the understanding of the church and the exercise of authority in the church. Parallels are easily drawn between what is happening in the political area and what is happening in the church.[47]

Titre Ande recognises, however, the influence of the urban youth movement in maintaining a sense of nationalism and actively defying ethnocentricism. He acknowledges their "work as agents of reconciliation. For instance in Bunia, youth have run seminars to bring together Hema and Ngiti who have been fighting for years."[48] The most recent round of fighting between Hema and Ngiti did not begin until 2001 but members of the Bunia church had already worked with internally displaced Gegere and Lendu. These peoples had sought refuge in Bunia from 1999 when Ugandan soldiers involved themselves in fraught land-right disputes and precipitated a bloody war.[49] Members of *Agape* and others visited internally displaced people, organised ethically mixed teams to visit areas of tension, and provided support for women who had been

---

[45] Alon Confino and Ajay Skaria, "The Local Life of Nationhood," *National Identities* 4 (2002), 9.

[46] Interview, Mbusa Bangau, Kampala, 28 July 2000.

[47] Titre Ande, "Authority in the Anglican Church in Congo: The Influence of Political Models of Authority and the Potential of 'Life-Community Ecclesiology,' for Good Governance" (PhD, Birmingham University, 2003), 176.

[48] Ibid., 183.

[49] Johan Pottier, "Roadblock Ethnography: Negotiating Humanitarian Access in Ituri, Eastern DR Congo, 1999–2004," *Africa* 76 (2006): 153.

raped and their children. Young, urban Hema and Ngiti courageously
went together to rural churches where mistrust of the other side ran very
deep. For them, the EAC could only be home if it was wide enough
to encompass all its members.

From its inception *Agape* was aware of the predominant influence of
the Hema and had deliberately taken leaders from a variety of ethnic
groups. Like many migrant clergy within the church, *Agape* leaders were
concerned about the potential for ethnic tension to escalate.

In rural areas, the network of groups allowed *vijana* from different
villages to meet and build relationships beyond immediate ethnic or
clan groups. One youth leader from Kumuru explained it thus:

> They get to know each other...Now the young people from here meet
> the young people from there. At first they will not like one another, they
> will say, 'What customs they have!' Then, after much interaction, they
> will understand.[50]

The poly-ethnic approach which arose as a result of the number of
ethnic groups which had Anglicans among them was further unified
in *Agape* discourse with reference to unity in Christ which intention-
ally challenged the norms of belonging. "There is neither Jew nor
Greek...all are one in Christ Jesus" (Gal. 3:28) was frequently quoted in
this regard. Ethnocentrism was considered by *Agape* to be unacceptable
for Christians and overcoming ethnic differences was one area in which
Agape's holistic *maendeleo* was brought to bear. *Agape* built on the urban
nationalism expressed by second generation migrants and was able to
provide an alternative narrative to the ethnocentric one espoused by
local warlords in local conflicts. For example, Ozua Samson aligned the
'call of God' to become a Christian with the assumption of a national
identity which encompassed one's ethnic identity:

> [When] someone hears the call of God...you will have the benefit of
> your tribe and, in addition, you will have the benefit of your whole coun-
> try. That's to say, I identify well as Lugbara...and also with the benefit
> of our country...Our country includes many tribes. These are all one
> people. We must unite and...work together.[51]

Ozua did not reject his Lugbara identity but he understood the value
of a larger unitary identity. He plotted Christian identity with national

---

[50] Interview, Atuku Abe, Kumuru, 19 August 2000.
[51] Interview, Ozua Samson, Aru, Swahili, 10 August 2000.

identity thus interpreting Christianity inclusively as belonging to a large network of ethnic groups united in order to work together within the nation state. In assessing identity thus he and other young people possessed a discourse of unity that would enable them to counter the violence. The fact that violent divisions appeared along ethnic lines demonstrated to interviewees the pertinence of their concern that the church should distance itself from anything that connected it with a particular ethnic cultural expression. *Agape*'s involvement in grassroots reconciliation work was born out of the ideology of holistic *maendeleo* that allowed *vijana* to respond more immediately and practically to ethnic conflict than did the EAC leadership. In these circumstances emphasis on nationalism and inclusive Christianity were attempts to negate deeply felt alternative identities.

The sense of unity in Christ that informed their cultural nationalism caused young people to act in the present as well as to hope for a better future. Another song composed about 1997 suggests that Christian *umoja* demanded actions of loyalty that went beyond the claims of ethnic allegiance. In words reminiscent of the armour metaphor in Ephesians 6 but also resonant in war-torn Congo, youth choir, *Gospel*, exhorted its listeners to engage in the present circumstances,

> ... Your clothes, soldier of Jesus,
> These are your actions
> Hold on to your belt
> Strengthen yourself for the fight
>
> Your bullets, soldier of Jesus,
> This is your faith
> Hold onto your faith
> You will win the battle.
>
> ... Our enemies will be confounded,
> Jesus alone will be chief.

A vision of a future heaven from the previous song is matched with the desire to overcome present divisions through faith and actions now. The aim is that all will unite under one divine authority instead of being violently split amongst local warlords.

Young, urban migrants asserted their identity as Christians over their ethnic loyalty, claiming a universal kinship that was immediately evident in their relationships across ethnic groups and in their subscription to national Christianity and culture. They sincerely expounded the inclusive rhetoric of Christianity and, in the Christian context, often portrayed ethnicity as divisive and unhelpful. Within the EAC the interpretation of nationalism was used to promote internal unity beyond the bounds of ethnicity at a time when the EAC was becoming increasingly ethnically diverse. It was also used increasingly to encourage unity beyond the bounds of denomination. Ethnocentrism was regarded as a hindrance in the perceived Christian duty of maintaining relationships within the EAC or among Christians of other denominations. Inclusivity and harmony were seen as attributes of true religion and thus there was a move towards identity signifiers that were seen to unite a wider group of people; nationalism served this purpose. For most migrant members, the nation—primarily as cultural community rather than dysfunctional state—provided the immediate context of Christian identity, in which worship and evangelism were to be carried out, and in which engagement with a variety of Christian communities was expected to take place. This nationalism was informed by a sense of transnationalism; the Anglican Communion offered a second locus of wider belonging with a group beyond national boundaries. The identification with the universal aspects of Anglicanism also enabled the youth movement to stand against the growing trend of ethnocentrism in Congo. Thus Congolese Christianity provided a group identity that intersected with membership of a transnational denomination and demonstrated that, in certain circumstances, religion and nationality can provide more persuasive narratives for identity than ethnicity.[52]

A Young Church

In 2000 the EAC in North-east Congo was predominantly a young church. It was young not simply because children under nineteen made up the majority of the congregations, nor because it was constantly spreading to new areas, but because young people were influencing change within it.[53] Tabu Abembe acknowledged this. When asked what change he had experienced in the EAC since his childhood, he said, "The development that I've seen in all the places I've worked is the spiritual growth of young people."[54] There were no groups for children

---

[52] William Miles, "Nationalism versus Ethnic Identity in Sub-Saharan Africa," *American Political Science Review* 85 (1991), 394 & 397.

[53] Titre Ande, "Authority in the Anglican Church of Congo," 185.

[54] Interview, Tabu Abembe, Bwakadi, French, 06 October 2000.

when Tabu was young and participation in church affairs was considered
to be the preserve of adults. The religious movement started by Apolo
Kivebulaya had been led by young men and women but an emphasis
on the conversion of elite families coupled with the adoption of the
Anglican system of church governance encouraged a gerontocratic
power structure within the EAC which had marginalised junior people.
In the 1990s the grip on the EAC by senior men from important families had been shaken and their influence in governance was no longer
exclusive. *Vijana* gained influence with relative ease and over a short
time span because of the flexibility of the EAC developed through the
migration of so many of its members. However, EAC identity did not
develop simply through change but through the contestation of change.
The activities of the youth movement in the EAC produced a variety
of reactions among those who were not part of it. Many of these held
positions of seniority in the EAC—the *wazee*; a term which denoted
not simply age but status, respect and the expectation of wisdom. The
reaction of *wazee* differed according to their personal circumstances and
positions within the church. Many hesitated to embrace change but
others were less reluctant. As Tinderya's description of *wazee* dancing
in church demonstrates, a simplistic equation of age with resistance to
change is inappropriate.

Wazee of the Semeliki escarpment who had not migrated and had a
stake in the socio-religious hierarchy of the village EAC were perhaps
most disturbed by change instigated by women and youth in the urban
and northern areas. They perceived it as a threat to the basic identity
of Anglicanism. The escarpment church remained a gerontocratic,
hierarchical institution that maintained *utaratibu, upole* and *heshima*
and was bewildered by and, at times, hostile to the change occurring
in other parts of the dioceses. It was proud of its Anglican tradition
and considered that change contravened its inheritance from Apolo
Kivebulaya. The *wazee*, however, continued to exert influence on the
EAC because Boga remained the administrative centre of its diocese
and many prominent clergy originally came from the escarpment. Their
senior positions enabled them to retard change but they were too few
and too isolated to halt it.

In 1990, just as Irene Bahemuka was enjoying the fellowship of
Agape and the growth of the church in Bunia, she married a man from
Boga and went to live there. After years of criticism of the identity
of her parents' church she found herself at its epicentre. There was
as yet no *Agape* group and she discovered to her dislike that not only

was the worship cold but "the culture and the religion were married together."[55] Some church services were surrounded by Hema traditions. The chief played a prominent role in church life as well as performing Hema ritual functions. For one who considered such a close association between the culture of one ethnic group and Christianity inappropriate this was an unhappy situation. She also criticised it for rarely promoting personal conversion, lacking lively worship and not teaching about the Holy Spirit. Beni Baataga, who grew up in the Boga area, also noticed a reluctance to change. He said of worship in 2000:

> The church in Boga is some how a traditionalist church, so they don't very much want a change—for instance, this jumping, clapping hands and dancing in the church, all those kinds of things...[56]

Nevertheless, the 1990s did see the beginnings of change on the escarpment. To polarise the areas from which migration took place and to which people migrated would be to over-simplify the argument. Migration is rarely entirely one way and connections between the escarpment and churches established through migration were never severed. Familial, trade and ecclesiastical links were continually maintained. Indeed, the institutional nature of the EAC formalised the continuous links between new parishes and old ones. Thus the escarpment church was increasingly influenced by the Christianity emerging in the urban and northern parishes. Bataaga also admitted visits from urban youth to the village played a part:

> They go with their youth spirit. What they have in the worship here (Bunia) they take it there. It becomes something new. And some young people there...are doing it.[57]

The national, urban culture appealed to village *vijana* too. Reverse migration played a further role in the process of rural change. During the war of 1996–7 some urban families thought the rural areas offered more security than the towns and returned to the escarpment, taking their urbanised ways of worship with them. The results of migration were starting to shape the identity of the entire EAC in the North-east.

The *Wokovu* were also initially critical of the charismatic *Agape* members. Their understanding of the Holy Spirit was primarily as an

---

[55] Irene Bahemuka.
[56] Interview, Bataaga Beni, Bunia, English, 15 September 2000.
[57] Ibid.

agent for salvation and sustaining and they were wary of the spiritual gifts. The gerontocratic revival leaders demanded strict observation of external codes of behaviour and expected worship and evangelism to be carried out in a particular way. The leaders initially felt threatened by *vijana* who they perceived as promoting a perverted form of revivalism. They were suspicious of *Agape's* provision of skills for young people, its emphasis on discussion rather than preaching and teaching, and its interest in charismatic phenomena. However, they could not fault the spiritual *maendeleo* promoted by the group which emphasised personal commitment reflected in an appropriate change of lifestyle and a desire to evangelise. Like *Wokovu*, *Agape* subverted the *utaratibu* of the EAC and promoted *uhuru* in worship. By 2000 most *Wokovu* had begun to understand *Agape* within a *Wokovu* frame of reference, to be a modern revival movement working completely within the EAC.[58] *Agape* demonstrated to *Wokovu* that other EAC members could experience revival in a similar way to them and re-enforced the internal *umoja* with other Congolese Anglicans.

The *wazee* who adapted the most were the first generation migrants to towns. They had seen great change in the chapels they had established. Rwakaikara Andre's reaction to change within the Bunia church is typical:

> There is *maendeleo*...we saw first that people began to go to church when [Judy Acheson] began that group of Agape. Then children began to go...So when she found the way of taking them to Europe, and they came back—even though there was a bit of disturbance from Satan—by the power of God everything was possible and it was good. Now the church became good and continues well.[59]

He had seen the church grow with the introduction of activities for young people. The mention of Satan suggests that in 1992 Rwakaikara felt horror at the charismatic activities introduced. Eight years later, however, his worse fears had *not* been realised. He still spoke of the EAC as his church and the church of his parents and he considered that the numerical growth of the church through the activities of the *vijana* was ultimately beneficial. The church established by first generation migrants had grown tenfold in thirty years. First generation migrants may not have liked all the innovation but they wanted to see the church

---

[58] Interview, Thumbe Ferdinand, Mahagi, Alur, 29 August 2000.
[59] Interview, Rwakaikara André, Bunia, Swahili, 23 September 2000.

continue for the next generation. The circumstances surrounding the initial migration of these people had encouraged them to replicate a familiar religious institution but the life changes which migration had brought them in the course of thirty or forty years also allowed them to accept the growth of the youthful EAC more easily than non-migrants.

In 2000 *wazee* and *vijana*, both men and women, still worshipped together. The old order remained but it was no longer the only option within the church. In order to chart change clearly, this chapter has explained change in terms of dichotomies: *uhuru* verses *utaratibu, furaha* verses *upole, inter alia.* Change is rarely so polarised and in the EAC in particular change was negotiated in such a way as to maintain internal *umoja* and avoid public division. *Utaratibu* did not vanish but it took a different position in the church. *Vijana* challenged the respectful, gentle *utaratibu* of hierarchy and liturgy as the paramount identity signifier. The challenge was not always direct but developed as a result of their alternative activities and structures. However, conversations with young people suggest that their loyalty to the EAC included an appreciation of hierarchy and ritual as seen in church governance and liturgy. *Utaratibu* continued to provide for *vijana* a sense of order, unity, power and security in an uncertain world. Nevertheless, its place in the EAC was altered. *Utaratibu* as interpreted by *upole* and *heshima* was no longer permitted to dominate Anglican identity in Congo. *Utaratibu*, interpreted by other identity signifiers of *maendeleo, uhuru, furaha* remained a framework of order around which corporate life and worship could be melded. The introduction of these new identity signifiers encouraged more informal and popular ways of being the EAC. In this identity flux, Anglican members emphasised *umoja*. If the EAC was to maintain internal unity by remaining a single enlarged institution, negotiation and compromise were vital. A stratified form of governance was maintained but dioc-esan appointed leaders had to work alongside leaders of choirs and *Agape* who represented a large percentage of the congregation. In its turn, the youth movement expressed mainstream identity, respecting hierarchical *utaratibu* and wanting to gain influence within the EAC power structure. As a result of the ability to compromise change was slowed and de-radicalised.

The EAC remained internally united. It also developed greater *umoja* with other denominations. Migration had encouraged diversity of Christian affiliation. Geographical spread of ECC members, new movements and internal disagreements, coupled with less state interference in church affairs, created a mix of denominations in North-east

Congo in the 1990s. Thus *umoja* among Christian churches in 2000 could be said, in some ways, to be more fragmented than in 1960. There was no suggestion that denominations might merge. However, such a picture is one-sided. The lines of unity that straddled divisions were drawn in the popular expressions of Christianity found in women's groups, choirs and youth groups. In the same way that some Anglican *vijana* in the 1970s attended the youth Bible studies of CECA 20 but remained members of their parents' church, in the 1990s *vijana* from CECA and the Catholics participated in the Anglican youth programme and introduced ideas learnt at *Agape* to their own churches.[60] In this pattern, loyalty to familiar tradition was apparent but for *vijana* an exploration of "best" Christian practice—whether that was involvement with peers, social skills, Bible study or charismatic phenomena—took initial precedence. At a time when Pentecostal churches exerted an influence on *vijana* a mainline church could appeal to them when it was perceived to be responding to their needs. Furthermore, through sharing communal events and recognising common evangelistic goals *vijana* encouraged an improved working unity amongst ECC members.[61] *Vijana* challenged the clearly bounded identities propounded by denominations and helped to further mix Christian identities. Although the number of different denominations rose significantly in North-east Congo, grassroots Christianities—expressed in terms of emotive, corporal and national forms of worship and a greater emphasis on the action of the Holy Spirit for pastoral care and healing—possessed greater mutual understanding and opportunities for collaboration in 2000 than they had done in 1960. They did so largely because women and young people met, worshipped and worked across denominational boundaries. Migration, which had been influential in the diversity of denominations, contributed to a greater popular tolerance and understanding of other denominations than was previously the case.

Conclusion

The identity of the EAC and its members had become increasingly hybrid by 2000 and included a variety of overlapping interpretations of religious belonging. The urban, migrant youth movement enabled the

---

[60] Interview, Judy Acheson, Bunia, English, 27 September 2000.
[61] Nyabongo Kwake, "Le Mouvement oecumenique dans la Cité de Bunia: Rêve ou Réalité?" (Diplôme de graduat diss., ISThA, 1994), 47–49.

church to embrace forms of Christianity which were becoming increasingly familiar throughout Congo. They fused this dynamic Christian expression with traditional EAC worship and governance. Effective power came to be shared more widely and thus internal *umoja* was maintained. The importance of *umoja* as identity signifier also enabled young people to engage in reconciliatory rather than violent action during the wars from 1996.

The EAC, whilst still retaining pride in its historic roots on the escarpment, improved its evangelical credentials and introduced Pentecostal elements, of a contemporary, national and transnational nature, in order to thrive in its local situation of economic decline, political disorder and ecclesiastical choice. These changes allowed opportunity for *vijana* to engage with contemporary Congolese forms of Christianity which were more national than ethnic in expression and—more importantly for those who practised them—were considered to be "more Christian" than those practised by their parents. In identifying themselves as Anglicans these *vijana* were firstly identifying themselves as Christians rather than members of a particular ethnic group. That the change was relatively peaceful, retained most of its original members, and gained more is a consequence of the large expansion by a small, marginalised church. The centre was too small to adequately control growth. Although, it had brought rapid and, for some, uncomfortable alterations, the increase in numbers, influence, and geographical spread were considered signs of success. Thus, obvious as the generational, gender and ethnic divisions were, they were less acute than might be expected in circumstances where migration was understood by the majority as dilution of identity rather than its *maendeleo*.

CHAPTER NINE

MIGRANT ANGLICAN IDENTITY IN CONGO

Introduction

[Ugandans] announce[d] Christ to the inhabitants of Boga... From there, the work expanded rapidly under African direction into many regions of Zaïre. Thus the prophetic word of Apolo on his deathbed was fulfilled, "Bury me with my head towards the West so that the work of the Lord will continue."... the Anglican Church of Zaïre has been planted through several waves of immigration.[1]

The reported prophetic last wish of Apolo Kivebulaya, "Bury me with my head towards the West..." are the words which began this book. They are found in all narratives of Apolo's life, including the EAC centenary pamphlet of 1996 quoted above where they are used to interpret the migratory nature and African agency of EAC growth since its inception. This final chapter analyses the use of this narrative by migrants to construct a new sense of 'home' as a place where meaning is grounded. It then presents an overview of the EAC migratory identity shifts indicating the importance of the conclusions for studies in Sub-Saharan Christian history.

Narrating Home

Throughout this book, the narration and re-interpretation of Apolo's life and death have been observed to shape and to reflect EAC identity. From early eyewitness accounts, through hagiography and oral myth, the founder of the EAC was used to supply meaning to the church as it developed. The influence of church founders and the myth-making of their lives has been acknowledged in African Initiated Churches[2] but less scholarly attention has been given to the founders of mainline churches. Founders give unique identity to their churches. The

---

[1] N.a. *Esquisse historique de l'Eglise Anglicane du Zaïre 1896–1996* (Bunia, ISThA, 1996), 1.

[2] Adrian Hastings, *The Church in Africa, 1450–1950* (Oxford, Oxford University Press, 1994), 535.

particularities of their lives provide the basis for narrating an identity that cannot be exactly replicated by other groups. Whereas the likes of Simon Kimbangu are remembered for their differences with mainline Christianity, even if those differences may have been less acute than the popular perception of them, Apolo is remembered for his successful introduction of a mainline mission church in a way which glosses over difference or difficulty.

The various interpretations of Apolo's burial story present a prime example of the use of narrative in constructing identity. Different groups interpreted his story in various ways, plotting it with significant hermeneutical terms in order to select and interpret their identity. The story was used to uphold escarpment *utaratibu* with its *upole* and *heshima* (chapter two), to implant escarpment *utaratibu* elsewhere and make a home-from-home (chapter three), to give credence to a previously unknown church (chapter four), to support revival and itinerant evangelism (*uhuru*) (chapter six), and to endorse women's ordination (*maendeleo*) (chapter seven). By the 1990s, migrant Anglicans no longer interpreted Apolo's story with hermeneutical terms that presented the church as a conservative, rural, gerontocratic institution, largely influenced by one ethnic group, in which hierarchy and liturgy mirrored dominant social powers to which others were expected to show due deference. Geographical spread, numerical growth, and the resultant variety of life experience by members altered the identity of the church. *Utaratibu* was plotted with events surrounding the northern migration and the experience of second-generation migrants, and thus interpreted by perceptions of *maendeleo, uhuru, umoja* and *furaha*, remaining an important identity signifier but challenged by the juxtaposition of other signifiers. So Apolo's story was employed to give meaning to the increasingly urbanised identity and the growing national, female- and youth-orientation. Apolo's role as identity signifier was no longer that of the guardian of escarpment *utaratibu*, he had become the symbol of EAC *umoja*. As a permanent symbol for EAC members, he mitigated the tension between continuity and change, or between *utaratibu* and *uhuru*.

The 1996 pamphlet narrates the story of Apolo in such a way as to imbue EAC history with unitary aim and a narrative *umoja* unique to the EAC and yet linking it to Uganda and beyond. The excerpt quoted above states that Africans brought the Christian message in an Anglican form to the Semeliki escarpment yet they were Africans who crossed cultural, linguistic and colonial boundaries to do so. This pattern repeated itself through migratory growth as Apolo himself expected it would. Apolo's dying wish is thus interpreted as a prophecy of expansion by plotting it with reference to subsequent migratory routes of the EAC. Apolo migrated to bring the EAC to Congo; thus migrants who establish EAC churches in their new locations are following their founder. In this contemporary interpretation, Congolese Anglican identity is given a base, not in the historical links with Apolo's work on the escarpment, but in the *spiritual and prophetic* connections made by linking Apolo's story to the migratory spread of the church. Thus it provided a narrative of common identity for the many EAC members whose personal histories included migration but for whom the Boga area had never been home.

Members used a variety of conceptions of 'home' in narrating their affiliation to the EAC. Analysing the EAC has given insights into the place of belonging and the importance of corporate and spiritual meaning. 'Home' was chosen as the best way of expressing their relationship with the EAC. They recognised in its corporate religious expression the locus for grounding their social, personal and spiritual meaning. The EAC provided them with a sense of belonging to others and to God. It gave them a construct of identity that enabled them to deal with migration. The way in which the EAC was home for migrants differed according to the interaction with other elements like gender and ethnicity that impacted upon identity. It also depended upon whether migrants attempted to maintain stable, settled, orderly ideas of home, viewing stability and continuity as their prime concern, or whether concepts of home had been reconstructed through travel and dislocation and thus their priority was flexibility to reorder their identity. In the centenary pamphlet the 'home' initiated by Apolo was connected with movement and change. The locus for social, personal and spiritual meaning was no longer constructed in terms of ethnic roots on the escarpment but in terms of a shared story of growth through migration.

Migration

Muhindo Tsongo goes some way to articulating the thesis that migration is a catalyst for religious change, when she links migration to renewed religious commitment and the resultant expansion of the church:

> The church... makes progress, she has many members because many people emigrated... and they were pleased to find anew their old church.[3]

---

[3] Interview, Muhindo Tsongo, Edinburgh, French, 17 December 1999.

Migration made EAC members more religiously observant and increased their loyalty to the Anglican Church. For Muhindo's family, however, "progress" was seen in terms of physical expansion rather than internal change: the "old church" was the home of escarpment values. Religious change was not intentional for the first migrants from the escarpment. Their religious identity was primarily located in life-experiences prior to migration and they wished to maintain the old set of religious experiences to sustain them in their new location. Thus they attempted to replicate the religious values and practices they had learnt from home in their new location. Anglican Christianity provided them with the familiar and homely as they adjusted to new social circumstances and so it proved a cohesive and sustaining force during migration. The fact that religious identity provides, in the first instance, a conservative influence in the flux of migration is attested in studies of immigrants in the United States. Jon Miller, for example, in his study of Koreans in Los Angeles demonstrates that first generation migrants adhere to what they call "authentic Korean culture" by which they mean " 'Koreanized', conservative Presbyterianism and conservative Methodism".[4] The study of the EAC suggests that an initial desire to retain a conservative form of religious belief from their place of origin might be common among many migrant Africans arising from both an increased Christian commitment and a desire for the familiar.

The specific details and speed with which adaptation to new circumstances takes place are affected by the peculiarities of each migration. The scale and variety of migration in North-east Congo coupled with a general assumption that the expansion and internal unity of the EAC was desirable, prevented the ghettoisation of Anglican practice by first generation migrants. The EAC offered stability during dislocation but it also permitted flexibility of practice to suit local circumstances. Northerners with different migratory circumstances presented alternative identities, which coalesced with escarpment values and practices at some points and diverged at others. The northern church developed through networks of Revivalists and returned-migrants rather than through replication of escarpment hierarchies. The mobility of the northerners introduced elements that increased the hybridity of the

---

[4] Jon Miller, "Missionaries and Migrants: The Importance of Religion in the Movement of Populations" (paper presented at the *Currents in World Christianity Conference*, Pretoria, 3–7 July, 2001), 7–8.

EAC. Members maintained an appreciation of *utaratibu*. However, faced with a dominant and hostile CECA 20, and their dislocation from traditional society as migrant labourers in Uganda, their expression of Anglican *utaratibu* contested customary social order rather than adjusting to it. They developed an EAC that grounded their identity but, in their religious home, some of the 'furniture' was different to that of the escarpment migrants. For the radical Revivalists, however, the EAC did not ultimately ground their identity. For the Chosen Evangelical Revival, membership of the EAC was of secondary importance to Christian witness and fellowship, that were properly attained through eschewing the importance of an earthly home. Although all EAC members were expectant of a heavenly home, the CER focused more wholeheartedly on the journey to it.

During the 1980s, migrants claiming allegiance to the same international institution but moving along different migratory routes widened local Anglican identity. As the hierarchical and liturgical *utaratibu* appreciated by members was plotted with different circumstances and interpreted by different expressions of Christian belief the EAC developed a hybrid identity. This was possible, not simply because the new-comers were numerically influential, but because church expansion was considered positive by church leaders on the escarpment. The guardians of escarpment tradition were confronted with a dilemma: change was often portrayed as rejecting the Anglican heritage brought by Apolo Kivebulaya and interpreted through escarpment values; on the other hand growth was perceived as fulfilling Apolo's dying words, interpreted as promoting the spread of the EAC. It was impossible to have one without the other. Whilst they had not expected growth to demand significant change they were willing to concede change in exchange for numerical growth, geographical spread, maintenance of unity and the ensuing higher profile for the Anglican Church in Congo. The ability of the EAC to manage these differences to the mutual satisfaction (albeit partial) of all parties gave the institution a greater chance of successfully negotiating change initiated by second-generation migrants. Young men and women were likely to experience difficulties with their parents' religious identity and strive for greater assimilation into the contemporary culture of the new location. If the new location was an urban one these difficulties were compounded by nationalist influences as a response to a variety of ethnic traditions. Young people were able to adapt most easily to migrant circumstances and—partly because the EAC could not maintain strong central control—were also able to alter the institution to which they had familial allegiance so that it more closely fitted their present needs of greater conformity to contemporary, national Congolese culture. As a result the EAC outside the escarpment was soon larger and more dynamic than in its original base. Its role as home for its members had been transformed and its boundaries were no longer so clearly delineated.

This study of a denomination undergoing rapid migratory change has presented a perspective of a mainline church from the grassroots upwards and provided insight into its altering identity when interfacing with social, political and religious developments around it. Identification with a particular church has been shown to provide members with a framework from which to respond to their changing circumstances and thus to affect the actions and adaptation of migrant members. Conversely, the shifting identity of migrants altered the identity of the church to which they belonged. It has been acknowledged that migration can influence the change of religious identity because particular migratory patterns in their historical and social context provided impetus for a shift in personal and corporate religious identity. Furthermore, the study has recognised that in a small church with expansionist ambition, migration induces greater heterogeneity within the institution and hastens ecclesiastical change because new life experiences, in dialogue with the old, provide material for altered identities.

Mobile Identities

Emphasis has been placed on the micro-informal, personal networks, social relations, beliefs and aspirations that impinge on migratory behaviour. Significant among these influences are popular perceptions of generational and gender norms and of ethnicity and nationalism. These identity features signify a complex of negotiated power relations which would benefit from greater research and analysis in the context of North-east Congo. Nevertheless, some conclusions that illuminate shifts in ecclesiastical authority structures may be drawn from the negotiated alteration of influence within the EAC.

Migratory-induced social change contested the gender and generation norms upheld within the EAC. Thus altering it from an institution which was largely led and oriented by gerontocratic men, to one in which younger and junior men were given positions of leadership, and in which women possessed increased opportunities to lead and a greater influence on the orientation of the church. In re-interpreting their religious identity *vis-à-vis* their membership of the EAC, women narrated their stories by selecting a hybrid range of elements—local and global, traditional and modern—that included a response to the alteration of the economic situation, knowledge of changes elsewhere in Africa, and meeting with women from other local denominations. These selected narratives encouraged women to take more prominent social and ecclesiastical roles and revived a charismatic orientation in worship that had connections with past religious practice.

This newly asserted identity was not a dramatic or sudden departure from pre-migrant identity. However, women began to negotiate practices within worship, pastoral care and the organisation of their own groups, often using covert tactics, which oriented the EAC towards the needs and aspirations of women. Elizabeth Isichei, in *A History of Christianity in Africa*, notes, "the strength and autonomy of women's church organizations" throughout the continent[5] and she sees in their corporate moral and financial influence on the churches an increased empowerment for women. The Mothers' Union complied with this description as it attempted to assert its internal independence and alter the orientation of the church to which it belonged, utilising changing social circumstances and altered expectations to further its goals.

Generational changes were evident from the arrival of the northern migrants. The rapid spread of the church was largely facilitated in this area by networks of junior members of society, who had little status or formal education. This contrasted with the urban growth of the EAC that was largely facilitated by influential laity and centrally appointed church workers who had a stake in maintaining the socio-religious power structures of the escarpment church. Nevertheless, the leadership of the EAC, pleased with the enlargement of the church in the north, responded by training many northerners, according them status through ordination, and attempting to absorb them into the escarpment model of church. The northerners responded positively to those elements that fitted their understanding of Anglicanism. They accepted training and ordination (unless they were radical Revivalists) but they remained critical of elements of worship or social custom within the EAC that they associated with escarpment culture. Institutional *umoja*

---

[5] Elizabeth Isichei, *A History of Christianity in Africa from Antiquity to the Present* (London, SPCK, 1995), 303 and 350.

was, nevertheless, desirable to both groups and was achieved through consensual interpretation of Anglican *utaratibu* and a willingness to accept some diversity of opinion in the way in which *utaratibu* was applied locally.

Second generation migrants in North-east Congo, like their counterparts in other parts of the globe,[6] often felt uncomfortable with the ethnic ambience of their parents' religion. They drew on a hybrid range of socio-religious influences. They were frequently more fluent in Swahili, Lingala and French than their parents' language, they accessed new opportunities and alternative forms of behaviour, and they considered Anglican services formal and dull. However, young people were able to find within the EAC a flexibility that permitted sufficient informality, multi-ethnicity and spiritual vibrancy to provide a form for engaging with contemporary society. Likewise, only a minority of *Wokovu* left the EAC. Unlike many of their counterparts in Kenya and Tanzania,[7] they remained within the EAC rather than joining the new Pentecostalist churches because the rapid migrant growth of the church prevented the central institution from exerting constraint upon them. These groups were able to narrate their own stories of belonging within the EAC. Active and meaningful participation within their own groups permitted them to instigate greater change affecting the entire EAC; a change that might not have been possible if migration had less impact and the EAC had greater centralised control. Church growth through widespread migration weakened the effective power of the centralised gerontocratic elite. Thus, in the 1990s, junior members gained influence within the EAC and were not inclined to leave their parents' church, either by forming a schismatic group or joining the growing number of Pentecostal churches. As a result, *vijana* too spoke of the EAC in affectionate terms, able to articulate loyalty to it, both for the new elements within it and for the familial association it held. They could appreciate *utaratibu* once it no longer monopolised identity within the EAC and, in doing so, they acknowledged the value of corporate *umoja*. The loosening of gerontocratic control through the

---

[6] Helen Rose Ebaugh and Janet Saltzman Chafetz, *Religion and the New Immigrants: Continuities and Adaptations in Immigrant Congregation* (Waltnut Creek, AltaMira, 2000), 129–130.

[7] Josiah Mlahagwa, "Contending for the Faith: Spiritual Revival and the Fellowship Church in Tanzania," in *East African Expressions of Christianity*, ed. Thomas Spear and Isaria Kimambo (Oxford, James Currey, 1999), 299.

historical process of migratory growth and adaptation made a practical, institutional *umoja* between different generations an obtainable reality.

During the forty-year period studied in this thesis, members of the EAC changed their understanding of ethnic identity *as it related to their religious identity*. It altered from one in which ethnicity was considered to provide familiarity and cohesion within the EAC to one in which ethnicity was more likely to be considered divisive and fragmentary. It was no longer acceptable that ethnicity and denominational loyalty should coalesce. Political nationalism in the 1970s fed the unifying discourse of "all one in Christ." Even in the 1990s when ethnic loyalty became more prominent in political and economic alliances there remained a belief in the symbiosis of cultural nationalism and Christian unity for overcoming ethnic differences. Gregory Maddox considers the tension between the universal and the local to be a familiar trait in African Christianity; "Christian practice acts as one factor that encourages a sense of community beyond the immediate setting. This element is what gives Christianity its power in Africa." Christianity impacts other loyalties and widens opportunities for belonging to encompass a greater number of people. Yet Christianity, Maddox says, has also "...become embedded in many African contexts,"[8] contexts that allow for indigenisation and in which local, small groups may have great influence on identity. That ethnic or clan loyalties continued to influence Christian expression both made for a greater commitment to the local church and for greater tension in the national church. The interplay of ethnic and national identities within Anglican identity in North-east Congo over a period of forty years demonstrates two things: that migration and Christianity are both forces which encourage the reassessment of some loyalties and the assertion of others; and that African Christianity affects and is affected by other identity choices.

Anglican Identity

The tension between the universal and the local that Maddox describes was also played out in the way in which EAC members identified themselves as Anglicans. Migrant members borrowed from the discourse of global Anglicanism by adopting the slogan, "unity in diversity," to

---

[8] Gregory Maddox, "African Theology and the Search for the Universal" in *East African Expressions of Christianity*, 35.

encourage a broad spectrum of belief and practice. When they applied the slogan, however, they were largely concerned with issues within the EAC. Migratory experience had caused EAC members to build a religious home that embraced a larger variety of people. The foundational sense of belonging, of home, for the EAC—*utaratibu* as interpreted by *upole* and *heshima*—usually meant others without the same collective memories could not belong; indeed, it threatened to create division. By insisting on "unity in diversity" the migrants claimed the foundational EAC identity was only one among others. The discourse of international Anglicanism was used to legitimise their local agenda.

The diversity migrants expected was twofold. Firstly, there was the EAC's ability to allow certain Anglican groups a degree of *uhuru* to worship as they wished. "We have internalised dissent. We have allowed battles . . . to be conducted within the Church, rather than exclude those with whom we disagree," were words written by an Archbishop of Canterbury in a book entitled *Anglicanism: A Global Communion*[9] and they express sentiment with which migrant members of the EAC could appreciate. They had compromised and collaborated because, ultimately, a united church was of paramount importance. The discourse of internal *umoja* was legitimised by recourse to global Anglican aims. By the 1990s expressions of migrant EAC identity still included reference to liturgy and episcopal hierarchy—regarded as universal elements despite their local re-coding—and reference to Apolo Kivebulaya who introduced these elements locally. They also frequently mentioned characteristics of Anglican Churches elsewhere that permitted difference, variety and change. The knowledge that Anglican practice deviated from the traditional EAC course permitted the choice of locally observed forms of Christian worship to be adopted by those whose power might otherwise have prevented it. Church leaders could negotiate with informal, popular networks of *Wokovu*, women and youth to legitimise the variant identities that were effectively re-shaping the function of the hierarchy, providing those networks did not launch a direct attack on hierarchical and liturgical *utaratibu*.

In the competing market place of denominations in Congo, Anglicans may well attempt to retain the distinctiveness of the EAC vis-à-vis other denominations by maintaining *utaratibu* whilst providing room for *maendeleo, uhuru* and *furaha* and *umoja*. Certainly, as the EAC continues

---

[9] George Carey, "Forward," *Anglicanism: A Global Communion* (Mowbray, London, 1998), vi.

to spread westwards and southwards throughout Congo and other dioceses impact upon its identity, "unity in diversity" will become an increasingly important aphorism in EAC discourse.

The second element to which "unity in diversity" could be applied was improved relationships with local denominations. The development of the EAC has demonstrated that denominational loyalty can enhance ethnic divisions, or it can replace them by providing a new set of divisions. However, by the 1990s, the discourse of Christian unity which had been used to challenge Hema dominance was seen to encompass other denominations in a way that it had not when CECA and the EAC were in conflict over local issues of growth and identity. By this time, 'mixed' Christianity was accepted to a greater extent and the ECC had largely abandoned its policy of separate spheres for different churches. Denominational identity remained acute; migrants continued to feel a sense of pride in their Anglican identity whilst meeting and worshipping with those from CECA and the Pentecostal movements. However, efforts were made to establish relations across church boundaries and to see church differences as secondary to wider Christian identity. In doing so, in the face of violent upheaval, Christians were attempting to steer a unitary course through the fragmentation of society.

Migration changed the way members perceived their Anglican identity. The expression of unity in diversity as a virtue of Anglicanism was not inevitable: had the EAC remained on the escarpment, or had its original power base been larger or more influential, altering the original codification of *utaratibu* might have been more problematic; had the EAC possessed an immutable doctrinal and ethical code, change would have come more slowly and might have resulted in schism. The particular historical and social circumstances surrounding migration, which weakened centralised authority, challenged prior assumptions about Anglican identity, and encouraged negotiation and compromise rather than division, both sustained and altered the EAC. This permitted change to take place in which the generation, gender and ethnic links with ecclesiastical power were configured to allow participation in leadership from a wider spectrum of the population and a greater variety of possible performances of the Prayer Book.

Contemporary African Christianity

Terence Ranger, in an article entitled "Religion, Development and African Identity," asserted that the entire Christian movement is an expression of African identity because of its huge significance in the twentieth century history of the continent. He called for a reassessment in which "...we should see mission churches as much less alien and independent churches as much less 'African' than has hitherto been the case."[10] Six years later he made a plea for "...a historiography which makes the mission churches as *interesting* as the independent ones."[11] This study is part of a growing trend of research that has taken such pleas seriously. It has addressed the grassroots historical development of a mission church rather than focus upon the seemingly exotic Christianities in Africa. By taking the migratory angle, integral to EAC growth, it has been freed from the institutional bias so often apparent in describing mainline churches. Thus a church, often perceived to be indivisibly linked to English identity, has been shown to imbue alien systems and traditions with local meaning obtained from indigenous experience in such a way that its members made their home within it. It is precisely this remoulding of originally foreign forms into the constantly shifting cultures of Africa that makes the study of mission churches so fascinating. In taking this angle, it is suggested that change engendered greater commonalities between different denominations, demonstrating that mission churches are less foreign than often imagined and just as interesting as independent churches.

The EAC started as a small church with a charismatic African founder whose memory remained precious and whose myths strengthened corporate identity. From its inception it relied upon African agency for its growth across boundaries of culture, language, missionary comity and state administration. It grew as a result of migrant lay initiative for church planting and evangelism. Because migration happened as a result of economic or political circumstance and was not a strategy of ecclesiastical leadership, those at the forefront of the geographical spread and accompanying identity change of the EAC were laity rather than clergy, lowly teachers rather than bishops and archdeacons, and, latterly, women and youth rather than older men. Many church leaders had a low level of education and little control over the growth of the

---

[10] Terence Ranger, "Religion, Development and African Christian Identity," in *Religion, Development and African Identity*, ed. Kirsten Holst-Peterson (Uppsala, Scandanavian Institute of African Studies, 1987), 31.

[11] Terence Ranger, "New Approaches to the History of Mission Christianity," in *African Historiography: Essays in honour of Jacob Ade Ajayi*, ed. Toyin Falola (London, Longman, 1993), 183. Italics mine.

church. By the 1990s, worship was characterised by vibrant, emotional praise, audience participation, a (contentious) interest in the power and gifts of the Holy Spirit which resonated with tradition popular religious expression, a desire to tackle the present and immediate problems of members through spiritual means and a willingness to study the Bible and apply it to daily life. Indeed, the EAC, as influenced by the women's and youth movements, could be described as "...exuberant, enthusiastic, experience-dominated Christianity," a description given to Pentecostal churches and AICs in Africa.[12] The EAC has responded to its contemporary context in ways similar to those of popular Christian movements throughout Africa. If Tinyiko Maluleke is correct in saying in a forward to a book on Pentecostal and AICs that:

> ...many Christians are dissatisfied with the faith diet provided by the so-called "historic mission churches." It is therefore, at the expense of these established churches that AIC type movements are emerging and growing...[13]

then this study, whilst not disagreeing with this statement entirely, provides a corrective nuance to it. It argues that some "historic mission churches" provided similar solutions to the contemporary social and religious situation, either by attempting to replicate some of the strengths of the newer churches or by arriving at the same answers through a different route. In doing so they retained members who required these solutions.

Of course, the above description of the EAC is selective. It does not mention that a written, formal, centralised liturgy remained a feature of EAC identity, nor that many members accepted centralised, hierarchical control, pursued skills and education-based development and would have liked to see better educated clergy who possessed a good grasp of theology; features more often associated with mainline churches. Furthermore EAC members, even youth who admired the Pentecostal movement, emphatically did not consider themselves pentecostal. The contemporary changes that took place within the EAC were not radical ones because many members remained sceptical of Pentecostalism. Radical change would have incurred the loss of members for whom the more formal identity still had resonance and meaning. Change was

---

[12] Allan Anderson, *Zion and Pentecost: The Spirituality and Experience of Pentecostal and Zionist/Apostolic Churches in South Africa* (Pretoria, UNISA, 2000), 146.

[13] Forward in ibid., x.

tempered by the need for order and unity provided by continuity with, what was understood as, a received tradition of Anglicanism.

I am not attempting to argue, therefore, that the EAC becomes "interesting" because it is, in some way, no longer an "historic mission church." Rather, I propose that there is a common contemporary Congolese—even African—expression of Christianity that is rendered invisible when denominations are rigidly grouped into mainline, AIC, and Pentecostal traditions. These titles reflect to a greater extent their historical paths and, possibly, their official doctrines, rather than the beliefs and practices of ordinary members that have greater lines of affinity between them than we have been led to believe. David Maxwell presents a similar argument in his article on the transnational growth of the Pentecostal Zimbabwe Assemblies of God Africa (ZAOGA). He describes the confidence, financial security and developmental language of African ZAOGA missionaries as analogous to the confidence, economic strength and imperial language of nineteenth century western missionaries and says that ZAOGA:

> . . . has evolved from a religious movement with strong links to Christian independency into a "territorial" organisation with a hierarchy of ordered centres resembling that of historic mission churches.[14]

If a Pentecostal Church can be partially compared to mainline churches then it is unsurprising that a mainline church can demonstrate some characteristics more frequently associated with Pentecostalism. What is apparent from this comparison of grassroots EAC and Pentecostal churches is not that they are identical but that they have similarities that suggest the emergence of common characteristics in African Christianity. Many denominations are developing hybrid identities that respond, to a greater or lesser extent, to contemporary social realities. This is seen in improved relations between denominations but it is also a cause, not just an effect, of better relations between some of them. Viewing the identity of a mainline church through the perspective of migratory spread and transformation has provided an image of the EAC that shares similar characteristics and concerns with other popular religious movements on the African continent.

---

[14] David Maxwell, "Christianity without Frontiers: Shona Missionaries and Transnational Pentecostalism in Africa," in *Christianity and the African Imagination*, ed. Maxwell and Ingrid Lawrie (Leiden, Brill, 2002), 329.

African Christianities are part of an ever-shifting cultural context and they undergo continual re-interpretation influenced by a variety of local and global forces, ancient and modern and reflective of change in society at large. Many of these Christianities display similar traits to each other whilst maintaining their individual identities. They select, reject, plot and reinterpret the influences available to them whether they are from the past or present, local or global contexts. In marrying diverse influences to meet present needs they produce hybrid identities that re-code the sources from which they gained their inspiration.

Conclusion

The migration into and throughout Congo of Africans who felt at home in an Anglican Church created the *Eglise Anglicane du Congo* on the Semeliki escarpment from 1896 and enabled its spread throughout the country from 1960. Migratory growth engendered a hybrid and mobile religious identity interconnected with local, regional, national and transnational influences, and reinterpreted to respond to present needs in a way that encouraged unity within the EAC and enabled a greater common expression of Christianity. Cohesive identity signifiers dominated those that might have provided smaller units of religious belonging and thus the EAC provided a locus of belonging for a growing variety of members. Congolese Anglican identity continued to be narrated through the Apolo story, but it was an interpretation of the story that plotted his ministry with subsequent migratory events. Thus, a common feeling of being at home within the EAC became rooted in the participation in the migrations that were the routes of growth of the EAC.

The migratory growth of the EAC supplies an example of African religious change that demonstrates that small-scale migration can enhance commitment to Christian faith, encourage denominational loyalty and also can produce rapid alterations to that specific Christian identity. Migration makes some change inevitable in any religious institution even one in which the forces for conservation of a received tradition are particularly strong. The EAC changed rapidly because it was a small church willing to exploit opportunities for expansion, which it understood to accord with the wishes of its African founder. Migratory expansion increased opportunities for change because migrant members rapidly outnumbered non-migrant members. The

EAC demonstrates that changes wrought by migration can enable the re-invention of a mainline church, turning it from a formal, geron-tocratic institution responsive to the societal norm of one particular area, to an organisation which accepts the increased involvement of societal juniors in order to meet the contemporary and local needs of the majority of its members. Migration allows a church the flexibility to respond to the criticism of a societal order of which it has become a part.

BIBLIOGRAPHY

Oral Sources

Interviews conducted and translated by Emma Wild-Wood unless otherwise stated.

Acheson, Judy (f), youth worker and CMS mission partner, Bunia, English, 27 September 2000.

Adili Janette (f), MU member, Kumuru, Swahili, 18 August 2000.

Adoroti Ombhabua David (m), pastor of Pazulu parish, Kumuru, Swahili, 17 August 2000.

Adubang'o Dieudonne (m), youth worker, Mahagi, Swahili, 29 August 2000.

Africa Jimmy (m), driver, church treasurer, Arua, English, 2 September 2000.

Agele Isaac (m), Aru Bible School director, Kampala, English, 26 July 2000.

Agupio Samuel (m), pastor of Isiro parish, Aru, Swahili, 9 August 2000.

Airene Ayike Agnes (f), MU member, Kumuru, Kakwa, 17 August 2000 [Wani Ezra and Agele Isaac, translators].

Aiye Joanne (f), MU member, Aru, Lugbara, Draru Leonora, (f) MU member, Aru, Swahili, 12 August 2000.

Akuso Dudu Elizabeti (f), MU member, Kumuru, Swahili, 17 August 2000.

Alio Samweli (m), pastor and student, Arua, English, 8 August 2000.

Alo Cecile (f), Anamwasi Paluku (f), Bhako Fibi (f), Pasa Therese (f), CECA 20 women's leaders, Bunia, Swahili, 18 September 2000.

Amodo Nghota, Dieudonné (m), Sunday School teacher, Kumuru, Swahili, 19 August 2000

Androsi Kasima (f), women's development worker, Boga, French, 8 October 2000.

Anguzu Alfred (m) night watchman, Aru, Swahili, 10 August 2000.

Anziko, Aser, Duria, Berocan, Bigule Tiru, Kiko, Mawanzo, Neema, Onzia, Seme, Usaru, (f), CECA 20 and Catholic women from EAC *Foyer Social* group, Aru, Lingala and French, 11 August 2000.

Anzu Asinata (f), Aru sub-parish M.U. leader, Lugbara, Asuɲe Ella Jesi (f) and O'daru Rada Monique (f), Aru sub-parish MU leaders, Swahili, 12 August 2000.

Anzukaru Marita (f), church founder and revivalist, Lugbara [Anguzu Georges and Titre Ande translators] 21 August 2000.

Arie Rose (f), MU member, Kumuru, Kakwa, 17August 2000 [Wani Ezra and Agele Isaac, translators].

Asiki David (m), Archdeacon of Mahagi, Aru, English, 22 August 2000.

Atuku Abe Nason (m), EAC member, Kumuru, Swahili, 19 August 2000.

Baba Atseko (m), Anglican Medical Service Administrator, Aru, French, 14 August 2000.

Balinda Tito (m), retired Archdeacon of Beni, Boga, Swahili, 2 October 2000.

Basimasi Kyakuhaire (f), early catechist in Boga, Komanda, Swahili, 21 September 2000.

Bataaga Beni (m), provincial communications officer, Bunia, English, 15 September 2000, also in May 1998.

Beatrice Kalumbi (f), Archdeaconry women's leader, Butembo, Swahili, 16 June 1998 [interview by Bitamara William].

Bileti Sila (m), founder of EAC, revival leader, Aru, Swahili, 10 August 2000.

Bitanihirwa Kamakama (m), Anglican schools co-ordinator, Bunia, French, 10 September 2000.

Bonabana Christina (f), Beni church benefactor and Canon, Swahili, 17 June 1998 [interview by Kalule Baudoin].

Buno Boaz (m), pastor of Linga, Mahagi, Swahili, 29 August 2000.

Byaruhanga Araly Isaka (m), choir leader, Bunia, Swahili, 13 September 2000.
Caroline Mwanga (f), Diocesan MU Secretary, Swahili, 16 June 1998 [interview by Bitamara William].
Damali Sabiti (f), MU provincial trainer, Mukono, English, 20 October 2000.
Damaria (f) and Esther (f) founders of Ombi sub-parish, Aru, Lugbara, 10 August 2000 [Anguzu Georges and Titre Ande translators].
Dezo Rasili (f), Toongo evangelist's wife, Aru, Swahili, Munduru Beti (f), Lugbara, 12 August 2000.
Etsea Ang'apoza Kila (m), CECA 20 president, Bunia, French, 18 September 2000.
Evasta Kasuna (f), ex MU leader, Bunia, Swahili, 16 September 2000.
Gboŋa Amuel (m), founder of Bongilo church, Kumuru, Swahili, 18 August 2000.
Grace Peter (f), member of MU, wife of pastor, Kumuru, Swahili, 19 August 2000.
Irene Bahemuka (f), diocesan MU worker, Boga, French, 30 September 2000.
Isingoma Kakwa Henri (m), Bishop of Katanga, Edinburgh, French, 7 June 2000.
Janette Sinziri (f), M.U. member, clergy wife, Kumuru, Swahili, 18 August 2000.
Joyce Babote (f), MU member, Komanda, Swahili, 21 September 2000.
Jurua Jonathan (m), elder of Aru-ville church, Aru, English, 11 August 2000.
Kabarole Baguma (m), Archdeacon of Aru, Aru, Swahili, 9 August 2000 [also in July 1998 by Yossa Way].
Kaheru Rosa (f), founder member of Bunia church, Bunia, Swahili, 16 September 2000.
Kalume Sivengire, (m), Development worker, Butembo, French, 11 June 1998 [interview by Ndungu Valihari].
Kamanyoha (f) and Isingoma (m) Chwa, church members, Bunia, Swahili, 23 September 2000.
Kapondombe Wiyajik Francois (m), pastor of Pathole, Mahagi, Swahili, 27 August 2000.
Kipindu Rachel (f), sub-parish leader of MU, Kumuru, Swahili, 19 August 2000.
Kiko Dudu (f), M.U. member, Kumuru, Lingala, 17 August 2000 [Wani Ezra, translator].
Kupajo Matatia Yobu (m), Imbokolo evangelist, Kakwa, 17 August 2000 [Wani Ezra and Agele Isaac, translators].
Kusika Kenyi Fredric (m), elder of Toongo church, Aru, Swahili, 11 August 2000.
Kyamulesere Geresomu (m), founder of Bunia and Komanda churches, Komanda, Swahili, 21 September 2000.
Leti Christophe (m), Head Christian of Ekanga parish, Swahili, Aru, 11 August 2000.
Likambo Tamaru (m), evangelist, Boga, French, 9 October 2000.
Lukumbula Kihandasikiri Elia (m), Director of Mbau Bible School, Swahili, 25 July 2000.
Mahirani Mustum Melena (f), EAC founder, Butembo, Swahili, 21 September 2000.
Mama Josephine (f), evangelist, founder member of Aru church, Swahili, 13 August 2000.
Mawa Isaac Remo (m), CECA 20 youth leader, Kumuru, French, 19 August 2000.
Mbusa Bangau Etienne (m), Vicar général of Bukavu Diocese, French, 28 July 2000.
Mukasa Nasanairi (m), Canon, Ugandan missionary to Congo, Luganda, 1998 [notes from several conversations with Bahemuka Mugeni].
Muhindo Tsongo Joyce (f), Tutor at ISThA, Edinburgh, French 17 December 1999 and Bristol 10 April 2000.
Munege Kabarole (m), Archdeacon of Bunia, Bunia, Swahili, 13September 2000 [also in June 1998 by Yossa Way].
Musubaho Ndaghaliwa (m), retired diocesan evangelist and Canon, Kaimana, Swahlili, 5 October 2000.
Ndirtho Paulo (m), Archdeaconry evangelist, Mahagi, Swahili, 29 August 2000.
Neema Adroro (f), M.U. member, Kumuru, Swahili, 17 August 2000.
Ngadjole Fredrick (m), Roman Catholic, Kampala, French, 22 October 2000.

Ngona (m) Phineas (m) and Richard Lombu (m), CECA 20 reformée members, Bunia, Swahili, 25 September 2000.

Njang'u Uzele Esther (f), church founder and revivalist, Mahagi, Alur, 28 August 2000. [Ubaya Uchaki and Udaga pi Mungu, translators].

Oloni Seth Walter (m), new pastor, English, Aru, 11 August 2000

Otuwa Simeon (m), founder of church and revival leader, Aru, Lugbara, 11 August 2000 [Anguzu Georges and Titre Ande translators].

Ozua Samson (m), Aru Archdeaconry Sunday School co-ordinator, Aru, Swahili, 10 August 2000.

Revival group meeting, Bunia, Swahili, 17 September 2000.

Ridsdale, Lucy (f), Deaconess, Bible School teacher in Boga and CMS Mission Partner, Cambridge, English, 15 January 1999.

Ridsdale, Philip (m), Bishop of Boga-Zaïre, 1972–1980, and CMS Mission Partner, Cambridge, English, 16 January 1999.

Rwakaikara Andre (m), trader and elder in Bunia church, Bunia, Swahili, 23 September 2000.

Sengi Lupanzula (m), pastor, Bwakadi, Swahili, 6 October 2000.

Sibanza Buleti Palini (m), ex-archdeacon of Rwenzori, Komanda, Swahili, 5 October 2000.

Sinziri Onadra Christophe (m), Archdeacon of Kumuru, Kumuru Swahili, 18 August 2000 [also in July 1998 by Yossa Way].

Tabu Abembe (m), Archdeacon of the Forest, Bwakadi, French, 6 October 2000.

Tchulu Dhelo (m), CECA 20 pastor, Bunia, Swahili, 20 September 2000.

Thumbe Ferdinand (m), church founder and revivalist, Mahagi, Swahili, 29 August 2000.

Tindyera Kabarole (f), MU leader and Archdeacon's wife, Bunia, Swahili, 19 September 2000.

Tingoli Kasuna Bunangana (m), EAC elder, Bunia, Swahili, 16 September 2000.

Titre Ande George (m), Principal of ISThA, Edinburgh, French, 25 September 1999 and 28 December 1999.

Tongo Joyce (f), MU member, Kumuru, Kakwa, 17 August 2000 [Wani Ezra and Agele Isaac, translators].

Tsongo Kima Abraham (m), Nord-Kivu Diocesan Secretary, French, Kampala, 29 July 2000

Tumusiime Drumo Rhoda (f), Kumuru Archdeaconry MU president, Kumuru, Swahili, 18 August 2000.

Ubotha Marthe (f), church founder and revivalist, Mahagi, Alur, 27 August 2000 [Uchaki Ubaya and Udaga pi Mungu, translators].

Uchaki Ubaya (m), pastor of Mahagi, Mahagi, Swahili, 30 August 2000.

Uketi Amosi (m), church founder and revivalist, Mahagi, Alur, 29 August 2000. [Uchaki Ubaya and Udaga pi Mungu, translators].

Uweka Marie (f), EAC member, Mahagi, Alur, 28 August 2000. [Uchaki Ubaya and Udaga pi Mungu, translators].

Ugen Lambert (m), church founder and revivalist, Swahili, 28 August 2000.

Uzele Salatiel (m), church founder and revivalist, Mahagi, Alur, 28 August 2000. [Uchaki Ubaya and Udaga pi Mungu, translators].

Wadhiko Dina (f), Aru Archdeaconry MU president, Aru, Swahili, 10 August 2000.

Wani Ezra (m) evangelist and archdeaconry secretary, Kumuru, French, 18 August 2000 [also July '98 by Yossa Way].

Yaka Warra Idroru (m), CECA 20 pastor, Kumuru, French, 19 August 2000.

Yobuta Peter (m), Pastor of Kumuru parish, Kumuru, Swahili, 19 August 2000.

Yossa Way (m), Academic Dean, ISThA, Kampala, French, 27 July 2000.

Yuma Ajule Hezekiah (m), EAC elder, Kumuru, Swahili, 18 August 2000.

Zamba Asu Hezron (m), catechist, Kumuru, Swahili, 18 August 2000.

Archival Sources

1. CECA 20 Central Offices, Bunia.
"CECA 20 Rapports Statistiques," 20 September 2000.

2. CMS, Crowther Centre Library, Oxford.
CMS Historical Record, London, CMS, 1955–6.
CMS Annual Report, London, CMS, 1934–35.
Fisher, A. B. in *Extracts from the Annual Letter of Missionaries, 1909*, London, CMS, 1910: 155.
Fisher, A. B. in *Extracts from the Annual Letter of Missionaries, 1912–1913*, London, CMS 1913: 87–88.
Tarrant, Ian. *A Brief History of the Anglican Church in Zaire*. Unpublished, 1988.
Tucker, A. "The Spiritual Expansion of Buganda; the Narrative of a Journey to Toro," *Intelligencier*, February, 1899: 105–111.

3. COU—Church of Uganda Archives, Uganda Christian University, Mukono.
Box 2bp10.1 Correspondence of Bishop of Uganda about Mboga.

4. MU—Africana Department Archives, Makerere University, Kampala.
Apolo Kivebulaya's Diaries in Luganda
Anne Luck's file, including English translations of Apolo Kivebulaya's diaries, letter from R. Fisher, 17 November1957, and *Bishop Balya's Account of Apolo Kivebulaya* (unpublished, n.d.).
The archives mentioned below are part of the continuing Oral History and Archive project of the EAC (supported by the Pew Charitable Trust and OMSC, New Haven). EAC archives are being copied on to microfilm by Yale University Divinity Library.

5. ArchA—Archdeaconry of Aru office
Parish and Archdeaconry statistics, 1985–1999.
1996. "Hadizi ya Archidiacone ya Aru."
Sila Bileti. 1988. "Historical Background of the Anglican Church in Leri."

6. ArchK—Archdeaconry of Kumuru office.
Parish and Archdeaconry statistics and maps, 1994–2000.
1996. "Hadizi ya Archidiacone ya Kumuru."

7. BP—Bunia Parish Office.
Parish registers—Marriages, baptisms, Sunday services.

8. DBg—Boga Diocesan Office.
Ridsdale, Philip and Ndahura Bezaleri, 'New Diocese in Zaïre.'
Ridsdale, Philip 'Journal de Bord (sic): Diocese de Boga-Zaïre.'
Musubaho Ndaghaliwa, "L'Eglise Anglicane du Zaïre" unpublished c. 1988.

9. DBk—Bukavu Diocesan Office.
"Bref Aperçu historique de l'Eglise Anglicane, Diocèse de Bukavu"

10. DNK—North-Kivu Diocesan Office.
Historique du Diocèse, NK960000.1

11. ISThA archives.
Histoire de la Paroisse Azangani, 1999
Yossa Way et al. "Eglise Independantes et Sectes Implantées à Bunia," report, April 2003.
Esquisse historique de l'Eglise Anglicane du Zaïre, 1896–1996, Bunia, ISThA, 1996.

12. PRP—Philip Ridsdale Papers Henry Martyn Centre, Cambridge.
"Report on Visit of Miss Diana Witts to the Dioceses of Boga and Bukavu, Zaïre, October 1979—May 1980".
"Unpublished account of life and work as CMS missionaries' Beryl Rendle, n.d."

13. RDO—Rwenzori Diocesan Offices
Baptismal Records from 1895.
Boga File, 1960–1972

Unpublished Theses and Dissertations

Adraa Mokili. "The Growth and Impact of Chosen Evangelical Revival (C.E.R.) in Ayivu County, Arua District, West Nile-Madi Diocese." Diploma, Makerere University, 1986.
Ang'omoko Tek'akwo Upio. "Mouvement des 'Barokole' dans le diocèse de Boga-Congo; cas de l'archidiacone d'Aru." Diplôme de Graduat, ISThA, 1997.
Bakengana Lukando. "Histoire de la Paroisse Anglicane de Kainama: Vue panoramique des origines à 1995." Diplôme de Graduat, ISThA, 1997.
Bampiga Bailensi. "Etude sur le Développement économique dans la Paroisse anglicane de Bunia." Diplôme de Graduat, ISThA, 1994.
Boliba Baba, James. "Adiyo: The coming of the Kakwa and the Development of their Institutions." B.A., Makerere University, 1971.
Buyana Mulungula. "Etude théologique du Boom charismatique de la Paroisse anglicane de Bunia." Diplôme de Graduat, ISThA, 1994.
———. "Conflit entre la Foi Chrétienne et le Ufumu dans le Milieu Urbain: Bukavu et Bunia." Licence, ISTB-Bunia, 1996.
Dirokpa Balufuga Fidèle. "Liturgie anglicane et Inculturation, Hier, Aujourd'hui et Demain: Regard sur la Célébration eucharistique en République Démocratique du Congo." PhD, Université Laval, 2001.
Edjidra Leko, J. B. "Histoire du Catholicisme dans la Zone d'Aru de 1925 à 1990." Licence, ISP-Bunia, 1996.
Embaga-Ujiga, Samson, R. "The Mission of the Church to the Lugbara Community of Lugazi Sugar Factory." Diploma of Theology, Bishop Tucker Theological College, 1981.
Isingoma Kahwa. "La Notion traditionelle de la Communauté en Afrique noire et son Integration dans la Vie ecclesiale (Cas de Banyoro en Republique du Zaïre)." Maitrise, Faculté de Théologie Evangélique de Bangui, 1989.
———. "La Monographie du Diocese de Boga-Zaïre." Diplôme de graduat, ISThA, 1984.
Kamba-Opima. "Evolution politique et économique separée des Lugbara au Congo belge et en Uganda sous le Regime colonial (1914–1956)." Licence, ISP-Bunia, 1991.
Kisembo Sumbuso. "Etude de Mouvement de la Jeunesse chrétienne 'Agape' dans le Diocèse anglican de Boga-Zaïre." Diplôme de Graduat, ISThA, 1994.
Kokole Idrng'i Loding'o. "Le Chrétien fâce au Mariage par Rapt (Cas de la Tribu Kakwa)." Diplôme de Graduat, ISTB-Bunia, 1986.
Lalima Tagamile Dhulembe. "L'Exercise de la Discipline dans une Eglise Africaine: Examen Théologique de l'Application de l'Article VII de R.O.I. de la CECA/AIM, Zaire." Maîtrise, Faculté de Théologie Evangelique de Bangui, 1984.
Lekeni, Mawa. "L'Exode des Lugbara vers Bunia de 1960 à nos Jours: les Facteurs determinants." Licence, ISP-Bunia, 1990.
Malherbe, Gerard. "La Mission au Lac Albert (Ituri-Zaïre) 1911–1934." PhD, Louvain la Neuve, 1976.
Mombo, Esther. "A History and Cultural Analysis of the Position of Abaluya Women in Kenyan Quaker Christianity, 1902–1979." PhD, Edinburgh University, 1998.
Morad, Stephen D. "The Founding Principles of the Africa Inland Mission and their Interaction with the African Context in Kenya." PhD, Edinburgh University, 1997.

Muhindo Tsongo, Joyce. "The Role of Women in the Anglican Church in Congo: A case of the Diocese of North Kivu." MA, Trinity College, Bristol, 2000.

Muzuro Kana Wai. "Croissance de l'Eglise locale de la Communauté évangelique an Centre de L'Afrique, Section de Bunia." Diplôme de Graduat, ISTB, 1982.

Ndahura Bezaleri. "L'Implantation de l'Anglicanisme au Zaïre, 1896–1972." Licence, Faculté Protestante de Kinshasa, 1974.

Niringiye, David Zac. "The Church in the World: A Historical-Ecclesiological Study of the Church of Uganda with particular reference to Post-Independence Uganda 1962–92." PhD, University of Edinburgh, 1997.

Nyabongo Kwake. "Le Mouvement oecumenique dans la Cité de Bunia: Rêve ou Réalité?" Diplôme de Graduat, ISThA, 1994.

Obitre Biya. "La Discipline ecclesiastique selon le Nouveau Testament et son Exercise dans le District de Aru." Diplôme de Graduat, ISTB, 1982.

Robins, C. E. "Tukutendereza: a study of social change and sectarian withdrawal in the Balokole Revival of Uganda." PhD, Columbia University, 1975.

Ruzinga Nobi. "Place et Valeur théologique des Chansons religieuses des Chorales dans l'Eglise (cas de la Paroisse anglicane de Bunia)," Diplôme de Graduat, ISThA, 1997.

Syaikomia Nganza. "Les Principes d'Organisation de la Communauté baptiste au Kivu." Diplôme de Graduat, ISTB, 1982.

Tabu Abembi J.-P. "Le Phenomène du Tribalisme au Sein de l'Eglise du Chirst au Republique Democratique du Congo; cas de la ville de Bunia." Diplôme de Graduat, ISThA, 1997.

Titre Ande. "Authority in the Anglican Church of Congo: The Influence of Political Models of Authority and the Potential of 'Life-Community Ecclesiology' for Good Governance." PhD Birmingham University, 2003.

Ucircan Adegitho. "Phenomène des Migrations alur: Cas de la Chefferie d'Anghal de 1933 à 1965." Diplôme de Graduat, ISP-Bunia, 1996.

Yeka Warra Idroru. "L'impact de la Penetration et de l'Expansion de l'Evangile sur le Peuple Kakwa." Diplôme de Graduat, ISTB, 1992.

Conference Papers

Miller, Jon. "Missionaries and Migrants: The Importance of Religion in the Movement of Populations." Presented at Currents in World Christianity Conference in Pretoria, South Africa, 3–7 July 2001.

Pottier, Johan. "Emergency in Ituri, DRC: Political Complexity, Land and Other Challenges in Restoring Food Security." Presented at the FAO International Workshop in Tivoli, Italy, 23–25 September 2003.

Published Sources

Adenaike, Carolyn Keyes. "Reading the Pursuit: An Introduction," in *In Pursuit of History: Fieldwork in Africa*, edited by Carolyn Keyes Adenaike and Jan Vansina, xvii–xliv. Portsmouth: Heinemann, 1996.

Adepoju, Aderanti. "Links between Internal and International Migration: the African Situation," in *International Migration Today*, edited by Charles Stahl, 34–44: UNESCO: University of Western Australia, 1988.

Al-Ali, Nadje and Khalid Koser. "Transnationalism, International Migration and Home," in *New Approaches to Migration? Transnational Communities and the Transformation of Home*, edited by Nadje Al-Ali and Khalid Koser, 1–13. London: Routledge, 2002.

Anderson, Allan. *Zion and Pentecost: The Spirituality and Experience of Pentecostal and Zionist/ Apostolic Churches in South Africa*. Pretoria: UNISA, 2000.

Anderson, Dick. *We Felt Like Grasshoppers*. Nottingham: Crossway Books, 1994.

Anderson, W. A. *The Church in East Africa, 1940–1974*. Dodoma: Central Tanganika Press, 1988.

Anthias, Floya, and Nira Yuval-Davis. "Contextualising feminism—gender, ethnic and class divisions." *Feminist Review* 15 (1983): 62–75.

Bagatagira, D. "Split in the Revival Movement in Uganda." *Occasional Papers in African Traditional Religion and Philosophy*, 4. Makerere University, Kampala, 1972: 1–5.

Barrett, David B., George T. Kurian and Todd. M. Johnson. *World Christian Encyclopaedia: A Comparative Study of Churches and Religions in the Modern World, AD 1900–2000*. Oxford: Oxford University Press, 2001.

Barrett, David, B. *Schism and Renewal in Africa; An Analysis of Six Thousand Contemporary Religious Movements*. Nairobi: Oxford University Press, 1968.

Baur, John. *2000 Years of Christianity in Africa: An African History 62–1992*. Nairobi: Paulines Publications, 1994.

Beattie, John. *The Nyoro State*. Oxford: Clarendon Press, 1971.

Bebbington, D. W. *Evangelicalism in Modern Britain: A History from the 1730s to the 1980s*. London: Unwin Hyman, 1989.

Biaya Tshikala K., 'Parallel Society in the Democratic Republic of Congo', in *Shifting African Identities*, edited by Simon Bekker et al. 41–69, Pretoria: Human Sciences Research Council, 2001.

Bokeleale, I. B. "From Missions to Missions." *International Review of Missions* 62 (1973): 433–436.

Boyd, Monica. "Family and Personal Networks in International Migration: Recent Developments and New Agendas." *International Migration Review* 23 (1989): 638–670.

Bozzoli, Belinda. *Women of Phokeng: Consciousness, Life Strategy and Migrancy in South Africa*. Portsmouth: Heinemann, 1991.

Braekman, E. M. *Histoire du Protestantisme au Congo, Histoire du Protestantisme en Belgique et au Congo Belge*. Bruxelles: Librarie des Eclaireurs Unionistes, 1961.

Bujo, Bénézet. *African Theology in its Social Context*. Nairobi: St. Paul Publications, 1992.

Byerlee, Derek. *Research on Migration in Africa: Past, Present and Future*. Michigan: Michigan State University, 1972.

Carey, George. "Forward" In *Anglicanism: A Global Communion*, edited by Andrew Wingate, Kevin Ward, Carrie Pemberton, Wilson Sitshebo, v–vi. London:Cassell, 1998.

Castles, Stephen, and Mark J. Millar. *The Age of Migration: International Population Movements in the Modern World*. London: MacMillan Press, 1998.

Chambers, Robert. "Rural Refugees in Africa: What the Eye Does Not See." *Disasters* 3 (1979): 381–392.

Chrétien, Jean Pierre. "Confronting the Unequal Exchange of the Oral and the Written," in *African Historiographies: What History for Which Africa?* edited by Bogumil Jewsiewicki and David Newbury, 75–90. Beverly Hills: Sage, 1986.

Comaroff, Jean & John. *Of Revelation and Revolution: Christianity, Colonialism and Consciousness in South Africa*. Chicago: University of Chicago, 1991.

Confino, Alon, and Ajay Skaria. "Viewed from the Locality: The Local, National and Global." *National Identities* 4 (2002): 5–6.

Cornell, Stephen. "That's the Story of our Life," in *We are a People: Narrative and Multiplicity in Constructing Ethnic Identity*, edited by Paul Spickard and Jeffrey W. Burroughs, 41–53. Philadelphia: Temple University Press, 2000.

Crisp, Jeff. "Ugandan Refugees in Sudan and Zaire: The Problem of Repatriation." *African Affairs* 85 (1986): 163–180.

De Boeck, Filip. "Postcolonialism, power and identity: Local and Global Perspectives from Zaire," in *Postcolonial Identities in Africa*, edited by Richard Werbner and Terence Ranger, 75–100. London: Zed, 1996.

De Vos, George, A. "Ethnic Pluralism: Conflict and Accommodation. The role of Ethnicity in Social History," in *Ethnic Identity: Creation, Conflict and Accommodation*, edited by Lola Romanucci-Ross and George De Vos, 15–47. Walnut Creek: AltaMira, 1995.

De Vos, George, A. and Lola Romanucci-Ross, "Ethnic Identity: A Psychocultural Persective," in *Ethnic Identity: Creation, Conflict and Accommodation*, edited by George A. De Vos and Lola Romanucci-Ross, 349–379, Walnut Creek: AltaMira, 1995.

Dobson, J. H. *Daybreak in West Nile*. London: Africa Inland Mission, 1967.

Dunaway, D. K. and W. K. Baum. *Oral History: An Interdisciplinary Anthology*, California: AltaMira, 1996.

Dunn, Kevin C. *Imagining the Congo: the International Relations of Identity*. New York: Palgrave Macmillan, 2003.

Ebaugh, Helen Rose, and Janet Saltzman Chafetz. *Religion and the New Immigrants: Continuities and Adaptations in Immigrant Congregations*. Waltnut Creek: AltaMira, 2000.

Eglise du Christ au Zaïre. "Dieu et le Monde: Procès Verbal du 4e Synode nationale de l'ECZ." Kinshasa: ECZ, 1977.

Ekechi, F. K. "Studies on Missions in Africa," in *African Historiography: Essays in Honour of Jacob Ade Ajayi*, edited by Toyin Falola, 145–165. Nigeria: Longman, 1993.

Eriksen, Thomas, *Ethnicity and Nationalism*, 2nd edition, London: Pluto Press, 2002.

Etherington, Norman. "Recent trends in the Historiography of Christianity in Southern Africa." *Journal of Southern African Studies* 22 (1996): 201–219.

Fabian, Johannes. "Potopot: Problems of Documenting the History of Spoken Swahili in Shaba," in *Swahili Studies: Essays in Honour of Marcel van Spaandonck*, edited by Jan Blommaert, 17–44. Ghent: Academia Press, 1991.

——. *Language and Colonial Power: The Appropriation of Swahili in the Former Belgian Congo*. Cambridge: Cambridge University Press, 1986.

Fog Olwig, Karen. "Contested Homes: Home making and the Making of Anthropology," in *Migrants of Identity: Perceptions of Home in a World Movement*, Rapport, Nigel; Dawson, A. 225–235. Oxford: Berg, 1998.

Gaitskell, Deborah. "Power in Prayer and Service: Women's Christian Organisations," in *Christianity in South Africa: A Political, Cultural and Social History*, edited by Richard Elphick and Rodney Davenport, 253–267. Claremont, S.A: David Philip, 1997.

Gatwa, Tharcisse. *Rwanda, Eglises: Victimes ou Coupables? Les Eglises et l'idéologie ethnique au Rwanda, 1900–1994*. Yaoundé: Editions CLE, 2001.

Gifford, Paul. *African Christianity: Its Public Role*. London: Hurst, 1998.

Gil-White, Francisco J. "The Cognition of Ethnicity: Native Category Systems under the Field Experimental Microscope." *Methods* 14 (2002): 161–189.

Gondola, Ch. Didier. "Popular Music, Urban Society and Changing Gender Relations in Kinshasa (1950–1990)," in *Gendered Encounters: Challenging Cultural Boundaries and Social Hierarchies in Africa*, edited by Maria Grosz-Ngaté and Omari H. Kokole, 65–84. New York: Routeledge, 1997.

Grimes, Babara F. "Ethnologue." English. http://www.sil.org/ethnologue/countries/Zair.html: SIL, 2000.

Grishick Ben-Amos, Paula. "The Promise of Greatness: Women and Power in an Edo Spirit Possession Cult," in *Religion in Africa*, edited by T. D. Blakley, W. E. A. van Beek and D. L. Thomson, 118–133. London: James Currey, 1994.

Hammersley, Martyn, and Paul Atkinson. *Ethnography: Principles in Practice*. London: Routledge, 1995.

Hastings, Adrian. *The Church in Africa, 1450—1950*. Oxford: Clarendon Press, 1994.

Henige, David. *Oral Historiography*. London: Longmans, 1982.

Hodgson, Dorothy L. "Of Modernity/Modernities, Gender, and Ethnography," in *Gendered Modernities: Ethnographic Perspectives*, edited by Dorothy L. Hodgson, 1–22. New York: Palgrave, 2001.

Hodgson, Dorothy L. and Sheryl A. McCurdy. "Introduction," in *'Wicked' women and the Reconfiguration of Gender in Africa*, edited by Dorothy L. Hodgson and Sheryl A. McCurdy, 1–24. Portsmouth: Heinemann, 2002.

Holstein, James A. and Jaber F. Grubrium. *The Self We Live By: Narrative Identity in a Postmodern World*. New York: Oxford University Press, 2000.

International Rescue Committee Report. "Mortality in the Democratic Republic of Congo: Results from a Nationwide Survey," April 2003.

Isichei, Elizabeth. *A History of Christianity in Africa from Antiquity to the Present.* London: SPCK, 1995.

——. "Does Christianity Empower Women? The Case of the Anaguta of Central Nigeria." In *Women and Missions: Past and Present*, edited by Fiona Bowie, Debora Kirkwood, Shirley Ardener, 209–226. Oxford: Berg, 1993.

ISThA, *Esquisse historique de l'Eglise Anglicane du Zaïre 1896–1996.* Bunia: 1996.

Jackson, John, A. *Migration.* London: Longman, 1986.

Jardin, Oliver. "The 'Mama Bakita' Centre for the Disabled at Aru." *Refugee* November (1987): 39–40.

Kabongo-Mbaya, Philippe B. *L'Eglise du Christ au Zaïre: Formation et adaption d'un protestantisme en situation de dictature,* Paris: Karthala, 1992.

Kalu, Ogbu, U. "African Church Historiography," in *African Historiography: Essays in Honour of Jacob Ade Ajayi*, edited by Toyin Falola, 166–179. London: Longman, 1993.

Kalu, Ogbu. "Pentecostal and Charismatic Reshaping of the African Religious Landscape in the 1990s." *Mission Studies* 20 (2003): 84–111.

Karanja, John. "The Role of Kikuyu Christians in Developing a Self-Conciously African Anglicanism," in *The Church Mission Society and World Christianity, 1799–1999*, edited by Kevin Ward and Brian Stanley, 254–282. Grand Rapids: Eerdmans, 2000.

Karugire, S. R. *A Political History of Uganda.* Nairobi: Heinemann, 1980.

Keyes, Charles F. "The Dialectics of Change," in *Ethnic Change*, edited by Charles Keyes, F. Seattle: University of Washington Press, 1981.

Landau, Paul Stuart. *The Realm of the Word: Language, Gender and Christianity in a Southern African Kingdom.* Cape Town: David Philip, 1995.

Leslie, Winsome, J. *Zaire: Continuity and Political Change in an Oppressive State.* Colorado: Westview, 1993.

Lloyd, A. B. *Apolo of the Pygmy Forest.* London: CMS, 1923.

——. *More about Apolo.* London: CMS, 1928.

——. *Apolo the Pathfinder—Who Follows?* London: CMS, 1934.

Lloyd, Margaret. *Wedge of Light: Revival in North West Uganda.* Rugby: private, n.d.

Luck, Anne. *African Saint: The Story of Apolo Kivebulaya.* London: SCM, 1963.

MacGaffey, Janet. "Long-distance Trade, Smuggling and the New Commercial Class: the Nande of North Kivu," in *Entrepreneurs and Parasites: The Struggle for Indigenous Capitalism in Zaire*, edited by Janet MacGaffey. 143–164. Cambridge: Cambridge University Press, 1987.

MacGaffey, Wyatt. *Religion and Society in Central Africa: The Bakongo of Lower Zaïre.* Chicago: Chicago University Press, 1986.

Maddox, Gregory H. "African Theology and the Search for the Universal," in *East African Expressions of Christianity*, edited by Thomas Spear and Isaria N. Kimambo, 25–36. Oxford: James Currey, 1999.

Manning, Patrick. *Francophone Sub-Saharan Africa, 1880–1995.* Cambridge: Cambridge University Press, 1998.

Markowitz, M. D. *Cross and Sword: The Political Role of Christian Missions in the Belgian Congo, 1908–1960.* Stanford: Hoover Institution Press, 1973.

Mason, Jennifer. *Qualitative Researching.* London: Sage, 1996.

Maxwell, David. *Christians and Chiefs in Zimbabwe: A Social History of the Hwesa People, c. 1870s–1990s.* Edinburgh: Edinburgh University Press, 1999.

——. "Christianity and the African Imagination." In *Christianity and the African Imagination*, edited by David Maxwell and Ingrid Lawrie, 1–24. Leiden: Brill, 2002.

——. "Christianity without Frontiers: Shona Missionaries and Transnational Pentecostalism in Africa," in *Christianity and the African Imagination*, edited by David Maxwell and Ingrid Lawrie, 295–332. Leiden: Brill, 2002.

——, *African Gifts of the Spirit: Pentecostalism and the Rise of a Zimbabwean Transnational Religious Movement*, Oxford, James Currey, 2006.

Mazrui, Ali A. and Alamin M. Mazrui. *Swahili State and Society: The Political Economy of an African Language*. Nairobi: East African Educational Publishers, 1995.

McKittrick, Meredith. *To Dwell Secure: Generation, Christianity and Colonialism in Ovamboland*. Portsmouth: Heinemann, 2002.

Meyer, Birgit. *Translating the Devil: Religion and Modernity Among the Ewe in Ghana*. Edinburgh: Edinburgh University Press, 1999.

Middleton, J. "Political Incorporation Among the Lugbara of Uganda." In *From Tribe to Nation in Africa*, edited by R. Cohen and J. Middleton. 55–70. USA: Chandler, 1970.

Middleton, John. *The Lugbara of Uganda*. New York: Holt, Rinehart & Winston, 1966.

———. "The Roles of Chiefs and Headmen Among the Lugbara." *Journal of African Administration* 8 (1956): 32–38.

Miles, William F. S. "Nationalism versus Ethnic Identity in Sub-Saharan Africa." *American Political Science Review* 85 (1991): 393–403.

———. "Self-Identity, Ethnic Affinity and National Consciousness: an example from rural Hausaland." *Ethnic and Racial Studies* 9 (1986): 427–444.

Mlahagwa, Josiah R. "Contending for the Faith: Spiritual Revival and the Fellowship Church in Tanzania." In *East African Expressions of Christianity*, edited by Thomas Spear and Isaria N. Kimambo, 296–306. Oxford: James Currey, 1999.

Mothers' Union. "About the MU." http://www.themothersunion.org/content: 2003.

Muller, Carol Ann, *Rituals of Fertility and the Sacrifice of Desire*, Chicago, University of Chicago Press, 1999.

Munayi, M.-M. "La Déportation et le Séjour des Kimbanguistes dans le Kasaï-Lukenie (1921–1960)." *Zaïre-Afrique* 119 (1977): 555–575.

Ndaywel é Nziem, Isidore. *Histoire Générale du Congo: De l'héritage ancien à la République Démocratique*. Paris: De Boeck & Larcier, 1998.

Nelson, J. E. *Christian Missionizing and Social Tranformation: A History of Conflict and Change in Eastern Zaire*. New York: Praeger, 1992.

Nugent, Paul and A. I. Asiwaju. "Introduction: The Paradox of African Boundaries," in *African Boundries: Barriers, Conduits and Opportunities*, edited by Paul Nugent & A. I. Asiwaju, 1–17. London: Pinter, 1996.

Nzongola-Ntalaja, Georges. *The Congo from Leopold to Kabila: A People's History*. London: Zed Books, 2002.

O'Connor, A. *The African City*. London: Hutchinson & Co., 1983.

Ojo, Matthews A. "Indigenous Gospel Music and Social Reconstruction in Modern Nigeria." *Missionalia* 26 (1998): 210–231.

Peel, J. D. Y. *Religious Encounter and the Making of the Yoruba*. Indiana: Indiana University Press, 2000.

———. "Gender in Yoruba Religious Change." *Journal of Religion in Africa* 32 (2002): 136–166.

Peterson, Derek. "Wordy Women: Gender Trouble and the Oral Politics of the East African Revival in Northern Gikuyuland." *Journal of African History* 42 (2001): 469–489.

Pirouet, Louise. *Black Evangelists, the spread of Christianity in Uganda: 1891–1914*. London: Rex Collings, 1978.

Pons, Valdo. *Stanleyville: An African Urban Community under Belgian Administration*. Oxford: Oxford University Press, 1969.

Johan Pottier, "Roadblock Ethnography: Negotiating Humanitarian Access in Ituri, Eastern DR Congo, 1999–2004," *Africa* 76 (2006), 151–179.

Pype, Katrien, "Dancing for God or the Devil: Pentecostal Discourse on Popular Dance in Kinshasa," *Journal of Religion in Africa*, 36 (2006): 296–399.

Ranger, Terence. "Religion, Development and African Christian Identity," in *Religion, Development and African Identity*, edited by Kirsten Holst-Peterson, 29–57. Uppsala: Scandanavian Institute of African Studies, 1987.

——. "New Approaches to the History of Mission Christianity," in *African Historiography: Essays in honour of Jacob Ade Ajayi*, edited by Toyin Falola, 180–194. London: Longman, 1993.

Rapport, Nigel, and A. Dawson. "Home and Movement: A Polemic," in *Migrants of Identity: Perceptions of Home in a World Movement*, edited by Nigel Rapport and A. Dawson, 19–26. Oxford: Berg, 1998.

Richardson, Kenneth. *Garden of Miracles: A History of the African Inland Mission*. London: Victory Press, 1968.

Rodriguez Toulis, Nicole. *Believing Identity: Pentecostalism and Mediation of Jamaican Ethnicity and Gender in England*. Oxford: Berg, 1997.

Roome, W. J. *Apolo, the Apostle to the Pygmies*. London: Morgan & Scott, 1934.

Samba Kaputo. *Phenomène d'Ethnicitie et Conflits ethno-politics en Afrique post-coloniale*. Kinshasa: Presse Universitaires du Zaire, 1982.

Samba, G. "Tolérance religieuse et Intérêts politiques belges au Kibali-Ituri (1900–1940)." *Etudes Zaïroises* 1 (1973): 92–112.

Sanneh, Lamin. *Translating the Message: The Missionary Impact on Culture*. Maryknoll: Orbis, 1989.

Schoffeleers, Matthew. "Pentecostalism and Neo-Traditionalism: The Religious Polarisation of a Rural District in Southern Malawi," in *Christianity and the African Imagination*, edited by David Maxwell and Ingrid Lawrie, 225–270. Leiden: Brill, 2002.

Southall, Aidan. "Ethnic Incorporation among the Alur," in *From Tribe to Nation in Africa*, edited by Ronald Cohen and John Middleton, 71–93. Scranton: Chandler, 1970.

Southall, Aidan W. *Alur Society: A Study in Processes and Types of Domination*. Cambridge: W. Heffer & Sons, 1953.

Southall, A. "Partitioned Alur," in *Partioned Africans: Ethnic Relations Across Africa's International Boundaries, 1884–1984*, edited by A. I. Asiwaju, 85–103. London: C. Hurst, 1985.

Spickard, Paul, and W. Jeffrey Burroughs. "We are a People: Narrative and Multiplicity in Constructing Ethnic Identity," in *We are a People*, edited by Paul Spickard and W. Jeffrey Burroughs. 1–29. Philadelphia: Temple University Press, 2000.

Stephan, Cookie White, and Walter G. Stephan. "What are the Functions of Ethnic Identity?" in *We are a People: Narrative and Multiplicity in Constructing Ethnic Identity*, edited by Paul Spickard and W. Jeffrey Burroughs, 229–243. Philadelphia: Temple University Press, 2000.

Sundkler, Bengt. "African Church History in a New Key," in *Religion, Development and African Identity* edited by Kirsten Holst-Peterson. 73–83. Uppsala: Scandinavian Institute of African Studies, 1987.

Tabu, Marie, Joyce Tsongo and Emma Wild. "Unity Must Adapt to Diversity: Congolese Women in Dialogue with Christianity and Culture." *Anvil* 15 (1998): 34–40.

Tasie, G. O. M. "Christian Awakening in West Africa 1914–18: A Study in the Significance of Native Agency," in *The History of Christianity in West Africa*, edited by O. U. Kalu, 293–308. London: Longman, 1980.

ter Haar, Gerrie. "Strangers and Sojourners: An Introduction," in *Strangers and Sojourners: Religious Communities in the Diaspora*, edited by Gerrie ter Haar, 1–12. Leuven: Peeters, 1998.

Turner, Thomas, *The Congo Wars, Conflict, Myth and Reality*, London: Zed Books, 2007

Uchendu, Victor C. "The Dilemma of Ethnicity and Polity Primacy in Black Africa," in *Ethnic Identity: Creation, Conflict and Accomodation*, edited by Lola Romanucci-Ross and George De Vos, 125–135: Walnut Creek, AltaMira, 1995.

van't Spijker, Gerard. "Credal Hymns as *Summa Theologiae*: New Credal Hymns in Rwanda after the 1994 War and Genocide." *Exchange* 30 (2001): 256–275.

Van Roy P. *Vie de son Excellence Mgr. Alphonse Matthijsen, Evêque de Bunia, 1890–1963*. Buina: Diocese of Bunia, 1970.

Vansina, Jan. *Introduction à l'ethnographie du Congo*: Universitaires du Congo, 1965.
——. *Oral Tradition: A Study in Historical Methodology*. London: Routledge, 1965.
——. "Afterthoughts on the Historiography of Oral Tradition," in *African Historiographies: What History for which Africa?* Edited by Bogumil Jewsiewicki and David Newbury. Beverly Hills: Sage, 1986.
Ward, Kevin. " 'Obedient Rebels'—the Relationship between the early 'Balokole' and the Church of Uganda: the Mukono Crisis of 1941." *Journal of Religion in Africa* 19 (1989): 194—227.
Ward, Kevin. A History of Global Anglicanism, Cambridge: Cambridge University Press, 2006
Welbourne, F. B. & B. A. Ogot, *A Place to Feel at Home, A study of Two Independent Churches in Western Kenya*, London, Oxford University Press, 1966.
Werbner, Richard. "Introduction: Multiple Identities, Plural Arenas," in *Postcolonial Identities in Africa*, edited by Richard Werbner and Terance Ranger, 1–25. London: Zed Books, 1996.
Wild, Emma. "Working with Women in Congo," in *Anglicanism; A Global Communion*, edited by Andrew Wingate, Kevin Ward, Carrie Pemberton, Wilson Sitshebo. 281–285. London: Mowbray, 1998.
——. " 'Is it Witchcraft? Is it Satan? It is a Miracle.' Mai-Mai Soldiers and Christian Concepts of Evil in North-east Congo." *Journal of Religion in Africa* 28 (1998): 450–467.
——. " 'Walking in the Light': The Liturgy of Fellowship in the Early Years of the East African Revival," in *Continuity and Change in Christian Worship*, edited by R. N. Swanson, 419–431. Suffolk: Boydell and Brewer, 1999.
Wild-Wood, Emma. "An Introduction to an Oral History and Archive Project by the Anglican Church of Congo." *History in Africa* 28 (2001): 445–462.
——. ' "Se Débrouiller" or the Art of Serendipity in Historical Research,' *History in Africa* 34 (2007): 367–381.
——, "Saint Apolo from Europe or 'What's in a Luganda Name?' " Church History, 77 (2008): 1–23.
Wilson, K. B. "Refugees and Returnees as Social Agents," in *When Refugees go Home*, edited by T. Allen and H. Morsink, 237–250. New Jersey: Africa World Press, 1994.
Wod'ukumu, Umvor Keno, Kaitenda Mulonda, and Chibenda Mulashi. "Les Measures coloniales belges contre l'Emigration des Indigènes du Territoire de Mahagi vers l'Uganda (1933–1955)." *Ujuvi* 12 (1990): 49–79.
Wood, Peter, and Emma Wild-Wood, " 'One Day we will Sing in God's Home': Hymns and Songs in the Anglican Church in North-east Congo (DRC)." *Journal of Religion in Africa* 34 (2004): 145–180.
Yates, Timothy. *Christian Mission in the Twentieth Century*. Cambridge: Cambridge University Press, 1994.
Young, M. Crawford. "Nationalism, Ethnicity and Class in Africa: A Retrospective." *Cahiers d'Etudes Africaines* 26 (1986): 421–495.

INDEX

Ajuku, Dronyi Sothenes   128–130
African Initiated Churches (AIC)   3, 7,
   15, 58, 173, 203
Al-Ali Nadje   7
Alur
   culture   106, 130, 138, 167, 183
   language   93, 105
   migration   81, 83
   people   6, 32, 51
Amin, Idi   17, 80, 83, 98
Anglican
   Church/es   55, 59, 71, 80, 81, 85,
      87, 93, 100, 101, 131, 137,
      203–218
   Communion   14, 55, 57, 89, 94,
      158–61, 196
   diocese   15, 74, 75, 80, 161, 177
   leaders   26, 34, 35–40, 41, 72, 74,
      77, 136, 175
   liturgy   13–14, 38, 60, 64, 68, 88,
      102, 106, 107, 158, 176
   hierarchy   13, 14, 46, 64, 88, 102,
      105, 106, 158, 197
   structure   62, 70, 106, 137, 142, 143
   tradition   42, 61, 63, 70, 142, 182, 197
Anglicans   12, 62, 87, 88, 95, 96, 115,
   117–120, 124, 126, 134–5, 138, 148,
   162, 187
Anglicanism
   UK   13, 29
   interpretation   37, 80, 89, 94, 187
   localisation   1, 40, 57–9, 88, 97,
      158–9
   universal   57–9, 61, 108, 106, 158–9
Apolo Kivebulaya
   burial request   1, 47–48, 77, 78,
      141–2, 203–5, 207
   influence   39–40, 61, 69, 70, 75, 76,
      160, 187, 217
   life   1, 14, 22–29, 36, 38, 41, 56, 87,
      114, 197
Archbishop   14, 129, 185, 187, 212
Aru
   church   85, 86–7, 118, 137, 161
   town   84, 103, 105
   zone   6, 16, 55, 81, 93, 115, 127,
      130, 146, 174
   Arua   128

Asiki David   iv, 94, 95, 97, 98, 99
AIM   3, 7, 15, 58

Balokole   45–46, 85–86, 128–129
   Baptism   24, 33, 87, 91, 115, 116,
      117–8, 132
      Basimasi Kyakuhaire   25–6, 40,
         44, 51, 52, 55, 145, 147, 161
      Belgian colonial rule   6, 14, 28, 29,
         51, 82, 83
Benezet Bujo   64
   Beni   16, 50, 51, 52, 53, 55, 57, 62
      Beni Bataaga   46, 75, 136, 198
Bezaleri Ndahura   74, 75, 176
Bible
   use of   98, 24, 40, 84, 97, 136, 141,
      175, 178, 182, 201
   translation   26, 32
Bible School   46, 95, 105, 122
Bishop
   person   26, 74, 136, 137, 176, 185
   position   13, 32, 214
Bileti Sila   86, 137, 140
   Boga
      area   36, 43, 55, 107, 198, 205
      EAC centre   35, 56, 57, 70, 74,
         77, 86, 95, 105, 107, 108, 109,
         114, 197
      culture   39, 59, 63, 68, 186
      inhabitants   22, 61, 108, 142
      village   1, 16, 24–30, 34, 41, 44,
         46, 53, 136, 177
Book of Common Prayer   24, 26, 32,
   37, 60, 68, 69, 70, 113, 140, 141, 182
Bunia   16, 32, 50–3, 61, 115, 156, 164,
   174–7, 181, 193
   church   54, 55, 154, 158, 184, 187, 199
Burundi   14
Butembo   16, 31, 50–55
   church   61, 71, 147–8, 161–2

Catholic
   Church   29–31, 32, 34, 59, 68, 174, 175
   members   15, 31, 48, 126, 201
   CECA 20 réformeé   124, 162
Chafetz, Janet Saltzman   49, 78, 171
Charismatic   175, 176, 184, 186–91,
   199, 201

Choirs   151, 163, 174, 179–184, 195,
   200, 201
Chosen Evangelical Revival (CER) *see*
   Revival *and* Revivalists
Christian belief   2, 37, 48, 62, 64, 114,
   117, 150, 163, 167, 207
Christianity
   African   2–4, 18, 50, 188–190, 211,
      213–6
   Anglican   13–15, 20, 109, 211–3
   contemporary expression   60, 170,
      171, 174, 177, 182, 186, 191,
      201–2
   conversion   3, 4, 26, 27, 37, 38, 85,
      97, 98, 99, 100, 117, 126, 133, 135
   inclusive   69, 94, 105, 195, 198
   local expression   35–6, 38, 40, 60,
      85, 91
   mixed   114–5
   and migration   65, 87
   and women   145, 153
Church of England   14, 33, 37, 38, 41,
   166, 182, 184, 186
Church of Uganda (COU)   14, 32, 41,
   43, 85, 89, 116, 117, 128, 166
   comparison with EAC   29, 48, 102,
      104, 108
Church Missionary Society (CMS)   14,
   22, 29, 32, 33, 34, 40, 42, 74, 95, 176
Comaroff, Jean and John   2
Communauté Evangelique du Centre de
   l'Afrique (CECA 20)
Communion, Holy   60, 91, 117–8, 123
Congo
   geography   6, 11, 15, 16
   history   27, 29–30, 34, 81–3, 111
   political situation   112, 118, 125,
      171, 172–3
Congolese Protestant Council (*See* Eglise
   du Christ au Congo)
Contextualisation   35, 63, 69, 91, 142,
   211
Conservative Baptist Foreign Missionary
   Society (CBFMS)   31, 33, 161

Damali Sabiti   156, 157, 159, 160
Dance   46, 128, 136, 140, 163, 166,
   182–3, 198
Denomination   4, 7
Denominational
   collaboration   69, 161–3, 164–5,
      184, 196, 200–1, 214–6
   conflict   34–5, 62, 92, 99, 114–5,
      116, 119, 121, 124, 136, 161

loyalty   11, 18, 56, 61–2, 68, 90,
   104, 120, 131, 176, 211, 212–3
   mix   3, 19, 54, 11–2, 147, 154, 174
Dislocation   1, 7, 14, 128, 146, 170,
   188

Ebaugh, Helen Rose   49, 78, 171
Education   10, 15, 43, 50, 53, 71–3,
   91, 104, 128, 133–4, 142, 179
   and women   44, 159, 168–9
Eglise du Christ au Congo (ECC)   34,
   58, 89, 112–3, 119, 136, 161, 162–5,
   174–5 200, 201
Ethnicity   3, 4, 9, 10–11, 13, 18, 66–9,
   75, 144, 154, 157, 172, 186, 189,
   192–6, 211
Eschatology   135–6, 191
Estella Mustum   71, 72, 162
Evasta Kusuna   56, 60, 148, 156–7

Fédération des Femmes Protestantes   163–5,
   169, 187
Furaha   163, 170, 181, 182, 190, 200

Gaitskell, Deborah   152
Ganda   1, 22, 27, 182
Generational
   conflict   169, 156, 186, 202
   issues   20, 41, 51, 72, 155, 157, 158,
      161, 171, 209–11
   relations   66–8, 150
Gerontocratic institution   142, 177,
   197, 210
   power   42, 43, 145, 151, 156, 158,
      189, 197, 199, 218
Gifford, Paul   172, 188
Global influence   96, 185, 188, 212,
   217
   institution   35, 88, 89, 94, 101, 102,
      158, 170, 186
   network   14, 158
Globalisation   188
God
   relationship with   123, 133, 167, 205
   supplication of   100, 152, 173
   understanding of   7, 25, 27, 32, 39,
      89, 98, 116, 119, 132, 134, 136,
      140, 161, 163, 194

Hastings, Adrian   56, 113, 114, 203
Healing   163, 165, 173–4, 185, 186,
   190, 201
Health care   15, 20, 25, 30, 43, 44, 50,
   73, 159, 173, 179

Hema
  culture   26–7, 35–8, 40, 44, 63, 68,
    108, 183, 198
  language   35–6
  people   5, 6, 17, 21, 46, 51, 68, 70,
    75, 156–7, 182, 189, 193–4
Heshima (respect)   38–40, 45, 57, 59,
    60, 212
  contested   47, 158, 165, 181, 185
  earned   89, 101
  for God   39, 140
  lack of   139, 55
Hodgson, Dorothy   144, 168
Home
  belonging   1, 7–9, 12, 20, 35, 48,
    49, 60–65, 68, 73, 83–4, 109, 111,
    114–5, 125–6
  heavenly   135–6
  physical   53, 56, 59, 72, 75, 77, 78,
    81, 87, 92, 99, 116
  re-ordering   70–1, 146–7, 150, 162,
    168, 171, 175, 194, 203–5
  Homeliness   8, 109, 135, 206
Homeless   143
Homelessness   127, 142

Identity   7–11, 111, 203–18
  African   66, 189
  Anglican   159, 161
  CECA   113, 124, 126
  Congolese   66–7, 76, 193
  contested   49, 50, 65, 70, 78, 197
  corporate   14, 27, 67, 109, 126, 127,
    129, 135, 196, 205
  EAC   17–9, 29, 47–8, 68, 70–1, 90,
    108–9, 126, 190–1, 200–1
  ethnic   3, 9–11, 18, 37, 63, 67, 176,
    192, 193, 194, 202
  gender   9, 11, 18, 144–5, 155, 169,
    208–9
  generational   9–11, 18, 144–5, 169,
    209–11
  migrant   9–11, 109, 116, 118, 193,
    195, 217
  national   9–11, 17, 139, 193, 194,
    195, 211
  personal   57, 62–3, 78, 99, 101, 135
  religious   2, 8, 13, 49, 54, 63, 70, 78,
    109, 116, 127, 130, 148, 170
  revivalist   127, 128, 131, 133, 138–142
  rural   17, 93, 49
  signifiers   12–3, 78, 80, 89, 106, 143,
    190, 196, 200, 201, 204
  urban   17, 50, 66–8, 71, 78

Immanuel Mission   31
Indigenisation (*see* contextualisation)
International church   11, 35, 37, 92,
    102, 207
  expression   191
  networks   129, 135, 139, 158–9, 169,
    186, 187
Irene Bahemuka   68, 70, 175–6, 197–8
Isichei, Elizabeth   145, 153
Itineration   135, 167
Ituri   5, 14–5, 29–31, 52, 67, 84, 115

Janette Sinziri   116, 144, 151
Jesus   47, 62, 91, 98, 99, 127, 130,
    132–3, 134, 154, 159

Kabarole Baguma   87, 95, 107, 118
Kabila, Laurent   173, 191
Kainama   16, 24, 36, 38, 40, 50–3, 56,
    57, 63, 176
Kakwa culture   130, 138, 82, 27, 106
  language   93, 105
  people   6, 32, 81, 83, 91, 102, 183
Kalu, Ogbu   3, 188, 190
Kenya   32, 45, 69, 159, 210
Kimbangu, Simon   15, 28, 204
Kimbanguists   174
Kinshasa   15, 50, 163, 174, 181, 183
Kisangani   15, 50, 51, 74, 176
Kumuru   16, 84, 93, 96, 105, 119

Landau, Paul   2, 3
Lese   21, 36, 46
Lingala/Bangala   85, 105, 163, 182,
    210
Local
  authority   185
  Christian expression   2, 14, 17,
    35–7, 39, 48, 60, 217
  culture   3, 37, 109–10, 128–9, 174
  influence   92, 188, 192–3, 211–2, 214
Lugbara – culture   82–3
  language   93, 105
  people   6, 32, 81, 85, 183, 194
Lukumbula Kinandsikiri   39, 45, 55,
    71, 72, 162
Luwum, Janani   129

Maddox Geoffrey   211
Maendeleo (development)   43–5, 50–1,
    63, 71–4, 89–90, 101–4, 158–61, 204
  contested   128, 134, 168
  wider interpretation   170–1, 173,
    177–9, 186, 194, 199, 202, 204

Mahagi church 136–8
 town 84, 86, 105, 131
 zone 6, 16, 81, 85, 87, 93, 97, 115, 127, 129, 130, 146
Mahirani Melena 55, 60, 61, 71, 147–8, 161
Maxwell, David 2, 3, 13, 87, 174, 175, 216
Mbuti 21, 24, 36, 77
McCurdy, Sheryl 144, 168
McKittrick, Meredith 5, 42, 65, 128
Meyer, Birgit 188, 190
Migrants 8–14, 17, 49, 53–4, 171–2
 first-generation 63, 69, 71–2, 74, 78, 147, 175, 189, 199
 returned migrants 85, 97, 89–92, 101, 104, 106, 116, 119
 second-generation 17, 50, 65–70, 71, 73, 76, 145, 160, 169, 176–7, 194, 210
Migration 1, 3, 4–7, 19, 65, 75, 78, 111, 134–6, 200, 205–8, 217–8
 economic 52, 134, 214
 forced 51, 87, 97
 colonial 21, 51–2, 82–3
 labour 17, 89, 106, 108, 125
 micro-factors 6–7, 208
 of Anglicans 50, 54, 57–8, 74, 109
 pre-colonial 21, 81–2
 rural-urban 17, 50–4, 58, 63, 145, 147, 177
 trans-border 17, 80–81, 83–5, 89, 124, 146
 urban-rural 198
Missionary/ies 21, 22, 28, 34, 77
 AIM 112, 117
 Catholic 30
 CMS 25, 29, 42, 95, 176
 policies 34, 59, 63, 69, 74, 77, 112, 113, 115
 societies 31–4, 125
Mlahagwa, Josiah 143, 210
Mobutu Sese Seko 15, 53, 56, 58, 59, 66, 11, 172, 173, 191
Mombo Esther 42
Mothers' Union (MU) 42, 44, 46, 56, 102–3, 107, 145–6, 148–61, 164–5, 169, 209
Muhindo Tsongo 7, 53, 152, 160, 161, 205–6
Mukasa Nasanari 39, 46, 47, 95, 137, 147
Munege Kabarole iv, 54–6, 62, 72, 86, 87, 95, 115, 136, 185

Music 11, 18, 46, 60, 67, 105, 174, 179, 181–3
Musubaho Ndaghaliwa 38, 50
Mwalimu/walimu (teachers) 25, 26, 41, 42, 57, 59, 60, 72, 87, 94–5, 96, 97–101, 107

Namibia 5, 42, 65
Nande culture 21
 people 5, 36, 51, 53, 71
Narrating identity 2, 12, 18, 63, 193, 203–5
Narratives 17, 66, 116, 131, 136, 155, 165, 209
 replotting 47–8, 70, 142, 145, 160, 194
Nationalism 11, 13, 74–6, 208
 cultural 67–8, 182, 192–6, 208
 political 66, 75, 211
Ngiti 21, 36, 193–4
Nord-Kivu 5, 15–6, 49–53, 67, 176
 church 55, 71, 73, 74, 177
Nyali 21, 36, 56, 156

Omukama (chief) 22, 27, 37, 38, 40
Otuwa Simeon 83, 85, 132, 136
Ovambo 5, 42
Ozua Samson 84, 85, 88, 99, 136

Peel, JDY 10, 38
Pentecostal
 churches 3, 163–4, 172, 173–5, 184, 210, 215–6
 influence 4, 18, 58, 88, 124, 181, 183, 186, 188, 190, 201–2, 213
Peripatetic evangelism 99, 135
Peterson, Derek 133, 166
Pottier Johan 192, 193
Prayer Book (*see* Book of Common Prayer)
Protestant
Pygmies (*see* Mbuti)

Quakers 42

Refugees 4, 5, 6, 80–3, 85–7, 109, 115, 116, 134
Revival 45–7, 165, 188, 199, 204
Revival, East African see *Balokole*
Revivalism 45–6, 86–7, 166
Revivalist
 belief 128, 130, 131, 133
 members 8, 18, 97–8, 100, 107, 126, 127–143, 148, 190, 198–9, 206–7
 women 46, 166–69, 183

Ridsdale, Philip   74, 176
Rwaikaikara André   61, 68, 199
Rwanda   14, 45, 128, 129, 173, 191

Semeliki escarpment   9, 17, 20–2, 27,
    Anglicanism on   35, 66, 73, 94, 145,
    183, 197
    migration from   50, 63
Silvanus Wani   129
Sinziri Onadra   iv, 93, 94, 116, 121
Spirit, Holy   184–7, 215
    healing   163, 164,
    inspiration   128, 134, 168–9, 182
    manifestation   143, 174, 176, 201
    power   166, 173, 191
    salvation   165, 198–9
Spirits, evil   185
Strivers   129
Sudan   15, 81, 82, 84, 87
Sundkler, Bengt   5
Swahili   12, 36, 38, 43, 105–6, 182, 102

Tabu Abembe   36, 138, 196
Talinga   21, 36
Tanzania   45, 98, 148, 210
Thumbe Ferdinand   86, 199
Tito Balinda   37, 76–7
Transnationalism   7, 139, 158, 161,
    186, 196, 202, 217
Trumpters   129

Ubaya Uchaki   132, 133, 140
Ubotha Marthe   97, 130, 136, 166–7
Uganda
    influence   25, 26–7, 37, 57, 66, 76,
        96, 98–101, 104, 118, 159
    migration to and from   6, 17, 52,
        80–6, 88, 92, 94, 109, 116, 130, 139
    political involvement   173, 191, 193
Uhuru (freedom)
    in society   101–3, 105–7, 125–6, 161
    in worship   45–7, 80, 89, 91–3,
        132–4, 143, 164, 166, 170, 181–2,
        190, 200, 212
Umoja (unity)   109, 116–7, 120, 200–2,
    204, 212

external   163, 164–5, 184
internal   127, 131, 141, 143, 193,
    195, 199
Upole (calm)   37–8, 60, 64
    contested   47, 89, 105–6, 182, 200
Utaratibu (order)   113, 118, 204, 210,
    212
    contested   47, 134, 158, 164–5, 172,
        175, 178, 184–5, 187, 199–200, 207
    with heshima and upole   37–8, 45, 47–9,
        59, 60, 63–4, 71, 73, 78–9, 146,
        151, 153
    with uhuru and maendeleo   80, 88, 89,
        92, 96, 101–2, 104–7

Vernacularisation   26, 36–7, 105
Vijana (see young people)

Walimu (see Mwalimu)
Wamama wa Habari Njema (Women of the
    Good News)   161–3
War   11, 15, 87, 171, 173, 191, 193,
    195, 198, 202
West Nile   32, 82, 117, 126, 129
White Fathers   30
Willis, J.J.   26
Wokovu (see revivalists)
Women   10, 52, 71–2, 122, 144–170,
    177, 193, 201, 205–9, 215
    leaders   26, 41–2, 97, 134, 150–1,
        155–6, 159–61, 166–8
    migrants   18, 145–7, 169
    roles   44, 46, 107
    old   145, 147, 156–7
    young   8, 156–7, 159, 185, 187, 197
Worship   72, 74, 85, 105, 107–8, 114,
    127, 140–1, 142
    contemporary   172, 178–84, 201
    escarpment   37–9, 60–2, 69, 78, 198
    pentecostal   174, 176

Young people/youth   18, 25, 70, 143,
    171–202, 210, 215

Zaïre   xvii, 203
Zimbabwe   3

STUDIES OF RELIGION
IN AFRICA

SUPPLEMENTS TO THE JOURNAL OF RELIGION IN AFRICA

1. MOBLEY, H.W. *The Ghanaian's Image of the Missionary*. An Analysis of the Published Critiques of Christian Missionaries by Ghanaians, 1897-1965. 1970. ISBN 90 04 01185 4
2. POBEE, J.S. (ed.). *Religion in a Pluralistic Society*. Essays Presented to Professor C.G. Baëta in Celebration of his Retirement from the Service of the University of Ghana, September 1971, by Friends and Colleagues Scattered over the Globe. 1976. ISBN 90 04 04556 2
3. TASIE, G.O.M. *Christian Missionary Enterprise in the Niger Delta, 1864-1918*. 1978. ISBN 90 04 05243 7
4. REECK,D. *Deep Mende*. Religious Interactions in a Changing African Rural Society. 1978. ISBN 90 04 04769 7
5. BUTSELAAR, J. VAN. *Africains, missionnaires et colonialistes*. Les origines de l'Église Presbytérienne de Mozambique (Mission Suisse), 1880-1896. 1984. ISBN 90 04 07481 3
6. OMENKA, N.I. *The School in the Service of Evangelization*. The Catholic Educational Impact in Eastern Nigeria 1886-1950. 1989. ISBN 90 04 08932 3
7. JĘDREJ, M.C. & SHAW, R. (eds.). *Dreaming, Religion and Society in Africa*. 1992. ISBN 90 04 08936 5
8. GARVEY, B. *Bembaland Church*. Religious and Social Change in South Central Africa, 1891-1964. 1994. ISBN 90 04 09957 3
9. OOSTHUIZEN, G.C., KITSHOFF, M.C. & DUBE, S.W.D. (eds.). Afro-Christianity at the Grassroots. Its Dynamics and Strategies. Foreword by Archbishop Desmond Tutu. 1994. ISBN 90 04 10035 0
10. SHANK, D.A. *Prophet Harris, the 'Black Elijah' of West Africa*. Abridged by Jocelyn Murray. 1994. ISBN 90 04 09980 8
11. HINFELAAR, H.F. *Bemba-speaking Women of Zambia in a Century of Religious Change (1892-1992)*. 1994. ISBN 90 04 10149 7
12. GIFFORD, P. (ed.). *The Christian Churches and the Democratisation of Africa*. 1995. ISBN 90 04 10324 4
13. JĘDREJ, M.C. *Ingessana*. The Religious Institutions of a People of the Sudan-Ethiopia Borderland. 1995. ISBN 90 04 10361 9
14. FIEDLER, K. *Christianity and African Culture*. Conservative German Protestant Missionaries in Tanzania, 1900-1940. 1996. ISBN 90 04 10497 6

15. OBENG, P. *Asante Catholicims.* Religious and Cultural Reproduction Among the Akan of Ghana. 1996. ISBN 90 04 10631 6
16. FARGHER, B.L. *The Origins of the New Churches Movement in Southern Ethiopia, 1927-1944.* 1996. ISBN 90 04 10661 8
17. TAYLOR, W.H. *Mission te Educate.* A History of the Educational Work of the Scottish Presbyterian Mission in East Nigeria, 1846-1960. 1996. ISBN 90 04 10713 4
18. RUEL, M. *Belief, Ritual and the Securing of Life.* Reflexive Essays on a Bantu Religion. 1996. ISBN 90 04 10640 5
19. McKENZIE, P. *Hail Orisha!* A Phenomenology of a West African Religion in the Mid-Nineteenth Century. 1997. ISBN 90 04 10942 0
20. MIDDLETON, K. *Ancestors, Power and History in Madagascar.* 1999. ISBN 90 04 11289 8
21. LUDWIG, F. *Church and State in Tanzania.* Aspects of a Changing Relationship, 1961-1994. 1999. 90 04 11506 4
22. BURKE, J.F. *These Catholic Sisters are all* Mamas! Towards the Inculturation of the Sisterhood in Africa, an Ethnographic Study. 2001. ISBN 90 04 11930 2
23. MAXWELL, D., with I. LAWRIE (eds.) *Christianity and the African Imagination.* Essays in Honour of Adrian Hastings. 2001. ISBN 90 04 11668 0
24. GUNNER, E. *The Man of Heaven and the Beautiful Ones of God.* 2003. *In preparation.* ISBN 90 04 12542 6
25. PEMBERTON, C. *Circle Thinking.* African Women Theologians in Dialogue with the West. 2003. ISBN 90 04 12441 1
26. WEISS, B. (ed.). *Producing African Futures.* Ritual and Reproduction in a Neoliberal Age. 2004. ISBN 90 04 13860 9
27. ASAMOAH-GYADU, J.K. *African Charismatics.* Current Developments within Independent Indigenous Pentecostalism in Ghana. 2004. ISBN 90 04 14089 1
28. WESTERLUND, D. *African Indigenous Religions and Disease Causation.* From Spriritual Beings to Living Humans. 2006. ISBN 90 04 14433 1
29. FAULKNER, M.R.J. *Overtly Muslim, Covertly Boni.* Competing Calls of Religious Allegiance on the Kenyan Coast. 2006. ISBN 90 04 14753 5
30. SOOTHILL, J.E. *Gender, Social Change and Spiritual Power.* Charismatic Christianity in Ghana. 2007. ISBN 978 90 04 15789 7
31. CLAFFEY, P. *Christian Churches in Dahomey-Benin.* A study of their socio-political role. 2007. ISBN 978 90 04 15572 5
32. WIT, H. DE and WEST, G.O. (eds.). *African and European Readers of the Bible in Dialogue.* In Quest Of a Shared Meaning. 2008. ISBN 978 90 04 16656 1
33. PALMIÉ, S. (ed.). *Africas of the Americas.* Beyond the Search for Origins in the Study of Afro-Atlantic Religions. 2008. ISBN 978 90 04 16472 7

34. WELCH, P. *Church and Settler in Colonial Zimbabwe.* A Study in the History of the Anglican Diocese of Mashonaland/Southern Rhodesia, 1890-1925. 2008. ISBN 978 90 04 16746 9
35. WILD-WOOD, E. *Migration and Christian Identity in Congo (DRC).* 2008. ISBN 978 90 04 16464 2